Morality and Revelation in Islamic Thought and Beyond

Morality and Revelation in Islamic Thought and Beyond

A New Problem of Evil

AMIR SAEMI

OXFORD
UNIVERSITY PRESS

Oxford University Press is a department of the University of Oxford. It furthers
the University's objective of excellence in research, scholarship, and education
by publishing worldwide. Oxford is a registered trade mark of Oxford University
Press in the UK and certain other countries.

Published in the United States of America by Oxford University Press
198 Madison Avenue, New York, NY 10016, United States of America.

© Oxford University Press 2024

All rights reserved. No part of this publication may be reproduced, stored in
a retrieval system, or transmitted, in any form or by any means, without the
prior permission in writing of Oxford University Press, or as expressly permitted
by law, by license, or under terms agreed with the appropriate reproduction
rights organization. Inquiries concerning reproduction outside the scope of the
above should be sent to the Rights Department, Oxford University Press, at the
address above.

You must not circulate this work in any other form
and you must impose this same condition on any acquirer.

Library of Congress Cataloging-in-Publication Data
Names: Saemi, Amir, author.
Title: Morality and revelation in Islamic thought and beyond :
a new problem of evil / Amir Saemi.
Description: 1. | New York : Oxford University Press, 2024. |
Includes index.
Identifiers: LCCN 2023040395 (print) | LCCN 2023040396 (ebook) |
ISBN 9780197686232 (hardback) | ISBN 9780197686249 (epub)
Subjects: LCSH: Islamic ethics—History. | Islam—Moral and ethical aspects. |
Qur'an—Ethics. | Good and evil—Religious aspects—Islam.
Classification: LCC BJ1291.S235 2024 (print) | LCC BJ1291 (ebook) |
DDC 297.5—dc23/eng/20230922
LC record available at https://lccn.loc.gov/2023040395
LC ebook record available at https://lccn.loc.gov/2023040396

DOI: 10.1093/oso/9780197686232.001.0001

Printed by Integrated Books International, United States of America

Is he who was dead, then We gave him life, and made for him a light by which he walks among the people, like he who is in total darkness, and cannot get out of it?

—The Qur'an (6:122)

>

To Omeed

Contents

Acknowledgments   xi

Prologue: Defining a New Problem of Evil   1
   Summary of the Chapter   1
   1. Two Stories   1
   2. Morally Controversial Scriptural Passages   4
   3. Seeming Prescribed Evil   8
   4. The New Problem of Evil and the Structure of the Book   23
   5. Historical Background   28

PART I: SCRIPTURE FIRST

1. The Consequentialism of the Late Ash'arites   37
   Summary of the Chapter   37
   1. Divine Command Theory of the Early Ash'arites   38
   2. The Consequentialism of al-Ghazālī   44
   3. The Moral Epistemology of al-Ghazālī   48
   4. The Argument for Strict Adherence to Scripture   52
   5. *Taqlīd* and the Rule of Figurative Interpretation   60

2. The Deontological Ethics of the Mu'tazilites   67
   Summary of the Chapter   67
   1. The Ash'arites and the Problem of Evil   68
   2. The Metaethics of the Mu'tazilites   70
   3. The Normative Theory of 'Abd al-Jabbār   82
   4. The Moral Epistemology of 'Abd al-Jabbār   86
   5. Natural Evil, Prescribed Evil, and Skeptical Theism   91

3. The Virtue Ethics of Islamic Philosophers   103
   Summary of the Chapter   103
   1. The Project of the Reconciliation of Reason and Religion   104
   2. Al-Fārābī's View on Epistemology and Religion   106
   3. Averroës's View on the Harmony of Religion and Philosophy   113
   4. The Virtue Ethics of al-Fārābī   121

PART II: ETHICS FIRST

4. The Impermissibility of Moral Deference — 137
   Summary of the Chapter — 137
   1. Moral Deference in Contemporary Philosophy — 138
   2. Al-Rāzī's Ethical Theory — 143
   3. Al-Rāzī on Moral Deference — 149
   4. Moses and Impermissibility of Pure Moral Deference — 157
   5. A Solution to the Problem of Prescribed Evil — 169

5. The Reliability of Our Moral Judgments — 171
   Summary of the Chapter — 171
   1. The Debate on Objective and Subjective Ought — 172
   2. Scripture, Ignorance, and Uncertainty — 179
   3. Ignorance Revisited — 185
   4. Kantian Arguments for the Accessibility Constraint — 190
   5. Moral Knowledge Optimism and the Muʿtazilites — 197
   6. The Case of Abraham — 202

6. The Hermeneutics of Scripture — 206
   Summary of the Chapter — 206
   1. Ethics-First Solutions to the Problem of Prescribed Evil — 206
   2. Lessons from a Philosophical Tale — 210
   3. The Nature of Law — 214
   4. Legal Interpretation Defended — 219
   5. The Moral Functions of Scripture — 223

Index — 235

Acknowledgments

This book was written with the help of many people. I can't thank them enough in these acknowledgments. All I can do is to mention a few names who have helped me the most.

I have been preoccupied with the main question of this book for many years. When I was in graduate school, I remember having long and incredibly insightful conversations with Arash Naraghi about how a conservative believer might appeal to hidden facts to resist our modern moral judgments. I feel a great sense of gratitude toward Arash. I kept thinking about this conservative argument and different ways around it. Mahmoud Morvarid and I often discussed the issue for days and hours; it was always his insight that taught me how to approach a problem in a better way. I gained valuable insight into the nature of moral testimony from Jeff McMahan, which enabled me to understand how the problem can be framed as a problem of moral testimony. Jeff also helped me in various ways during the writing of the book. I am very grateful to him.

When I decided to write a book about morality and revelation, Peter Adamson suggested that I should write the book as a historically informed work in the philosophy of religion and moral philosophy. Not only did Peter help me to think about the structure of the book, but his comments and insights on the historical aspects of the book were also always enlightening. I am indebted to Peter for all his help.

From the moment I started writing the book, I discussed its ideas with many people, and their comments and ideas, whether they realize it or not, have helped me immensely in completing it. These people include, but are not limited to, Hamid Vahid, Gianfranco Soldati, Larry Temkin, Sajed Tayebi, Arash Abazari, Saleh Zarepour, Matthew Griffin, Philip Atkins, Sara Aronowitz, Marilie Coetsee, Dean Zimmerman, Nasir Mousavian, Mohsen Zamani, Mostafa Mohajeri, Kelly Clark, Scott Davison, Shahriar Khosravai, Zahra Sarkarpour, Marilie Coetsee, and Alex Guerrero. I am especially thankful to Arash Abazari, Saleh Zarepour, and Scott Davison for their continuous support and encouragement.

I am also very grateful to Kelly Clark who supported the book with his John Templeton grant. His support really helped me to be able to spend time on writing. I presented some of the ideas in a class at Rutgers and in a summer school at IPM. I found the comments and questions of my students at Rutgers and those of the participants of the IPM summer school hugely beneficial. I am grateful to all of them.

I would like to thank especially Philip Atkins, Scott Davison, and Matthew Griffin. Philip and Scott copyedited some chapters of the book and provided excellent comments on the last draft. Matthew Griffin not only provided inspiration, motivation, and support throughout the writing process, but also carefully copyedited the entire work. It is simply impossible for me to express my gratitude to him in words.

I would also like to express my gratitude to the Oxford University Press editors, Lucy Randall and Lauralee Yeary, for guiding the editorial process in a gracious, kind, and professional manner. In addition, I am also very thankful to OUP reviewers for their very helpful comments. They helped me to significantly improve the manuscript. I feel very much indebted to the reviewers for this improvement.

When I was writing this book, I was reading *Lord of the Rings* with my wonderful son Omeed, my light and love in life. The epilogue of Part II, which reflects, in a way, the central point of the book, is chosen partly in commemoration of that memory. I wish to convey to him, and to the reader, that while we might be living in trying times, if I am right in this book, to be human is, in part, to be able to discern good and ill, as much in the Golden Wood as in our own homes. I am everlastingly thankful to Omeed for all kindness, hope, and joy he brought into my life.

Prologue

Defining a New Problem of Evil

Summary of the Chapter

Section 1. This section describes the story of the Prophet's uncle's conversion to Islam as well as that of Iblis's disobedience to God. In both stories the question of the conflict between morality and revelation arises.

Section 2. Some examples of morally controversial Scriptural passages are presented.

Section 3. A seemingly prescribed evil is an action prescribed by Scripture which is deemed immoral by our independent moral judgments. Some contemporary Islamic scholars deny the existence of any seemingly prescribed evil by using the reinterpretation strategy or the contextualization strategy. I will argue that neither of those strategies works.

Section 4. The new problem of evil, that is, the problem of divinely prescribed evil, is presented as a tension between three theses: the divinity of Scripture, the existence of seemingly prescribed evil, and the reliability of our independent moral judgments. The section ends with an explanation of the book's structure, which represents different approaches to solving the problem.

Section 5. This section explains the value of finding a historically informed solution to the problem of prescribed evil. The section also presents a preliminary historical background for readers unfamiliar with the Islamic tradition.

1. Two Stories

Let me begin with two stories about morality and revelation and their potential conflict.

The First Story

The epigraph of the book is a verse from the Qur'an, reportedly revealed to describe the moral dissimilitude of two leaders of the Meccan community: Abū Jahl, one of the Prophet's most determined enemies, and Hamzah, the Prophet's uncle and a strong supporter.[1] The verse seems to refer to Hamzah's conversion to Islam. Hamzah was in disbelief, but God made him a light by which he could walk among the people. Abū Jahl, on the other hand, is in total darkness and cannot get out of it. Hamzah's conversion has a curious element, however.

While Hamzah was a powerful man in the community, he did not accept Islam for several years, even after he was personally approached by the Prophet to accept the Prophet's message. What helped him to see the truth was witnessing severe harassment of the Prophet (and early Muslims) by the majority, under the leadership of Abū Jahl. Disturbed by what he saw, he took the side of the weak and the vulnerable. In this famous story, it is first and foremost Hamzah's sense of justice, and not the content of revelation, that helped him to see the truth. What, then, is the light by which he came back from the dead and walked among people? Is it his sense of justice or the Prophet's message? It looks like the former. Hamzah's sense of justice paved the way for him to see the truth in the Prophet's message.

But now imagine this hypothetical scenario: years after his conversion to Islam, he comes across a verse that seems to be asking him to do something that goes against his sense of justice. Suppose that Scripture asks him to harass the weak and the vulnerable. What should he do then? While it looks intuitively very plausible that he should again take the side of the weak and the vulnerable, the answer to the question is not so straightforward. Believers have always thought that God works in mysterious ways. We have witnessed countless disasters: earthquakes, flooding, volcanic eruptions, hurricanes, diseases, and so on. Despite great tragedies that we can't find meaning in, believers have kept their faith, holding that God works in ways that we cannot understand, and so cannot judge God's acts with our limited intellect. The same might be said in the hypothetical scenario: we cannot judge Scripture by our limited intellect.

---

[1] See Seyyed Hossein Nasr, editor-in-chief, *The Study Quran: A New Translation and Commentary* (New York: Harper One, 2015), 38.

The Second Story

The Qur'an tells us the story of Iblis's disobedience: When God created Adam, He "said to the angels: 'Bow yourselves to Adam'; so they bowed themselves, save Iblis—he was not of those that bowed themselves" (7:11). Iblis's disobedience brought him eternal damnation. The Qur'an describes the reason for his disobedience as follows: "Said He, 'What prevented thee to bow thyself, when I commanded thee?' Said he, 'I am better than he; Thou createdst me of fire, and him Thou createdst of clay'" (7:12). According to the orthodox reading of the story, Iblis had too much pride to bow to Adam, and this pride is the cause of his ruin. However, there is an alternative reading of the story, suggested by the Persian Sufi al-Hallaj and his followers.[2] On their reading of the story, Iblis was the supreme monotheist, an unwavering lover of God who could not bring himself to worship anything but God. Interpreting bowing to Adam as an expression of worship, Iblis decides that his refusal to worship anyone but God is more valuable than avoiding any penalty or curse bestowed on him for his disobedience.

My goal is not to evaluate this alternative interpretation. But let's imagine for a moment that the alternative interpretation is correct. On this alternative reading, Iblis's independent moral principle of worshiping no one but God was in conflict with God's command, and he decided to take sides with his own moral principle. Should he have done so? What would you do if you were in Iblis's shoes? Imagine a case in which you are commanded by God to do something that goes against your conscience. What should you do in this hypothetical situation? On the one hand, you have to stick to your morals and principles. But on the other hand, who are you to judge what is moral and what is not, when God tells you what to do?[3]

---

[2] See Whitney S. Bodman, *The Poetics of Iblīs: Narrative Theology in the Qur'ān*. Vol. 62 (Harvard University Press, 2011), 262–67. Hud Hudson's paper "Iblis, Abraham, and Teleological Suspensions," *The Monist* 104.3 (2021): 281–99, drew my attention to this example. I was inspired by him to begin the book with this story. Al-Hallaj's position on Iblis is not, of course, orthodox. Nevertheless, it inspired later Sufis, some of whom adopted it. A notable example is Ayn al-Qudat al-Hamadani (interestingly al-Hallaj and Ayn al-Qudat are the two early Sufi martyrs—though they were not killed for their views on Iblis). See C. W. Ernst, *Words of Ecstasy in Sufism* (Albany: State University of New York Press, 1985), 77–80.

[3] I chose these two stories to introduce the problem of the book, but there are two other well-known Qur'anic stories about the clash between our moral principles and revelation, namely, the story of Moses and Khidr, and the story of Abraham's sacrifice. I will talk about those stories in Chapters 4, 5, and 6.

2. Morally Controversial Scriptural Passages

The hypothetical scenarios discussed in the last section might not be purely hypothetical. Many believers from different faiths today are in a situation very much like the hypothetical scenarios I described. While believers take Scripture to be the word of God, they find Scriptural passages that seem incompatible with their modern moral sensibilities. The examples are abundant. Let me give a few examples from the Qur'an.[4]

- Men are the protectors and maintainers of women, as God has given some of them an advantage over others, and because they spend out of their wealth. The good women are obedient, guarding what God would have them guard. As for those from whom you fear disloyalty, admonish them, and abandon them in their beds, then strike them. But if they obey you, seek no way against them (4:34)
- God instructs you regarding your children: The male receives the equivalent of the share of two females. (4:11)
- And call to witness two men from among you. If two men are not available, then one man and two women whose testimony is acceptable to all—if one of them fails to remember, the other would remind her. (2:282)
- As for the thief, whether male or female, cut their hands as a penalty for what they have reaped. (5:38)
- The adulteress and the adulterer—whip each one of them a hundred lashes, and let no pity towards them overcome you regarding God's Law, if you believe in God and the Last Day. And let a group of believers witness their punishment. (24:2)
- And all married women [are forbidden unto you] except those [slaves] you rightfully possess. (4:24)

The passages cited from the Qur'an, taken literally, seem to suggest that a woman has a strong duty to be obedient to her husband, that men are allowed to punish their wives when they fear that their wives may not be obedient, that the norms governing inheritance should be discriminatory against women, that women's testimony is not as worthy as men's, that there should be severe corporal punishments for theft and adultery, that slavery is permissible, and that having a sexual relation with a slave is permitted. According

---

[4] The translations are from Talal Itani.

to modern moral sensibilities, these prescriptions violate various norms of justice and fairness.

It is not only the Qur'an which contains morally counterintuitive passages. We can find morally controversial passages in Scripture of other religions. For example, the following passages are from the Bible.[5]

- Wives, submit to your own husbands as you do to the Lord. For the husband is the head of the wife as Christ is the head of the church, his body, of which he is the Savior. Now as the church submits to Christ, so also wives should submit to their husbands in everything. (Ephesians 5:22–25)
- If anyone curses his father or mother, he must be put to death. (Leviticus 20:9)
- If a man commits adultery with another man's wife—with the wife of his neighbor—both the adulterer and the adulteress must be put to death. (Leviticus 20:10)
- If a man lies with a man as one lies with a woman, both of them have done what is detestable. They must be put to death. (Leviticus 20:13)
- If, however, the charge is true and no proof of the girl's virginity can be found, she shall be brought to the door of her father's house and there the men of her town shall stone her to death. She has done a disgraceful thing in Israel by being promiscuous while still in her father's house. (Deuteronomy 22:20–21)

The passages cited from the Bible, taken literally, have morally objectionable content. Let's call Scriptural passages whose apparent meaning seems morally questionable *morally controversial passages*. Morally controversial passages can and have been used in efforts to show that either God is immoral or Scripture is not divine.[6] In other words, morally controversial passages are taken as evidence against the following claim:

Divinity of Scripture. Scripture is the words of an omnibenevolent, omniscient and omnipotent God.

---

[5] The translations of the Bible are from New International Version.
[6] E.g., Louise Anthony, "Does God Love Us," in *Divine Evil*, edited by Michael Bergman, Michael J. Murray and Michael C. Rea (New York: Oxford University Press, 2011), 29–47; Edwin Curley, "The God of Abraham, Isaac and Jacob," in Bergman, Murray, and Rea, *Divine Evil*, 58–79; Evan Fales, "Satanic Verses, Moral Chaos in Holy Writ," in Bergman, Murray, and Rea, *Divine Evil*, 91–109.

Many devout Jews, Christians, and Muslims accept the divinity of Scripture. I think it would be even harder for Muslims to deny the divinity of Scripture than it is for Jews and Christians. After all, it is widely accepted that the Bible consists of *reports* of various prophets' sayings and deeds. Orthodox Jews and Christians, of course, think that the authors of the Bible were divinely inspired. But it is at the core of Islamic belief that the Qur'an is God's direct revelation to the Prophet. The Qur'an is what God has said to the Prophet Muhammad. Therefore, denying the divinity of Scripture is not a viable option for a Muslim believer.

The counterpart of the Bible in the Islamic world might be Hadith, that is, the collection of the sayings of the Prophet Mohammad.[7] Hadith is not the direct words of God. Accordingly, one might think that there is room for error in Hadith in a way that there is not in the Qur'an. However, the received view in the Islamic tradition is that Hadith has the same status as the Qur'an. Neither can be mistaken. Muslims believe that the Prophet is infallible, at least with regard to issues pertaining to religion, and so the sayings of the Prophet with regard to religious matters cannot be mistaken.[8]

The orthodox Islamic position on the authority of Hadith (when they are found to be historically authentic) is very similar to the orthodox position of Jews and Christians on the authority of the Bible. Christians and Jews believe that while the Bible might not be the direct words of God, the authors of the Bible were divinely inspired, and thus they believe that there is no room for mistake in the Bible. Similarly, Muslims predominately believe that while the sayings of the Prophet are not directly God's words, there can't be any mistake in them. So, as long as a Hadith is authentic, that is, it accurately presents the Prophet's words, its content must be true. Of course, there is always room to question the authenticity of a particular Hadith. That is, one may deny that this reported saying of the Prophet is *in fact* a saying of the Prophet. But when it is established that this saying is such, the majority of Muslims do not allow for any possible error in terms of the *content* of the saying. Accordingly,

---

[7] According to the Shia, Hadith also includes the sayings of imams.
[8] For example, in a textbook in Islamic seminaries, entitled *The Authority of the Tradition*, we read, "On the question of the authority of the Prophet, we did not find in the books of theologians such as al-Ghazali, al-Bazdawi, al-Amidi, and those who follow their paths, including the scholars of jurisprudence, any *explicit or implicit disagreement*. Those people are the people who have studied the books of their predecessors rigorously and have examined even the minor differences thoroughly. They don't even see the need to present reasons to justify the authority of the tradition. All they do is to briefly discuss the question of infallibility before addressing the authority of the tradition." 'Abd al-Khāliq, 'Abd al-Ghanī, *The Authority of the Tradition* (حجية السنة) (Dār al-wafā', Egypt, 1993), 248.

a thesis similar to the divinity of Scripture can be formulated with regard to Hadith.

Infallibility of the Prophet. Hadiths, if authentic, are the words of an infallible morally perfect Prophet.

The infallibility of the Prophet and the divinity of Scripture are very similar. If the Prophet, as traditionally conceived, is infallible and morally perfect, there would be no difference between God's words and the Prophet's words with respect to the possibility of error. The epistemic status of the Prophet's words would be the same as that of the Qur'an. In other words, on the traditional understanding of Hadith, Hadith is part of Scripture. Scripture is divided into two parts: one part is the direct words of God, while the other part is the words of the Prophet, who is divinely inspired. The second part, thus, is the indirect words of God and enjoys the same epistemic and moral status as the first part.

There are many well-established Hadiths which seem incompatible with modern moral sensibilities. Just to give a few examples, there are many well-established Hadiths prescribing the execution of apostates and the stoning of the adulterers, adulteresses, and homosexuals.

- Allah's Messenger said, "The blood of a Muslim who confesses that none has the right to be worshipped but Allah and that I am His Apostle, cannot be shed except in three cases: In Qisas [i.e., retaliation] for murder, a married person who commits illegal sexual intercourse and the one who reverts from Islam (apostate) and leaves the Muslims." (*Sahih al-Bukhari*, vol. 9, book 83, Hadith 17). (Similar Hadiths can be found in *Sahih al-Bukhari* 4:52:260, 9:84:57, 9:89:271, 9:84:58, 9:84:64.)[9]
- A man from Bani Aslam came to Allah's Messenger while he was in the mosque and called [the Prophet] saying, "O Allah's Messenger! I have committed illegal sexual intercourse." On that the Prophet turned his face from him to the other side, whereupon the man moved to the side towards which the Prophet had turned his face, and said, "O Allah's Messenger! I have committed illegal sexual intercourse." The Prophet turned his face (from him) to the other side whereupon the man moved to the side towards which the Prophet had turned his face, and repeated

---

[9] The translations are from Dr. M. Muhsin Khan.

his statement. The Prophet turned his face (from him) to the other side again. The man moved again (and repeated his statement) for the fourth time. So when the man had given witness four times against himself, the Prophet called him and said, "Are you insane?" He replied, "No." The Prophet then said (to his companions), "Go and stone him to death." The man was a married one. Jabir bin `Abdullah Al-Ansari said: I was one of those who stoned him. We stoned him at the Musalla in Medina. When the stones hit him with their sharp edges, he fled, but we caught him at Al-Harra and stoned him till he died. (*Sahih al-Bukhari* 7:63: 196) (Similar Hadiths can be found in *Sahih al-Bukhari* 2:23:413, 3:34–421, 3:49:860, 3:50:885, 4:56:829, 6:60:79, 7:63:195.)

- If a man who is not married is seized committing sodomy, he will be stoned to death. (*Sunan Abi Dawud*, book 39, Hadith 4448)

According to our modern moral sensibilities, these Hadiths are morally counterintuitive. Of course, with respect to any reported Hadith, including the ones I mentioned, there is always room to deny their authenticity. That is, one might say that they do not report accurately what the Prophet has *in fact* said. However, some morally controversial Hadiths like the ones mentioned here are very well established. They are mentioned in all major books of Hadith and have been accepted by the Muslim community for centuries. It is hard to deny their authenticity based on historical records.

If Islamic Scripture includes Hadith, as the Islamic community predominantly holds, the number of morally controversial passages increases tremendously. However, to address the main problem of the book, I don't need even to assume the orthodox view that Islamic Scripture includes Hadith. The problem arises as long as we accept that there are some morally controversial passages in Scripture, be it the Qur'an, the Bible, or Hadith.

3. Seeming Prescribed Evil

The existence of morally controversial passages may generate a problem for the divinity of Scripture. What makes morally controversial passages problematic for the divinity of Scripture is that they seem to prescribe actions that a perfect God would not prescribe. These passages, taken in their apparent meaning, prescribe actions which are immoral according to our modern independent moral judgments. By *our independent moral judgments*, I mean *moral judgments obtained through careful a priori moral reflections and sufficient empirical observations, independent of Scripture*. The following are some examples of the independent moral judgments that we make in modern times:

> A woman does not have a strong duty to be obedient to her husband.
> Men are not allowed to beat their wives.
> The norms governing inheritance should not discriminate against women.
> Discrimination against women and sexual minorities is always wrong.
> Women's testimony is as trustworthy as men's.
> There should never be corporal punishments for theft and adultery.
> Slavery is never permissible.
> Apostates should never be killed because of their unbelief.

Surely we might say if God is perfectly just, He should not prescribe or permit immoral actions. God's perfect nature is in tension with what we may call *seemingly prescribed evil by Scripture*. Let's define "seemingly prescribed evil" as follows:

> *Seemingly Prescribed Evil* describes *by definition* an action prescribed or permitted by the best interpretation of a Scriptural passage which seems immoral, according to our independent moral judgments.

Note that the definition of seemingly prescribed evil is broad enough to include not only seemingly immoral acts prescribed by the best interpretation of Scriptural passage, but also seemingly immoral acts that are deemed *permissible* by Scripture. The morally controversial passages cited in the last section, when taken in their apparent meaning, seem to prescribe or permit actions which are immoral according to our independent moral judgments.

The existence of *some* seemingly prescribed evil is sufficient to generate the new problem of evil which I am concerned with in the book. While the classical problem of evil involves the conflict between a perfect God and immoral events in the world, the new problem of evil arises from a conflict between the divinity of Scripture and seemingly prescribed evil. That is, if God is just and the Scripture is God's words, He should not prescribe or permit evil actions. If so, seemingly prescribed evil is evidence against either God or the divinity of Scripture (I will explain the problem more carefully in the next section). As Plantinga explains in the following, the theist could respond to this problem in two different ways:

> There are fundamentally two ways to respond to this difficulty. First, take the passages at face value: God did issue these commands, and had good reason to do so. And second, take it that God did not in fact issue those commands. The first is perhaps the majority Christian response.[10]

There are problems with both of Plantinga's ways of dealing with the problem. His first way to resist the problem is to insist that seemingly prescribed evil is in fact consistent with the divinity of Scripture. I will come back to this possibility in the next section. The second way to respond to the problem is to deny the existence of seemingly prescribed evil, that is, to say that *no* Scriptural passage, when interpreted correctly, prescribes actions that are immoral according to our independent moral judgments. The theist might hold that the best interpretation of morally controversial passages is not their apparent meaning, since the interpretation of an ancient text, the context of which is radically different from our own, is difficult. Eleonore Stump explains the difficulty as follows:

> Even a carefully supported interpretation of narratives is, in effect, only a recommendation to look at a text in a certain way. It invites readers to consider that text and ask themselves whether after all they do not see the text in the way the interpretation recommends. Interpretations present, suggest, offer, and invite; unlike philosophical arguments, they cannot attempt to compel.... These remarks apply to narrative texts in our own culture and language, but they are especially pertinent when the narratives in question are written in a language very different from our own and stem from a culture very different from our own.[11]

There is a long debate as to whether there are sufficient textual reasons to deny the literal interpretation of morally controversial passages. The opponents of the divinity of Scripture hold that some of those passages are very clear and unambiguous, and that there are no adequate textual reasons to depart from

---

[10] Alvin Plantinga, "Comments on 'Satanic Verses, Moral Chaos in Holy Writ,'" in Bergman, Murray, and Rea, *Divine Evil*, 111.

[11] Eleonore Stump, "Comments on 'Does God Love Us,'" in Bergman, Murray, and Rea, *Divine Evil*, 49–50.

the literal meaning of the text. This response is even more plausible in the case of passages with moral injunctions, as those passages have very clear and specific content. This is evidenced by the fact that the dominant contemporary views in Islamic jurisprudence (including the Sunni schools of law and the Imāmiyya—Shia—school) regarding many of the morally controversial passages are in line with the literal reading of the passages. In other words, throughout centuries, those passages are understood by scholars with their literal meaning. Just to give an example, the dominant view regarding the penalty for adultery is that it should be severe (it is either one hundred stripes or stoning, depending on the case). The difference among the various schools of law concerns what constitutes adultery, what are the epistemic criteria to establish its occurrence, who has the authority to execute the penalty, and perhaps whether stoning is textually justified. But there is virtually *no* disagreement among different schools of Islamic jurisprudence about the core belief that adultery should be severely and corporally punished. The same holds for the penalties for theft and homosexuality, and for differential treatment of men and women in various subjects.

In modern times, however, some Islamic scholars (who could be categorized as *modern Islamic reformers*) have attempted to *deny* the existence of seemingly prescribed evil. They deny that there is *any* action prescribed or permitted by the best interpretation of a Scriptural passage which seems immoral, according to our independent moral judgments. In what follows, I will discuss two general strategies, that is, reinterpretation and contextualization, used to deny the existence of seemingly prescribed evil, and explain why these strategies do not look promising.[12]

Reinterpretation

According to the reinterpretation view, exegetical considerations and *linguistic reasoning* can help us see that the correct interpretation of morally controversial passages is in fact *consistent* with our independent moral judgments. Amina Wadud and Asma Barlas are two modern Islamic scholars whose project is to show that the Qur'anic passages, when understood correctly, are consistent with our independent moral judgments with regard

---

[12] I am indebted to Fatema Amijee for the presentation of these two views in her excellent paper "How to Be a Feminist Muslim," *Journal of the American Philosophical Association* 9.2 (2023): 193–213, https://doi.org/10.1017/apa.2022.9.

to the relation between men and women. To this aim, they sometimes use linguistic reasoning and sometimes employ the contextualization method. I will use some of their discussions to demonstrate how linguistic reinterpretation is supposed to work.

The Qur'an (4:34) seems to imply that men are in charge of the affairs of women, that wives have a strong duty to be obedient to their husbands, and that husbands can punish wives by beating them when they think that their wives are rebellious. Wadud argues that this prescription is mainly limited to family affairs and is consistent with our independent moral judgments:

> For obvious biological reasons, a primary responsibility for the woman is child-bearing ... [W]hile this responsibility is so obvious and important, what is the responsibility of the male in this family and society at large? The Qur'an establishes his responsibility as *qiwamah* [i.e., in charge of / managers]: seeing to it that the woman is not burdened with additional responsibilities which jeopardize that primary demanding responsibility that only she can fulfill. Ideally, everything she needs to fulfill her primary responsibility comfortably should be supplied in society, by the male: this means physical protection as well as material sustenance. Otherwise, it would be a serious oppression against the woman.[13]

With regard to the issue of women's duty of obedience and men's permission to beat their wives who, they fear, are rebellious, she says:

> The word *qanitat* used here to describe "good" women, is too often falsely translated to mean "obedient," and then assumed to mean "obedient to the husband." In the context of the whole Qur'an, this word is used with regard to both males (2:238, 3:17, 33:35) and females (4:34, 33:34, 66:5, 66:12). It describes a characteristic or personality trait of believers towards Allah. They are inclined towards being co-operative with one another and subservient before Allah.... As for those (feminine plural) from whom you fear *nushuz* ..., it should first be noted that the word *nushuz* likewise is used with both males (4:128) and females (4:34), although it has been defined differently for each. When applied to the wife, the term is usually defined as "disobedience to the husband." Others have said this verse indicates that

---

[13] Amina Wadud, *Qur'an and Woman: Rereading the Sacred Text from a Woman's Perspective* (Oxford: Oxford University Press, 1999), 72.

the wife must obey the husband.... However, since the Qur'an uses *nushuz* for both the male and the female, it cannot mean "disobedience to the husband." Sayyid Qutb explains it as a state of disorder between the married couple. In case of disorder, what suggestions does the Qur'an give as possible solutions? There is 1. A verbal solution.... If open discussion fails, then a more drastic solution: 2. Separation is indicated. Only in extreme cases a final measure: 3. The "scourge" is permitted.[14]

As we can see, Wadud seeks linguistic reasons to weaken the counterintuitive implication of the Qur'anic passage. One immediate worry that I shall come back to is that Wadud's exegesis is in contrast with the traditional understanding of the passage assumed throughout centuries. Another important problem is that although Wadud claims that the weakened implications are consistent with our independent moral judgments, they are clearly not. For example, regarding whether or not men should be in charge, Wadud assumes that it is appropriate to assign the role of child-raising to women, and that the Qur'anic passage determines the role of males to be materially supporting women to fulfill their primary responsibility. However, many feminists argue that justice in family and society requires a weakening of traditional ideas about gender. Various studies have shown that the traditional assignment of role in the family leads to an unjust division of domestic labor, unjust division of labor in society, the lack of access of women to high-paid jobs, an increase in domestic violence, and insecurity for women.[15]

The issue of men's permission to beat their wives also remains unsolved in Wadud's exegetical remarks. She says that "only in extreme cases ... the 'scourge' is permitted." While it is not clear what Wadud's linguistic justification is to limit the application of the passage to "only extreme cases," a permission to beat women even in extreme cases goes against our moral judgments. To make the passage more in line with our moral judgments, Barlas, following some commentators, suggests that *daraba* (i.e., to strike) can be translated as "holding in confinement" in certain legal contexts.[16] But the permission to hold one's wife in confinement, when one fears that there is "a state of disorder," is still morally counterintuitive. With regard to this

---

[14] Wadud, *Qur'an and Woman*, 74–75.

[15] See Susan Moller Okin, *Justice, Gender, and the Family* (New York: Basic Books, 1989). See also Claudia Geist, "The Welfare State and the Home: Regime Differences in the Domestic Division of Labour," *European Sociological Review* 21.1 (2005): 23–41.

[16] Asma Barlas, *"Believing Women" in Islam: Unreading Patriarchal Interpretations of the Qur'an* (Austin: University of Texas Press, 2002), 189.

passage, then, the exegetical effort to depart from the literal meaning and to make the passage morally palatable might not be entirely successful, and so we might still think the passage provides us good reasons to believe that there is some seemingly prescribed evil.

Regarding testimonial injustice, Barlas says that the Qur'an 2:282 does not give us a permission to discount the value of women's testimony across the board:

> There are a total of five cases of evidence giving in the Qur'an, and in only one does it make the provision about two women, for very specific social reasons. Had this been an across-the-board formula in the Qur'an, it would not have attached greater weight to a wife's evidence than to the husband's in the far more consequential matter of adultery.[17]

On the question of discrimination against women in inheritance, Wadud writes:

> Qur'anic statement, in verses 4:11–12, makes "the share of the male . . . equivalent to the portion of two female (siblings)," [yet] a complete look at this same verse enumerates a variety of proportional divisions between males and females. In fact, if there is one female child, her share is half the inheritance. In addition, the consideration of parents, siblings, distant relatives, as well as offspring is discussed in a variety of different combinations to indicate that the proportion for the female of one-half the proportion for the male is not the sole mode of property division, but one of several proportional arrangements possible.[18]

I worry that those exegetical remarks are often not sufficient to make morally controversial passages consistent with our independent moral judgments. Concerning testimonial injustice, even if Barlas is right that there is no across-the-board formula in the Qur'an to discount the value of women's testimony, the mere fact that in some cases, such as in the case of financial matters as suggested in 2:282, women's testimony is not considered to be as worthy as men's makes it the case that the Scriptural passage seems to permit an unjust act (according to our independent moral judgments) and is sufficient for us

---

[17] Barlas, *"Believing Women" in Islam*, 190.
[18] Wadud, *Qur'an and Woman*, 87.

to believe in the existence of seemingly prescribed evil. Regarding the question of inheritance, the problem is that, even if Wadud is right that the Qur'an approves of a variety of different modes of property division, the fact that the passage also holds that the sexist mode of property division is "one of several *proportional* arrangements possible" creates a tension between the passage and our independent moral judgments.

Wadud and Barlas do not discuss corporal punishment for theft and adultery. However, the general strategy of Islamic scholars to reconcile the Qur'anic passages with our independent moral reasoning is to minimize the cases in which corporal punishment is allowed. For example, regarding 5:38, Ramon Harvey writes:

> Jurists have discussed the conditions required for a person to be considered a sāriq (thief) in the legal sense. They generally act to circumscribe the concept to the minimum number of possible offenders by requiring the stolen item to have been guarded and specifying a minimum value for it, treating these as ambiguous (mujmal) aspects requiring further explanation (bayān). Abū Zahra provides an alternative to the classical view by arguing that the fact that the verse mentions "the thief" is an indication that the punishment is only to be applied to the repeat offender who truly deserves this epithet.[19]

The same strategy is also employed in the case of adultery. Modern scholars usually seek to minimize the cases in which corporal punishment is appropriate by, among other things, raising the bar for establishing that adultery has happened. Yet the problem is that a permission for the use of corporal punishment for theft and adultery even in exceptional cases goes against our independent moral judgments.

While the recent attempts to reinterpret Scripture to make it in line with our independent moral judgments are not entirely successful, there are *three general reasons* to think that the reinterpretation view *in principle* cannot work, or at least is inadequate.

First, our moral judgments evolve over time. Our moral consciousness has broadened through the years. We make moral progress, refining our moral judgments and discovering instances of injustice to which we were blind before. If we look at human history, many moral judgments that seem

---

[19] Ramon Harvey, *Qur'an and the Just Society* (Edinburgh: Edinburgh University Press, 2018), 184.

obviously true today were not considered so a hundred years ago. It might be the case that at some point in history, maybe at the time of revelation, our moral judgments *did* accord with our understanding of Scripture. Our moral judgments, however, have changed enormously in the last thousand years, and so it is inevitable that *some* of our moral judgments today will differ from the judgments assumed in Scripture. The discrepancy between our moral judgments today and canonical historical texts is not even peculiar to religious Scripture. Commenting on the US Constitution, especially the so-called "three-fifths compromise," Noam Chomsky says:

> There is a definite broadening of our moral consciousness over the ages. Things that were considered entirely legitimate two hundred years ago are considered Nazi-like today. For example, if some Third World country were to produce something like the US Constitution, which was a revolutionary and highly libertarian document at the time, we would call it a reversion of Nazism.[20]

While our moral judgments change, the text does not. There are various linguistic, syntactic, and semantic constraints that limit our interpretation of an existing text. We are not at liberty to interpret a text in any way we like. Given the stark discrepancy between Scripture and our moral judgments today, it requires a *radical* reinterpretation of Scripture to make it consistent with our moral judgments. It would be too optimistic to think that we could engage in a radical reinterpretation of the text without straying from a faithful reading of the text. I have provided a couple of examples of morally controversial passages, and reviewed some recent attempts to reinterpret those passages. We noted that those attempts could not remove *all* moral objections to the passages. Modern scholars have too many linguistic constraints to be able to reinterpret the passages in a way that it resists all contemporary moral objections to them. They can mitigate the moral objections, but they can't remove them altogether.

Second, as our moral judgments evolve over time, the problem of divinely prescribed evil is bound to arise, if not today, tomorrow. If one holds that exegetical reinterpretation can show that there is *no* seemingly prescribed evil today *or ever*, one holds that at *any given time* in human history one can

---

[20] "Moral Consciousness | Noam Chomsky," https://www.youtube.com/watch?v=JJucBx7ZF5M, accessed August 3, 2023.

reinterpret Scripture to make it consistent with moral judgments *of that time*. But if we think that we have always the power to reinterpret Scripture in a way that makes it consistent with our moral judgments at any given time, we should think that Scripture has no determinate meaning; the meaning of the text is *underdetermined*. But this makes Scripture morally and religiously unimportant. Moreover, it is just not true that Scripture has no meaning of its own and is so malleable that could take any form we want.

Third, bringing Scripture in line with our contemporary moral judgments requires a *radical departure* from the apparent meaning of the text and from the way that the text has been understood throughout centuries.[21] There are two different reasons *not* to take morally controversial passages at face value:

> *Textual Justification.* There are textual reasons (e.g., ambiguity, contextual elements) to interpret morally controversial passages nonliterally.
> *Moral Justification.* There are moral reasons to interpret morally controversial passages nonliterally, as the literal understanding of the passages is inconsistent with a morally perfect God.

---

[21] To give just one example of the traditional understanding of the Qur'an, the following is Ibn Kathir's exegesis of Qur'an 4:34. *Tafsir* (i.e., Qur'anic exegesis) by Ibn Kathir is considered among the best commentaries on the Qur'an by the Muslim community (translated into English by a group of scholars under the supervision of Sheikh Safiur-Rahman Al-Mubarakpuri). As we can see, Ibn Kathir's understanding is very close to the apparent meaning of the passage. The same goes for other controversial passages. "Men are the protectors and maintainers of women," meaning, the man is responsible for the woman, and he is her maintainer, caretaker, and leader who disciplines her if she deviates; "because Allah has made one of them to excel the other," meaning, because men excel over women and are better than they for certain tasks. This is why prophethood, as well as other important positions of leadership, was exclusive to men. The Prophet said, "People who appoint a woman to be their leader, will never achieve success." "As to those women on whose part you see ill conduct," meaning, the woman from whom you see ill conduct with her husband, such as when she acts as if she is above her husband, disobeys him, ignores him, dislikes him, and so forth. When these signs appear in a woman, her husband should advise her and remind her of Allah's torment if she disobeys him. Indeed, Allah ordered the wife to obey her husband and prohibited her from disobeying him, because of the enormity of his rights and all that he does for her. Al-Bukhari recorded that Abu Hurayrah said that the Messenger of Allah said, "If the man asks his wife to come to his bed and she declines, the angels will keep cursing her until the morning." "As to those women on whose part you see ill conduct, admonish them (first)." With regard to Allah's statement, "Abandon them in their beds," `Ali bin Abi Talhah reported that Ibn `Abbas said, "The abandonment refers to not having intercourse with her, to lie on her bed with his back to her." Several others said similarly that Allah's statement, "Beat them" means, if advice and ignoring her in bed do not produce the desired results, you are allowed to discipline the wife, without severe beating. Muslim recorded that Jabir said that during the Farewell Hajj, the Prophet said: "Fear Allah regarding women, for they are your assistants. You have the right on them that they do not allow any person whom you dislike to step on your mat. However, if they do that, you are allowed to discipline them lightly. They have a right on you that you provide them with their provision and clothes, in a reasonable manner." Ibn `Abbas and several others said that the Ayah refers to a beating that is not violent. Al-Hasan Al-Basri said that it means a beating that is not severe.

The radical departure from the traditional understanding of the text cannot be authorized by textual reasons alone. The traditional scholars of Scripture were not ignorant about what the text apparently means and what the linguistic rules are. The reinterpretation view, if successful at all, can suggest a new *possibility* for understanding the text. But to vindicate this possible reading as the *correct* reading of the text we need to appeal to Moral Justification. But, then, one might ask why we should take our contemporary moral judgments for granted. Why can't Scripture guide us about what is morally correct? The reinterpretation view often takes our contemporary moral judgments for granted without providing an argument to justify this assumption.[22] I will argue in the first part of the book that there are powerful arguments to the effect that Scripture should inform the correct understanding of morality, and not the other way around. Therefore, the reinterpretation strategy cannot succeed unless it provides a principled argument to explain why Moral Justification is correct.

Contextualization

According to the contextualization view, to understand a Scriptural passage, especially a morally controversial one, we have to consider the historical context of the passage, which includes the values and practices of the people to whom Scripture is revealed. The contextualization view holds that when we take into account the context of Scripture, we can see that the following claims are true:

(C1) The conduct prescribed by the Qur'an is in general an improvement in the practices that were culturally dominant at the time.

---

[22] In "How to Be a Feminist Muslim," Amijee rejects the reinterpretation view on the grounds that it is theologically undesirable for our understanding of Scripture to be influenced by our independent moral thinking. I agree that one can't just *assume* that our independent moral judgments are correct, and we will see in Part I of the book that many Islamic thinkers hold that our moral judgments need to follow Scripture. However, if my arguments in Part II of the book can establish that our independent moral judgments are reliable, I don't find the attempt to make God's words compatible with our independent moral judgments in principle *theologically* undesirable (I will come back to this issue in the last chapter of the book). As I explained, the problem with such an attempt is that (1) it is doubtful that it can succeed, (2) given the constant change in our moral judgments, it might deprive Scripture from having any content, and (3) it presupposes the validity of our independent moral thinking without providing any justification for it.

(C2) Given the vast difference between our culture and that of Scripture, the conduct prescribed in morally controversial passages applies only to people within the culture of Scripture.

Barlas explains (C1) in the following way:

> We can only address these types of issues if . . . we . . . keep in mind the historical context of its revelation in a seventh-century (Arab) tribal patriarchy (much like the Taliban in Afghanistan today). Contextualizing the Qur'an's teachings (i.e., explaining them with reference to the immediate audience and social conditions to which they were addressed), shows that, far from being oppressive, they were profoundly egalitarian.[23]

Barlas also approvingly quotes Wadud to state the second claim:

> The mere fact that the Qur'an was revealed in seventh-century Arabia when the Arabs held certain perceptions and misconceptions about women and were involved in certain specific lewd practices against them resulted in some injunctions specific to that culture.[24]

We might apply this strategy to all controversial passages cited in section 2. For example, we can apply it to the wife-beating passage (4:34). Wadud says that "in the light of the excessive violence towards women indicated in the biographies of the Companions and by practices condemned in the Qur'an (like female infanticide), this verse should be taken as prohibiting unchecked violence against females. Thus, this is not permission, but a severe restriction of existing practices."[25] The main idea is that the Qur'anic passage functions to restrict (and thus makes an improvement in) the existing practice of unchecked violence against women. Barlas makes a similar claim:

> We also can deduce that the Qur'an uses *daraba* [i.e., to strike] in a restrictive rather than in a prescriptive sense by examining the historical context of this teaching. At a time when men did not need permission to abuse

---

[23] Barlas, *"Believing Women" in Islam*, 6.
[24] Wadud, *Qur'an and Woman*, 9.
[25] Wadud, *Qur'an and Woman*, 74–75.

women, this Ayah [i.e., verse] simply could not have functioned as a license; in such a context, it could only have been a restriction insofar as the Qur'an made *daraba* the measure of last, not the first, or even the second, resort. And if the Qur'an meant to restrict abuse even during those most abusive of times, there is no reason to regard this Ayah as an authorization at a time when we claim to have become more, not less, civilized.[26]

Barlas, then, claims that the Qur'anic passage does not give permission to men in our time to beat their wives. The permission described in the verse is only limited to a specific time and culture. I am sympathetic with both of the claims made by the contextualization view. But the question is whether the contextualization view can show that there is no seemingly prescribed evil, and the answer is no. It is important to know that (C1) and (C2) do not entail that there is no seemingly prescribed evil. While it might be the case that permission to beat one's wife only as a last resort was substantial progress on the practice of abusing women by men, this does not imply that the act of beating one's wife was justified back then. To show that there is no prescribed evil, the contextualization view needs to show that the action prescribed by Scripture is *justified*, not that it is better than some very worse alternatives.

It is true that an action might be justified in one circumstance, but not in another. There can be cases where the contextualization of an action shows that the action was *justified in the context of its occurrence*. For example, it may be okay to kill a person in self-defense, but it is not okay to kill a person to protect one's shoes. The contextualization view sometimes seems to claim that actions which can be described as seemingly prescribed evil *were not evil in the context in which Scripture is revealed*. For example, regarding the case of testimonial injustice, Wadud says:

> Considering that women could be coerced in that society, if one witness was female, she would be easy prey for some male who wanted to force her to disclaim her testimony. When there are two women, they can support each other—especially in view of the term chosen: if she (*tudilla*) "goes astray," the other can (*tudhakkira*) "remind" her, or "recall her attention" to the terms of agreement.[27]

---

[26] Barlas, *"Believing Women" in Islam*, 188.
[27] Wadud, *Qur'an and Woman*, 86.

The claim here is that in a society in which women could be coerced to testify, the requirement of having two females to witness is not unjust. While this justification has some merit, one might think that this justification is not sufficient to remove the charge of imposing epistemic injustice to women by this requirement. After all, enforcing this rule makes it the case that a sole woman has less chance of being heard in society.

The claim that, according to our independent moral judgments, *all* instances of seemingly prescribed evil were justified in the context of Scripture is independent of (C1) and (C2) and does not follow from them. While it might be true that our independent moral judgments deem *some* instances of seemingly prescribed evil as justified in the context of Scripture, it is unlikely that the contextualization view can show that *all* instances of seemingly prescribed evil should be deemed justified in the context of Scripture by our independent moral judgments. For example, we hold that one may not beat one's wife even in a society in which violence against women is dominant. One should not beat one's wife, *period*. It is morally wrong to beat one's wife at any time or in any culture. Similarly, we might think that treating women unfairly (regarding inheritance or testimony) is *always* wrong, that severe corporal punishment for theft or adultery is *always* wrong, and that holding slaves has *always* been wrong, and so on. If we hold to these moral judgments, it is unlikely that we can deem all instances of seemingly prescribed evil to be morally justified in the context of their prescription.

Similar to the reinterpretation view, the contextualization view, through endorsing (C2), seek to make morally controversial passages morally more palatable by weakening their implications. It blocks the generalization of the moral rule prescribed by the passage by indexing it to a particular time and culture. In the last chapter of the book, I will explain that there is a grain of truth in the contextualization view. However, as a strategy to deny the existence of seemingly prescribed evil, the contextualization view cannot work as long as we hold to moral judgments such as the prohibition of beating one's wife in all times and cultures. On this view, the best interpretation of morally controversial passages in Scripture will still be regarded as prescribing or permitting actions which seem immoral to our contemporary moral judgments. It would just show that the prescription or permission was restricted to a certain audience.

There is also another important worry for the contextualization view. In fact, the third worry for the reinterpretation view applies to the contextualization view. The traditional view regarding morally controversial passages is not to restrict them to a specific time and culture. According to the traditional view, all Scriptural injunctions are universal injunctions valid for all times and cultures. As we have seen, textual reasons by itself does not justify a rejection of the traditional view, and the motivation behind the contextualization view is Moral Justification. The contextualization view assumes that we have moral reasons to remove the tension between morally controversial passages and our independent moral judgments. However, we might ask, again, why our contemporary moral judgments should guide our interpretation of Scripture and its implications, and not the other way around. Why should we take Moral Justification for granted? Similar to the reinterpretation view, the contextualization view needs to defend Moral Justification.

In sum, for the reinterpretation view and the contextualization view to be preferable to the traditional view, we need to show that Moral Justification is correct, but as we will see in Part I of the book, this is not an easy job. Moreover, it looks like the reinterpretation view and the contextualization view fail to show that there is no seemingly prescribed evil. The problem of divinely prescribed evil arises if there is at least *one* instance of seemingly prescribed evil. There are many morally controversial passages in the Qur'an and the Bible. There are a great number of morally controversial passages in Hadith. I don't need to claim that the reinterpretation view or the contextualization view works for no controversial passage; as long as there is at least *one* passage in Scripture whose best interpretation goes against our moral judgment, we face the problem of divinely prescribed evil. Finally, based on the limited degree of freedom in interpretation and the substantial change in our moral judgments over a thousand years, I have presented a general argument to the effect that it is very unlikely that all seemingly prescribed evil can be explained away.

I will assume henceforth that there are some seemingly prescribed evils; that is, there are some actions permitted or prescribed by the best interpretation of a Scriptural passage which our independent moral judgments deem immoral. For the sake of simplicity, I will use wife-beating (as it seems to be prescribed by the Qur'an 4:34) as my central example of a seemingly prescribed evil.[28] If it turns out that there are sufficient textual reasons for

---

[28] This example has the advantage of having a biblical counterpart. Ephesians (5:22–25) says wives should submit to their husbands in everything.

a successful exegetical reinterpretation of this particular verse, all my arguments can apply to other examples of seemingly prescribed evil for which we don't have appropriate exegesis.

4. The New Problem of Evil and the Structure of the Book

The new problem of evil that I address in the book consists of the fact that there is a tension between the following three theses:

Divinity of Scripture. Scripture is the words of an omnibenevolent, omniscient, and omnipotent God.
Existence of Seemingly Prescribed Evil. There are some actions prescribed or permitted by the best interpretation of a Scriptural passage which seem immoral, according to our independent moral judgments.
Reliability of Our Independent Moral Judgments. Our independent moral judgments reliably represent moral values, moral duties, and moral permissions.

We can call this problem *the problem of Scriptural evil*, or *the problem of divinely prescribed evil* (or for short, *the problem of prescribed evil*).

While believers want to maintain *the divinity of Scripture*, they should find the other two theses very plausible too. I have argued for *the existence of seemingly prescribed evil* in the last section. Regarding *the reliability of our independent moral judgments*, think about our independent moral judgments that I mentioned in the last section: our judgments about the wrongness of violence against women, the wrongness of sexism and slavery, the wrongness of corporal punishment, the wrongness of discrimination against religious and sexual minorities, and so on. These judgments look true to us. We live by these moral judgments, and we are very confident that they are true. However, there is a tension between those three theses.

Although the divinity of Scripture is consistent with the existence of seemingly prescribed evil, their conjunction is in tension with the reliability of our independent moral judgments. To see the tension, suppose a believer takes the divinity of Scripture to be true. Let's also suppose that the person believes that there is some seemingly prescribed evil. Given belief in the divinity of Scripture, the person should believe that God wouldn't permit or prescribe conducts that are in fact immoral, and thus that seemingly prescribed evil is not really evil. It merely looks evil. If our independent moral judgments deem an action prescribed by Scripture to be evil, it is because our independent moral judgments are not correct. On the other hand, if a believer accepts the reliability of our independent moral judgments, and the existence of seemingly prescribed evil, then that person should believe that some seemingly prescribed evil is really evil, and thus that Scripture prescribes evil. This would undermine belief in the divinity of Scripture.

We can in fact compare the problem of divinely prescribed evil to the classical problem of evil. The existence of seemingly prescribed evil is similar to the existence of seemingly pointless evil. The theist responds to the classical problem of evil by maintaining that God works in mysterious ways. For theists, natural evil is not evidence for God's inexistence because God has sufficient reasons to allow evil to occur in the world. We cannot judge God's acts with our limited intellect. The believer might want to say the same for the problem of prescribed evil. We may not, the believer would say, judge Scripture by our limited intellect. A seemingly prescribed evil such as beating one's wife or discrimination against women *looks* morally objectionable, given our limited knowledge of the moral realm. Yet we are never in a position to *justifiably believe* whether these actions are in fact wrong, *everything considered*. We can't justifiably believe that seemingly prescribed evil is in fact evil because the reliability of our independent moral judgments cannot be taken for granted. In fact, many contemporary Islamic, Christian, and Jew conservatives actually hold this position and behave accordingly. They believe that Scripture can reveal to us a morality hidden from our reason, a morality possibly quite different from our modern moral judgments.

The new problem of evil, that is, the problem of divinely prescribed evil, is more difficult for a theist to overcome than the classical problem of evil at least in three ways. First, the classical problem of evil can be resolved by denying that pointless evil exists. The theist can deny the existence of *pointless* evil by saying that we cannot know about God's reasons, and that He may in fact have sufficient reasons to allow evil to occur in the world. As I will explain in Chapter 2, holding a skeptical view about our knowledge of God's reasoning does not lead to skepticism about our everyday morality. However, if theists want to solve the problem of divinely prescribed evil *in just the same way*, they should deny the reliability of our independent moral judgments, which entails skepticism about modern moral beliefs (including beliefs about the wrongness of slavery, discrimination against women and sexual minorities, corporal punishment, etc.); it is a price that theists don't have to pay if they only care about solving the classical problem of evil. Second, the problem of prescribed evil creates a difficulty for the theist's solution to the classical problem of evil. The theist's solution to this problem on its own might not have any implication for everyday morality, but when combined with Scripture's divinity and the existence of seemingly prescribed evil, it would. For, as I will explain in Part I, the theist's solution to the classical problem of evil seems to entail that Moral Justification (defined in the previous section) is false. But, as we will see, if Moral Justification is false, then it will be very hard for the theist to defend our modern moral beliefs. Third, while there is a large literature on the classical problem of evil, the problem of prescribed evil is underexplored. Even philosophers who have addressed the problem have taken the reliability of our independent moral judgments for granted.[29] While conservative theists frequently invoke hidden moral facts to question some of our modern moral intuitions, this skeptical argument has received little philosophical study.

The problem of prescribed evil can be approached in two ways. There are also two parts in this book, "Scripture First" and "Ethics First," each dealing with the problem in one of these two ways (see table 1 for a very brief description of the structure of the book). The first part of the book deals with the position of Islamic scholars who hold that when forming moral judgments, Scripture takes priority over our moral reason. Scripture comes first. Scripture, taken at face value, has the power of defeating our independent moral judgments. Let's call this *the Scripture-first view*. According to the Scripture-first view, we can solve the problem of prescribed evil by denying the reliability of our independent moral judgments. Part I shows that the Scripture-first view is the *dominant view* in the history of Islamic philosophy, which has been held and argued for from the early days of Islam until today.

Part I consists of three chapters. In each chapter, I explore arguments for rejecting the reliability of our independent moral judgments when they are in conflict with Scriptural injunctions. These arguments are offered by three major schools of Islamic philosophy that is, the Ashʿarites (Chapter 1), the Muʿtazilites (Chapter 2), and the Greek-influenced philosophers, *falāsifa* (Chapter 3). Each chapter also explains the normative moral theory endorsed by each Islamic school as well as the moral epistemology implied by that theory. I will argue that each of school's moral theories corresponds roughly to one of the three major theories in contemporary moral philosophy, that

---

[29] See, for instance, Alvin Plantinga, "Comments on 'Satanic Verses.'" The same assumption is present in other essays of this anthology.

Table 1 The structure of the book

	Prologue	Defines the problem of prescribed evil as a tension between three theses: *the divinity of Scripture, the existence of seemingly prescribed evil,* and *the reliability of our independent moral judgments.* The prologue also explains why there are some seemingly prescribed evils despite some recent attempts to deny them.
Part I: Scripture First	Chapter 1	Explains how one can deny the reliability of our independent moral judgments by appealing to consequentialism. The argument against the reliability of our independent moral judgments is called *the argument for strict adherence.*
	Chapter 2	Explains how one might reconstruct the argument for strict adherence without appealing to consequentialism. This presents a final case for denying the reliability of our independent moral judgments.
	Chapter 3	Explains how Islamic philosophers reject the reliability of our independent moral judgments through their intellectualized epistemology and theological virtue ethics.
Part II: Ethics First	Chapter 4	Explains how one might withhold judgment regarding the reliability of our independent moral judgments while simultaneously maintaining that our independent moral judgments are *rationally* binding. This presents an ethics-first solution to the problem of prescribed evil.
	Chapter 5	Explores various ways to defend the reliability of our independent moral judgments against hidden moral facts.
	Chapter 6	Explains how we can make the three main theses consistent through adopting a legal interpretation of Scriptural injunctions. The chapter also gives an account of the moral function of Scripture.

is, consequentialism, deontological ethics, and virtue ethics. Chapter 1, then, explains how one can deny the reliability of our independent moral judgments by appealing to consequentialism. I will call the argument for rejecting the reliability of our moral judgments in favor of accepting Scriptural injunctions at face value *the argument for strict adherence.* I will argue that this argument, as formulated in accordance with the ideas of the Ashʿarite theologian al-Ghazālī, has certain problems.

On the basis of the moral theory of the Muʿtazilites, Chapter 2 explains how we one might reconstruct the argument for strict adherence without appealing to consequentialism. This presents a final case for denying the reliability of our independent moral judgments. *Chapter 3* explains how Islamic philosophers dismiss our independent moral judgments through their theological virtue ethics.

It is hard for conscientious modern Muslims to question the reliability of their own independent moral judgments (about slavery, sexism, discrimination against minorities, fairness, etc.). In fact, it is part of the identity of progressive Muslims to maintain their independent moral judgments. But the conclusion of Part I is that we can't simply assume the reliability of our independent moral judgments (despite the fact that many philosophers of religion simply do so). The reliability of our independent moral judgments needs to be *defended*. This is what I undertake to do in Part II, called "Ethics First." An ethics-first solution to the problem of prescribed evil has two goals:

> *First*, it aims to *defend* the reliability of our independent moral judgments against the argument for strict adherence.
> *Second*, it aims to *reconcile* seemingly prescribed evil with our independent moral judgments without renouncing our independent moral judgments.

Part II consists of three chapters. The first two chapters present the case for the reliability of our independent moral judgments. Chapter 4 concerns the (ir)rationality of moral deference to Scripture. I will argue that *even if* we take our independent moral judgments *not* to be *objectively* reliable, *rationality* requires us to act based on our own moral judgments, especially in asymmetrically high-stake situations, that is, in high-stake situations in which we are in the dark about the consequences of following Scripture's injunctions. The chapter presents, then, an unapologetic ethics-first solution to the problem of prescribed evil. According to this solution, while the problem of prescribed evil can be dissolved by withholding judgment regarding the objective reliability of our independent moral judgments, when it comes to our everyday life we rationally ought to act on the basis of our independent moral judgments.

Chapter 5 presents a defense of the reliability of our independent moral judgments. Broadly speaking, there are two ways of viewing morality: philosophical utilitarianism takes facts about happiness as the starting point of morality, whereas the Kantian view holds that morality is about how we will or how we justify ourselves to others. Chapter 5 argues that, if philosophical utilitarianism is accepted, the thesis of the reliability of our independent moral judgments can be justified on the basis of our uncertainty about hidden moral facts and that, if the Kantian view is accepted, the thesis can be justified on the basis of the inaccessibility of hidden facts. Either way, human morality cannot be affected by hidden moral facts whose existence can only be hinted at by divine means.

Establishing the truth of the reliability of our Independent moral judgments is not adequate to solve the problem of divinely prescribed evil, assuming that the divinity of Scripture and the existence of seemingly prescribed evil are true. Chapter 6 argues that these three theses look inconsistent because of the implicit assumption that actions prescribed or permitted by God are *morally* obligatory or permitted. The inconsistency will be removed once we hold that while actions prescribed or permitted by the best interpretation of a Scriptural passage are *legally* obligatory or permitted, according to religious law, they don't need not be morally obligatory or permitted. In fact, a perfect God can be *morally justified* in legislating *legal laws* that deviate from morality. Based on ideas of philosopher Ibn Tufayl, I will suggest an understating of Scriptural injunctions which is compatible with the reliability of our independent moral judgments. This constitutes a second unapologetic solution to the problem of prescribed evil. I will end the book by offering some suggestions for the moral function of Scripture in the modern world.

5. Historical Background

While this monograph is a book in contemporary philosophy of religion and moral philosophy, it involves a fair amount of historical discussion (especially in Part I). The goal of the monograph is to look at history in order to draw from it ideas that can be used to address a pressing problem for our contemporary world. The chapters of Part I begin with a historical discussion of one (or more) important historical figure(s) and end by considering what implication this history has for addressing the problem of prescribed evil. In the chapters of Part II, I will show that the arguments offered either have their roots in the ideas of one (or more) historical figure(s) or are in line with the spirit of their ideas.

Given that the problem of prescribed evil is a general problem in the philosophy of religion, one might wonder why a historically informed solution is valuable. The answer is threefold. First, the relation between revelation and reason is a central topic in Islamic thought. This book is about the relation between revelation and reason in the moral realm. Exploring various ways that Islamic scholars have understood this relation gives us a fundamental insight into understanding their moral theory and moral epistemology. By connecting the moral theory and moral epistemology of Islamic thinkers to a vexing contemporary problem, I hope that the reader will gain a fresh and contemporary perspective on the history of ethics in Islamic philosophy.

Second, most problems in philosophy are not new. The problem of prescribed evil is not entirely new either. It is true that most of the Islamic philosophers and theologians we discuss in the book did not believe that direct injunctions on ethical matters in the Qur'an had ever pushed *against* our moral intuitions. For them, wife-beating, corporal punishment for theft or adultery, and discrimination against women and sexual minorities, sadly, would have not been morally concerning, and there would be almost no other cases of counterintuitive moral injunctions in the Qur'an. However, the issue of harmony between reason and revelation is a central theme in Islamic thought, and most Islamic thinkers have constructed their theological theories to explain why there is ultimately an agreement between reason and revelation. It is an intellectual mistake to ignore what a rich historical tradition has to offer on a central contemporary problem.

Third, the question of violence and discrimination against women and religious and sexual minorities has a unique importance in our contemporary world, especially when the relation of Islam to violence is concerned. Progressive Muslims today need to be able to understand the problem of prescribed evil, trust their moral intuitions, and find an adequate solution for seemingly questionable injunctions in Scripture. A solution to a central Islamic problem has a better chance of being accepted by the Muslim community if it is informed by the Islamic tradition. This is in part why I present my solution to the problem through critical engagement with the ideas of classic Islamic scholars, and by reconstructing a narrative, grounded in the Islamic tradition, in which the problem is addressed.

While the ultimate goal of the book is to find a historically informed solution to the problem of prescribed evil, a subsidiary goal of the book is to provide a contemporary overview of moral theory and moral epistemology in Islamic thought. I also hope that my historical discussions of moral theory in Islamic thought help the reader to find a deeper insight into the nature of the problem of prescribed evil. Nonetheless, in order to make the book more accessible to readers who are not particularly interested in historical discussions of the Islamic tradition, I provide instructions in *the first note of each chapter* on which sections can be skipped without losing sight of the discussion of the problem of prescribed evil.

Before we proceed to Part I, a very brief historical background for a reader who has no familiarity with the Islamic tradition might be helpful. The cursory historical background I provide here only aims to help the reader to be able to put our discussions into a historical perspective. The reader who is not particularly interested in a very general historical background can skip the rest of the prologue.

Islamic theology is divided into two main schools: the *Mu'tazilites* and the *Ash'arites*. The Mu'tazilites formed the earliest school of theology in Islamic thought, emerging within a hundred years from the death of the Prophet. It consisted of a group of theologians who called themselves "the upholders of justice and oneness." The creation of the school can be traced back to Wāṣil ibn 'Atā (699–749) and flourished in Basra and Baghdad. The Mu'tazilites developed a rationalistic theology holding that reason is a new source of religious knowledge. They also argued against divine command theory, holding that there are intrinsic moral properties that can be discovered by reason. The Mu'tazilites were firm advocates of free will, as they believed free will is a necessary condition for moral responsibility.

The main Mu'tazilite figure we will discuss in the book (especially in Chapter 2 and Chapter 5) is Qadi 'Abd al-Jabbār al-Hamadi (935–1025). 'Abd al-Jabbār is regarded as the culmination of the Mu'tazilite school. 'Abd al-Jabbār's theological summa, *al-Mughnī*, is the comprehensive handbook of the Mu'tazilite school.

The Mu'tazilite school died out, mainly due to political factors. Earlier caliphs were instrumental for the rise of the Mu'tazilites, but later caliphs oppressed them. There are very few Muslims today who identify themselves as Mu'tazilites. The Mu'tazilites, however, survived in the form of the Imāmiyya school (i.e., the Shia school). The Imāmiyya school adopted many of the Mu'tazilites' views, including their outlook on morality.

The rival school of the Mu'tazilites is the Ash'arites. The Ash'arite school of Islamic thought can be seen as a reaction to overly rationalistic views of the Mu'tazilites; it was founded by Abu al-Hasan al-Ash'ari (873/874–935/936). The early Ash'arites espoused divine command theory. They downplayed the role of reason in discovering religious truths. The Ash'arite school is the dominant school of thought in the Islamic world, and its dominance is, again, partly due to political factors. The great minister of Saljuks, Nizām al-Mulk, established Nizāmiyya universities throughout the Islamic world. The Ash'arite theology was included in the standard curriculum of the Nizāmiyya universities. The Saljuks helped the Ash'arite theology to become dominant across the Islamic empire. Most of the Sunni world today accepts the main Ash'arite theological doctrines.

The Persian theologian Abū Hāmid al-Ghazālī (1058–1011) is the most prominent Ash'arite thinker. We discuss his works throughout the book (but especially in Chapter 1). Al-Ghazālī studied under another prominent Ash'arite thinker, Imam al-Haramayn al-Juwayni (discussed in the same chapter) and became the head of the Baghdad Nizāmīyya University. It is not an exaggeration to say that al-Ghazālī's views become the orthodox Ash'arite doctrines and influenced the whole Islamic world up until now.

The third school of Islamic thought that we will discuss is the "Philosophers" ("*Falāsifa*"), as they liked to call themselves. They called themselves the philosophers (or *falāsifa*) because they saw their works as a continuation of Greek philosophy. The translation movement started in the mid-eighth century, and from the ninth century onward Muslims found many important philosophical books in Arabic written by Greek philosophers such as Plato and Aristotle. Already, the rationalistic mood of Islamic theology was set by the Mu'tazilites. When the Greek works were translated into Arabic, Islamic thinkers, under the influence of the Mu'tazilites, regarded reason as a source of knowledge, and found a new and incredibly rich source of knowledge.

Islamic philosophers (*falāsifa*) such as al-Kindi, al-Rāzī, al-Fārābī, Avicenna, and Averroës took themselves to be developing and perhaps revising the works of Plato and Aristotle. Similar to their predecessors, *falāsifa* spent a large amount of time studying logic, science, and the works of earlier Greek philosophers. The Islamic philosophers were not very concerned about the differences among the views of Greek philosophers; rather, they regarded Greek philosophy as a scientific tradition that could be advanced by careful rational discussion and Islamic insight. Philosophy was considered an accumulative way of acquiring knowledge about the universe. Even though Islamic philosophers such as al-Fārābī and Avicenna sought to make Aristotelian philosophy religion-friendly, their Aristotelian-Platonic views about the nature of reality looked very different from theological views at the time. The Ash'arite movement was a reaction not only to the rational theology of the Mu'tazilites, but also to overly rationalist views of Islamic philosophers. The Ash'arites resented the views of Islamic philosophers to the extent that al-Ghazālī claimed some of their views amount to the disbelief in Islam.

Here an important terminological decision is in order. While this might sound strange to our ear, the Mu'tazilites and the Ash'arites who do not build their theories on Greek philosophy are not called *philosophers* in the Islamic tradition; instead, they practice *theology* (*kalām*), and they are called theologians (*mutakallimūn*). Al-Ghazālī is a very interesting case in this regard. While al-Ghazālī was certainly very familiar with Greek philosophy (and at times incorporated some of Avicenna's view into his own), he would not call himself a philosopher, given his lack of sympathy for Greek philosophy. Given the way we use the term "philosopher" today, Mu'tazilite and the Ash'arite theologians would certainly be considered philosophers. However, in harmony with the strange but prevalent use of the term "philosopher" in the Islamic tradition, I will use the term "philosopher" only for *falāsifa*. I will avoid using the term "philosopher" to describe theologians discussed in this book.

The four main Islamic philosophers that we discuss in the book are al-Rāzī (854–925), al-Fārābī (872–950), Averroës (1126–1198), and Ibn Tufayl (1105–1185). Al-Fārābī probably had the most influence on the moral theory of Islamic philosophers. He was closely familiar with Aristotle's *Nicomachean Ethics*. Chapter 3 discusses how al-Fārābī transformed Aristotelian virtue ethics into a theological virtue ethics that set the tone for all of his successors. This virtue ethics is accepted almost universally by his successors, such as Avicenna and Averroës.

We therefore don't discuss Avicenna in the monograph; insofar as we are concerned with the problem of prescribed evil, there is no substantial difference between the moral epistemology of al-Fārābī and that of Avicenna.[30] However, Chapter 3 does briefly discuss Averroës, since his famous essay on the harmony of philosophy and religion is a clear statement of the al-Fārābīan view on the subject.

Two other major Islamic philosophers that we will discuss in Part II are al-Rāzī and Ibn Tufayl. Abū Bakr Muhammad ibn Zakariyyā al-Rāzī is one of the earliest Islamic philosophers who practiced *falāsifa* under the influence of Greek philosophers. Al-Rāzī is most famous for his medical works. His philosophical works are mostly lost and underappreciated. Even contemporary Islamic philosophers such as al-Fārābī and Avicenna did not engage with al-Rāzī's philosophical works substantively. However, as Chapter 4

---

[30] See Deborah Black, "Practical Wisdom, Moral Virtue, and Theoretical Knowledge: The Problem of the Autonomy of the Practical Realm in Arabic Philosophy," in *Moral and Political Philosophies in the Middle Ages: Proceedings of the Ninth International Congress of Medieval Philosophy*, ed. B. Carlos Bazán, Eduardo Andújar, and Leonard G. Sbrocchi, 3 vols. (New York: Legas, 1995), 1:451–65. Black provides evidence that there is no substantial difference between the moral epistemology of al-Fārābī and that of Avicenna.

explains, his nonorthodox attitude toward the function of morality promises a satisfying solution to the problem of prescribed evil.

The other major Islamic philosopher discussed in Part II is Ibn Tufayl. Like al-Rāzī, Ibn Tufayl was also the physician and counselor of the caliph of his age. He cherished Avicenna's works and met young Averroës when he was old (his introducing Averroës to the caliph significantly helped Averroës in his later career). Chapter 6 argues that Ibn Tufayl's philosophical tale *Hayy ibn Haqzān*, opens up a new hermeneutical possibility in interpreting morally controversial passages in Scripture.

PART I
SCRIPTURE FIRST

He who is satisfied with reason alone, without the light of the Qur'an and the Tradition, is deluded... the diseases of the heart can be treated only by medicines derived from the religious law.
—Al-Ghazālī, *Ihyā*, vol. 3, book 1

1
The Consequentialism of the Late Ash'arites

Summary of the Chapter

Section 1. This section presents al-Juwainī's divine command theory. It also discusses al-Juwainī's argument that we don't have intuitive moral knowledge.

Section 2. This section is about al-Ghazālī's normative theory. It discusses al-Ghazālī's semantics for ethical terms such as "obligation" and "good" as well as how he uses this semantics to develop a version of self-centered consequentialism.

Section 3. The section overviews al-Ghazālī's moral epistemology. According to al-Ghazālī, given that it is God who determines the consequences of actions, reason has no power in discovering the moral status of actions. The intellect's only role is to understand the Prophet's statements as well as moral terms.

Section 4. Based on al-Ghazālī's ideas, the argument for strict adherence is reconstructed to reject the reliability of our independent moral judgments. The argument implies that we have to follow Scriptural injunctions in their literal sense. The argument's reliance on consequentialism, however, generates some worries for the argument.

Section 5. Al-Ghazālī's rule of figurative interpretation permits a departure from the literal interpretation of the Qur'an when there is a logical proof that the literal interpretation is impossible. I'll argue that neither al-Ghazālī's critical stance on *taqlīd* nor his allowance for nonliteral interpretation of Scripture undermines the strict adherence argument.[1]

---

[1] The reader who is not interested in *historical* discussions of al-Ghazālī's moral theory may skip sections 1, 2, and 3. The main section that discusses the problem of prescribed evil is section 4. Section 3 functions as an introduction to section 4.

1. Divine Command Theory of the Early Ash'arites

According to divine command theory, an action is wrong because God has prohibited it; an action is morally obligatory because God has commanded it. In other words, God has absolute power to make any action He wishes right or wrong by commanding or prohibiting it. Actions in themselves have no moral property. The moral status of actions is entirely dependent on God's volition. If divine command theory is correct, to know about the moral status of an action, we must know about God's commands and prohibitions, and Scripture, the proponents of the divinity of Scripture would assume, is the only way to have epistemic access to God's volitions. The truth of divine command theory makes it the case, then, that independent of Scripture, we would have no reliable way to know about a variety of God's volitions and thus about morality. Therefore, divine command theory implies that our moral judgments independent of revelation are not reliable.

The early Ash'arites espouse divine command theory.[2] Imām al-Haramayn al-Juwainī (1028–1085), commonly known as Imām al-Haramayn (the leading master of the two holy cities, i.e., Mecca and Medina), is an important Ash'arite thinker who represents the orthodox Ash'arite view on the matter as follows:

> Goodness or badness do not derive from a genus or an essential attribute, the meaning of goodness is that for the doing of which the law confers praise, and what is meant by the bad is that for the doing of which the law confers censure.... When we describe an act as being either obligatory or prohibited, we do not mean to imply that, by specifying this, we are distinguishing the quality in an act that is obligatory from another in the one that is not obligatory. What is meant by "obligatory" refers merely to the act which, because the law commands it, is obligatory. What is meant by "prohibited" is the act which, because the law forbids it, is prohibited.[3]

---

[2] The Ash'arites are the dominant theological school of Sunni Islam, founded by Abu'l Hassan al-Ash'arī (874–936). One of the most famous tenets of the Ash'arites is divine command theory. For a short general introduction to the Ash'arites see Peter Adamson, *Philosophy in the Islamic World* (New York: Oxford University Press, 2016), chapter 15. See Richard M. Frank, *Early Islamic Theology: The Mu'tazilites and al-Ash'arī* (Aldershot: Ashgate, 2007) for the history of early Islamic theology. See also Mariam Attar's *Islamic Ethics: Divine Command Theory in Arabo-Islamic Thought* (London: Taylor & Francis, 2010).

[3] For a biography of Abu'l-M'aālī 'Abd al-Malik 'al-Juwaynī see the introduction to the English translation of *Kitab al-irshād ila qawati Al-Adilla fi usul al-i'tiqad* by Paul Walker published under the title *A Guide to Conclusive Proofs for the Principles of Belief* (Reading: Garnet Publishing, 2000). I use Walker's translation for the passages I quote from *Irshād*, here 140–41.

According to al-Juwainī, there are no intrinsic moral properties. Moral properties are *extrinsic* properties which must be understood in terms of God's commands. An action is good only if the law (i.e., God's law) praises doing it. The action is good because of the law's praising it. The goodness is not intrinsic to the action. Moreover, the *meaning* of moral predicates is determined by the law. This view entails that reason, independent of the law, plays no role in discovering the moral attributes of our actions. For independent of the law, there is no moral property to be discovered. On this view, moral intuitions are not specific judgments about whether an action instantiates an intrinsic moral property. They are, at best, judgments about specific commands in the law, and thus they can never justifiably be in conflict with the law. In other words, reason has no independent standing to question the moral claims of the law.

This orthodox Ash'arite way of denying the power of reason in the moral realm is not promising. For it rests on a very implausible semantics for moral terms. If the semantics of moral terms were to be understood in terms of the law, people who have no belief about the law should lack moral concepts altogether. If 'wrong' and 'prohibited by God' were synonymous, we could not coherently deny that 'wrong' means 'prohibited by God' unless we don't understand the meaning of the term 'wrong'. But this is quite implausible. Rational people can have the concept of moral wrongness while denying that it is synonymous with 'prohibited by God'. One who denies that 'wrong' means 'prohibited by God' is not *conceptually* confused.

Moreover, on this theory, moral terms used by someone who denies the existence of God would be empty. That is, if 'wrongness' by definition means "what is prohibited by God," then someone who thinks that there is no God should think that there is nothing prohibited by God and thus nothing is wrong. In other words, even if atheists have moral concepts, they should think that, as a matter of *conceptual analysis*, moral concepts are empty that is, they are not instantiated by anything. But it is very implausible to think that an atheist *must* think that nothing is morally wrong, on pain of being conceptually confused. An atheist might be able to use moral terms properly and judge that such and such is right or wrong, without having beliefs about God's commands and prohibition. The theist might think that the moral beliefs of atheists are false. But this is not the issue. The issue is whether an atheist can possess moral concepts, form various moral beliefs, understand moral terms, and use them. If so, moral terms do not have a theological definition.

Later Ashʿarites, such as al-Ghazālī, despite maintaining the skeptical stance of the early Ashʿarites toward the power of reason in discovering moral truth, reject the crude semantical view of early Ashʿarites, precisely because it does not capture the ordinary meaning of our moral terms. Al-Ghazālī knew that nonbelievers could use moral terms properly and that they could have various moral beliefs. According to al-Ghazālī, while many of the moral beliefs of nonbelievers might be mistaken, for reasons I will explain shortly, there is nothing *conceptually* incoherent in saying that nonbelievers have various moral beliefs. Nonbelievers, on al-Ghazālī's view, may well be morally mistaken, but they are not conceptually confused.

I find al-Ghazālī's objection valid, and I think that divine command theory as formulated by al-Juwainī is too crude to be true. *Throughout the book, I assume that divine command theory is false.* But before turning to al-Ghazālī's views (in the next section), let's take a little digression and consider al-Juwainī's objection to the view that reason can discover moral matters. He takes his Muʿtazilite opponent to hold a view according to which moral claims are intuitive, and thus reason has the power of discovering those moral truths by intuition. But this view, he thinks, cannot be right for the following reason:

> About what you insist is self-evidently good or bad, it is under contention and [thus] your assertions are rejected . . . why did you claim an intuitive knowledge of the good and the bad, when you knew that those in opposition to you in this matter cover the face of the earth. . . . It is not acceptable to distinguish one group of scholars as those who, despite all being equally to perceive it, have a special kind of intuitive knowledge. (*Irshād*, 142)

A quick terminological point before getting to al-Juwainī's objection. Al-Juwainī uses 'self-evident' and 'intuitive' interchangeably. I am not sure if these two terms are equivalent. Given that the view that our moral knowledge is intuitive may be more plausible than the view that it is self-evident, I will use the term 'intuitive' to characterize the Muʿtazilite view. Now, how should we understand al-Juwainī's objection? He asks why his opponent would "claim an intuitive knowledge of the good and the bad" when "those in opposition to you in this matter cover the face of the earth." The objection here is that the fact that many people (including the Ashʿarites) do not believe that we have intuitive moral knowledge is in tension with the view that we have intuitive moral knowledge. Al-Juwainī then claims that the only option for his opponent is to say that only a special group of scholars, presumably the proponents of the intuitive moral knowledge view, have intuitive moral knowledge. But he takes this to be implausible: if there is such a thing as intuitive moral knowledge, everyone should be able to have it. We can formulate al-Juwainī's objection as follows:

(1) Many people deny that we have intuitive moral knowledge.
(2) If many people deny that we have intuitive moral knowledge, then only a special group of scholars, who don't deny this, can have intuitive moral knowledge.
(3) But if there is such a thing as intuitive moral knowledge, everyone is able to have it.
(4) Therefore, there is no intuitive knowledge of morality.

Let's just grant premises (1) and (3). But why should al-Juwainī's opponent accept premise (2), which is the crucial premise of this argument? To be able to assess premise (2), we need to be clearer on what the denial of intuitive moral knowledge amounts to. Suppose that a proponent of intuitive moral knowledge says that we know the moral proposition that P (e.g., that torturing a baby is wrong) on the basis of intuition. There are two different ways to deny this view.

> First, one might deny one's intuitive moral knowledge of P by denying that one knows that P; for example, one might deny that P is true. (And so it cannot be known at all.)
> Second, one might deny one's intuitive moral knowledge of P by denying that the *source* of one's knowledge is intuition (while still maintaining that one knows that P).

Muʿtazilites and Ashʿarites for the most part agree on the *instances* of moral knowledge. For now, let's suppose that the deniers of intuitive moral knowledge that al-Juwainī has in mind are from the second category; that is, they agree on instances of moral knowledge but disagree on whether moral knowledge is intuitive.[4] I will get back to the first category later.

---

[4] George F. Hourani discusses al-Juwainī's objections to the Muʿtazilites in chapter 10 of his *Reason and Tradition in Islamic Ethics* (New York: Cambridge University Press, 1985), 124–35. With regard to this argument, Hourani says that agreement on first-order moral claims might be sufficient for attribution of intuitive knowledge, but he does not explain why it is so.

Al-Juwainī holds that the Ashʿarites do not have intuitive knowledge because they deny that their moral knowledge is intuitive. But does the capacity to have intuitive knowledge require that knowers believe the basis of their knowledge is intuition? A comparison with perceptual knowledge might be helpful here. Many people think that we can have perceptual knowledge on the basis of our perceptual experience. For example, suppose someone knows by perception that there is a tree within view. But if you ask about the basis of that knowledge, the person might not be able to identify the source correctly. Inability to correctly identify the source of one's knowledge, however, does not remove one's knowledge that there is a tree within view. Now, suppose that people have a mistaken view about the source of their perceptual belief. While they believe that there is a tree in front of them on the basis of their perceptual experience, they think that the belief came to them as a revelation from God. One might think that their mistake in identifying the grounds of their belief deprives them of perceptual knowledge. I am not sure if this is true. I think that they have perceptual knowledge as long as their belief is properly grounded. But even if they do not have perceptual knowledge in this case, it is still *possible* for them to have perceptual knowledge on the basis of perception.

Al-Juwainī seems to read the intuitive moral knowledge view as requiring too much. Not only does he require the knower to be aware of the basis of her knowledge, but he also requires the knower to actually think of the basis of her knowledge *as* the basis of her knowledge. However, the intuitive moral knowledge view can be understood in a weaker way: while the knower should have some kind of epistemic access to the basis of her knowledge, she does not need to actually identify that *as* the basis of her knowledge. The intuitive moral knowledge view, when understood in this weaker way, says that we *can* have intuitive knowledge of moral matters just in case we have intuitions about those moral matters, and those intuitions can ground our knowledge of them. We can have intuitive moral knowledge even if we don't identify the grounds of our knowledge correctly. When we understand the intuitive moral knowledge view in this weaker way, it is clear that premise (2) of al-Juwainī's argument fails. The fact that the Ashʿarites deny intuitive moral knowledge does not show that they can't have intuitive moral knowledge on the basis of their intuitions.

Let's return to the first way of denying intuitive moral knowledge mentioned earlier. Suppose a denier of the intuitive moral knowledge view holds that its proponents get the *instances* of moral knowledge wrong; that is, what they take to be intuitive moral knowledge is not knowledge at all, let alone intuitive knowledge. I am not sure whether al-Juwainī thinks that the Ash'arites deny intuitive moral knowledge for that reason. But al-Juwainī thinks that there is another group of people, that is, non-Muslims, who deny the Mu'tazlites' instances of intuitive moral knowledge:

> What conforms our point here is that the Barahima, who, like, the Mu'tazilites, hold, according to their own claim, that the determination of the good and the bad is a rational matter, would therefore believe that the slaughtering of animals, subjecting them to pain, and exposing them to hardship and overwork is bad. Their believing this, however, does not represent true knowledge, but rather ignorance. (*Irshād*, 144)[5]

Islamic law does not prohibit the killing of animals. In the same vein, many Muslims do not find the killing of animals morally objectionable. One might respond to this objection by using the weaker understanding of the intuitive moral knowledge view. It might be the case that everybody shares the same intuition about the wrongness of the killing of animals, while some people, say, under the influence of Islamic law, do not form the belief that the killing of animals is impermissible. The fact that different people have different moral *beliefs* does not undermine the intuitive moral knowledge view as long as there are universal moral *intuitions*, and those intuitions *can give rise to* moral knowledge. However, al-Juwainī's might insist that some people do not have the same intuition that killing animals is wrong, and if, on fundamental moral issues, people have different intuitions, we should be skeptical about the intuitive moral knowledge view.[6] In the next chapter, we will see that the Mu'tazilites concede that intuition supports Barahima's judgments; that is, there is a rational intuition for animal slaughtering's being morally

---

[5] The term *Barahima* is used in the Islamic context to refer to theists who did not believe in a prophet or revelation. The group may have no connection to Indian Barahima. Some think that the identity is created to conceal the true identity of heretics; for example, see Nadjet Zouggar, "The Philosophers in Sunni Prophetology," trans. Daphne Granot, *Bulletin du Centre de recherche français à Jérusalem 23* (2012), http://journals.openedition.org/bcrfj/7279, accessed August 4, 2023.

[6] Hourani also mentions this argument by al-Juwainī but dismisses it as "irrelevant, because the Mu'tazilites had never claimed that *all* Brahmin judgments of ethics were sound, and they did not have to maintain that the Brahmin prohibition of animal slaughter was a genuine intuition" (*Reason and Tradition*, 129). However, al-Juwainī's point here might be that it is implausible to dismiss the intuition of a large amount of people on a very basic matter of morality. If humans have the power of acquiring moral knowledge by using intuitions, why should we think that only certain people can use this power correctly in a very basic matter? Moreover, the Mu'tazilites concede that intuition supports Barahima's judgments (see Chapter 2, section 4).

wrong. It is just they argue that this intuition does not provide justification for animal slaughtering's being morally wrong, for reasons to be explained in the next chapter.

In sum, according to al-Juwainī, there are only two alternatives: either morality comes from God or it does not. If it does, moral properties and concepts are characterized by God's volitions, and thus we have no intuitive moral knowledge and all our moral knowledge comes from God. If morality does not come from God, there are intrinsic moral properties of which we have intuitive knowledge. He rejects the second view because he thinks the intuitive moral knowledge view is incorrect. As we will see in the next section, al-Ghazālī thinks that this is a false dilemma. The Ash'arites do not need to espouse an implausible semantical view about moral terms, and they don't need to reject the possibility of rational moral knowledge altogether. Moral properties and concepts are not characterized by God's volitions, and we might have some very limited rational moral knowledge. Yet God has the power to determine our moral obligations in whatever way He wishes, and, thus, our knowledge of our obligations comes from our knowledge of God's commands.

2. The Consequentialism of al-Ghazālī

Al-Juwainī was a brilliant theologian and legal scholar. But his gifted student, Abu Ḥāmid Muhammad al-Ghazālī (1058–1111), surpassed him in almost all respects and overshadowed his influence.[7] When al-Ghazālī was the head of the Baghdad Nizāmiyya University, the main university in the Islamic world, he wrote *al-Iqtisād fi l'itiqad* to formulate and defend the main doctrines of the Ash'arites. To explain al-Ghazālī's view on the relation between reason and revelation I will mostly use *al-Iqtisād*.[8] *Al-Iqtisād* is a rather early book by al-Ghazālī, and he wrote other ethical books, but he never changed his view on the relation between reason and revelation, and in his later ethical books, he had a more practical goal, that is, how to develop

---

[7] The life and works of al-Ghazālī have been well studied. For a good review of al-Ghazālī life see the first two chapters of Frank Griffel, *Al-Ghazālī's Philosophical Theology* (New York: Oxford University Press, 2000), 19–87. For the chronology of his works see George F. Hourani, "A Revised Chronology of Ghazālī's Writings," *Journal of the American Oriental Society* 104.2 (1984): 289–302.

[8] I use Yaqub's translation of al-Iqtisād, and make reference to this work for my citations. Abu Hamid M. b. M. al-Ghazālī, Al-Ghazālī's "Moderation in Belief," trans. Aladdin M. Yaqub (Chicago: University of Chicago Press, 2014).

inner and religious virtues. Al-Ghazālī wrote *al-Iqtisād* to defend Ash'arite doctrines, although his formulations of them sometimes are different from the orthodox Ash'arite view.[9] The ethical view he espouses in *al-Iqtisād* is a case in point. His view here changed the ethical views of the Ash'arites. Late Ash'arite thinkers such as Fakhr al-din al-Rāzī are heavily influenced by al-Ghazālī' in their ethical views.[10]

Al-Ghazālī held that the skepticism of the Ash'arites toward the power of reason in discovering moral truth was fundamentally correct. But he was aware of the fact that the semantics for moral terms provided by the Ash'arites was not plausible. For it couldn't capture the meaning of moral terms as used in ordinary linguistic practices. Moral terms and concepts are not peculiar to believers: nonbelievers use the same terms and have the same concepts. We can't expect revelation to determine the content of a concept which is possessed by both believers and nonbelievers. In the following passage, al-Ghazālī expresses his dissatisfaction with early Ash'arite semantics for moral terms and presents his alternative.

> What is specifically called "obligatory" is that act the refraining of which leads to definite harm [to oneself]. If this harm obtains in the next life—I mean the hereafter—and is known through the revelation, we call the act "obligatory," and if the harm obtains in this worldly life and is known through reason, in this case too the act might be called "obligatory." The one who does not affirm the revelation might say it is obligatory for a hungry person who is dying of hunger to eat if he finds bread. He means by "eating is obligatory" that performing it is preponderant over refraining from it because of the harm that is caused by refraining from it. We do not forbid this convention according to the law. The terms are open to all and there are no restrictions on them either due to revelation or due to reason. Linguistic practice would bar the usage of a term if it fails to describe the subject matter as it is known. (*al-Iqtisād*, 159)

Contrary to classic Ash'arite thinkers such as his teacher al-Juwainī, al-Ghazālī thinks that Islamic law can't impose restrictions on the meaning

---

[9] See Richard M. Frank, *Al-Ghazālī and the Ash'ari School* (Durham, NC: Duke University Press, 1994), for an exposition of the Al-Ghazālī's outlook on Ash'arism. See also Frank Griffel's *Al-Ghazālī's Philosophical Theology* on whether Al-Ghazālī's later view on cosmology is consistent with his earlier views expressed in *al-Iqtisād*.

[10] See Ayman Shihadeh, *The Teleological Ethics of Fakhr al-Dīn al-Rāzī* (Boston: Brill, 2006), for a very thorough presentation of al-Rāzī view.

of moral terms: "The terms are open to all." On the alternative semantical view al-Ghazālī proposes, the concept of obligation should be understood in terms of harms and benefits to the agent. This implies, first, that we have a rationalist definition of obligation, and second, that *ethical egoism* is true in virtue of the meaning of 'obligation'. Ethical egoism is the view which says one ought to maximize one's benefits. Ethical egoism is a form of consequentialism. According to consequentialism, obligations are determined solely by the consequences of actions. Ethical egoism, which we may call *self-centered consequentialism*, is different from *universal consequentialism* in that while universal consequentialism says that obligations are determined by consequences that an action has for *all* sentient beings, self-centered consequentialism limits the scope of consequences that should be taken into account in evaluation of an action to consequences that the action has for the agent.[11]

The difference between universal consequentialism and al-Ghazālī's view can also be seen through al-Ghazālī's account of the concept of *goodness*. According to consequentialism, *deontological* concepts, such as the concept of *obligation*, are to be understood in terms of axiological concepts, such as the concept of goodness. An obligatory action is an action which brings about the optimum amount of goodness in the world. Universal consequentialism is often formulated in terms of the notion of *goodness simpliciter*. We can understand the notion of *good simpliciter* in contrast with the notion of *good for*. For instance, we might say my pleasure is not good only for me, but it is *simply good*. Accordingly, the right action, on a universal consequentialist view, is the one which would bring about the optimum amount of goodness simpliciter. Al-Ghazālī, however, does not think that the concept of good *simpliciter* is a valid notion. For him, the only legitimate way for something to be good is to be *good for* someone. He defines the meaning of 'good' in the following way:

---

[11] When I refer to universal consequentialism throughout the book, I mean *agent-neutral* universal consequentialism, that is, a consequentialism whose value theory admits *only agent-neutral values*. There is a new wave of consequentialists, called consequentializers, who think we can combine agent-relative values with universal consequentialism. For example, see James Dreier, "In Defense of Consequentializing," in *Oxford Studies in Normative Ethics*, vol. 1, ed. Mark Timmons (Oxford: Oxford University Press, 2011), 97–119, and Douglas W. Portmore, "Consequentializing Moral Theories," *Pacific Philosophical Quarterly* 88 (2007): 39–73. No matter whether it is possible to accept agent-relative consequentialism conceptually, I refer to agent-neutral consequentialism simply as "consequentialism" in this book.

As for the term "good," the basis of its meaning is that the act in relation to the agent divides into three categories. One of them is that it is in accordance with him, that is, it serves his purpose, the second is that it is contrary to his purpose, and the third is that there is no purpose in performing it or refraining from it. The division is established by the intellect. The act that is in accordance with the agent is called "good" for him; *there is no meaning to its being good other than its accord with his purpose*.... If [the act] relates to someone other than the agent and it is in accordance with this other person's purpose, then it is called "good" for the one with whose purpose it accords... the terms 'good' and 'bad' are based on whether there is accord or contrariety, and these are *relational matters* that vary with people.... [G]ood and bad, for all mankind, are descriptions of two relational qualities that vary with that which they relate, and not of qualities of essences, which do not vary with relations. (*al-Iqtisād*, 160–61)

Al-Ghazālī departs from the early Ash'arites by maintaining that the meaning of axiological terms can be discovered by reason. He defines goodness in terms of one's aims and purposes. If something satisfies my desire, it is good for me. Reason alone tells me that pleasure is good for me. On the other hand, he denies that anything can be simply good. Things are good relative to certain purposes. Thus, something can be good for me and bad for you, and nothing is nonrelationally good. The nonrelational concept of goodness is not a legitimate notion on al-Ghazālī's view.

Universal consequentialism, on the other hand, is conceptually dependent on the nonrelational notion of goodness simpliciter. The right action is the one which maximizes the aggregate amount of goodness simpliciter. The right action on this view is *not* determined by what is *good for* the agent. Rather, every state which is simply good (or bad), such as the pleasure of any sentient being, contributes to making an action right or wrong. On the other hand, al-Ghazālī defines his self-centered consequentialism with the relational notion of *good for*.[12] The right action is the one which maximizes the

---

[12] Later Ash'ari thinkers such as Fakhr al-din al-Rāzī adopt al-Ghazālī's account of axiological notions and follow him in rejecting the notion of good simpliciter. See Shihadeh, *Teleological Ethics*. Shihadeh's presentation of Fakhr al-Rāzī's view, however, is sometimes confusing. While he says that al-Rāzī's view is an "emotivist theory" (59 and 62), he calls al-Rāzī view "self-centered consequentialism," that is, "the view that an act is good if it serves the agent's own interests" (62). Shihadeh's definition of consequentialism is unusual, as it is not formulated in terms of deontic notions. Moreover, emotivism and consequentialism, standardly understood, are inconsistent metaethical views (i.e., one denies that ethical statements have truth-value, while the other does not), so it is unclear how he can ascribe both views to late al-Rāzī. Moreover, he says al-Ghazālī's view "results in a standard

aggregate amount of goodness for me. What is good for others is not relevant to whether my action is right or wrong.

Ethical egoism or self-centered consequentialism is not very plausible. The moral status of my killing another person is not determined only by the benefits and harms that this killing has for me. It would still be wrong for me to kill someone even when this killing would have only good consequences for me. However, universal consequentialism and self-centered consequentialism are structurally parallel. As far as we are concerned with the moral epistemology of al-Ghazālī, the difference between these two types of consequentialism is not particularly important. For epistemological theses of al-Ghazālī are not dependent on a specific form of consequentialism.

3. The Moral Epistemology of al-Ghazālī

Al-Ghazālī is skeptical about the epistemic power of reason in the moral realm. The main idea behind his skepticism is very simple: in the evaluation of an action, *all* consequences, including otherworldly consequences of the action, matter, and given our ignorance about many of those consequences, reason alone would be unable to discover the deontic status of our actions.

> The meaning of being obligatory is that there is a preponderance in favor of performing a given act over refraining from it in light of the prevention of harm that it is estimated or known to occur by refraining from the act. If this is what being obligatory means, then that which obligates is what gives preponderance, and that is God (Exalted is He). . . . The meaning of the prophet's statement that it is obligatory is that it is made preponderant by God's attaching punishment to one of the options. . . . Understanding can come only through the intellect. The intellect does not understand by

---

divine command ethics. By contrast, al-Rāzī endorses a thoroughly consequentialist stance in his *usul al-fiqh*, which he clearly bases on his philosophical and theological metaethics" (73). Shihadeh justifies his claim by saying that, on al-Rāzī's view, "if scripture does not present an explicit rule in relation to a given act, other normative methods and procedures may apply to it. Yet the most important ones are consequentialist, and may be summarized as follows. . . . If the act is beneficial, it will be *prima facie* permitted; if harmful, it will be *prima facie* proscribed" (73). For one thing, in cases in which Scripture presents an explicit rule, there is no difference between al-Rāzī and al-Ghazālī. For another thing, the difference between al-Rāzī and al-Ghazālī stems from the fact that al-Rāzī thinks that in cases in which there is no explicit rule in Scripture we might be in an epistemic position to know about the benefits and harms of our actions, while al-Ghazālī is more skeptical. This difference can hardly make one a consequentialist and the other a divine command theorist. This difference says nothing about the normative view they adopt (which is the same, i.e., ethical egoism).

itself that there is preponderance; rather it must hear this from a messenger. The messenger does not give preponderance to performing an act rather than refraining from it; but God is the giver of preponderance, and the messenger is an informer. The truthfulness of a messenger is not made evident through itself but through a miracle. (*al-Iqtisād*, 188)

According to al-Ghazālī, the intellect or reason cannot know whether an action is obligatory because reason cannot know *all the consequences* of the action. The intellect's role is to understand the Prophet's statements as well as ethical concepts. But the intellect cannot play any role in knowing right and wrong actions independent of revelation, for the intellect is ignorant about the consequences of actions. God determines the consequences of one's actions. Reason alone has no epistemic access to what God has attached to actions in this world and the other world. The only way for us to know whether our actions are right or wrong is to know about their consequences *through revelation*. Hence, while al-Ghazālī departs from the orthodox Ash'arites on the semantics of moral terms, he is very much in agreement with them about the fact that reason has no say when it comes to discovering moral truths.

Given the structural similarity between self-centered consequentialism and universal consequentialism, al-Ghazālī's skepticism can be expressed in terms of universal consequentialism as well. That is, suppose that the right action is the one that brings about a maximum amount of good (simpliciter). It is God who determines the consequences of actions, and thus in order to know which action is right and which action wrong, we should rely on the Prophet. So, if universal consequentialism is correct, and if we believe that God exists and that He creates this world as well as the hereafter, we should be skeptical about the power of reason in knowing right and wrong.

One might object to al-Ghazālī's argument by saying that even though God creates the consequences of actions, He is not at liberty to create them in whatever manner He wishes. There are constraints that God's creation must satisfy. For example, His wisdom and justice would be constraints on His creation; that is, the creation of heaven and hell must be just and wise; and we might have intuitive knowledge about what kinds of rewards or punishments are just and wise.

Regarding God's wisdom, al-Ghazālī maintains that God's wisdom consists in the knowledge of the order of universe, and this by itself has no normative consequence for God's act of creating the universe.

If by "wisdom" it is intended, as previously stated, the knowledge of the order of things and the power to produce this order, then there is nothing [in refraining from compensating the suffering of an animal in the afterlife] that is contrary to wisdom. If another sense [by "wisdom"] is intended, the only form of wisdom that is due to God is what we mentioned; anything other than that is a meaningless expression. (*al-Iqtisād*, 178)

As for justice, al-Ghazālī explains, if self-centered consequentialism is true, the only norm governing God's creation would be self-centered consequentialism. But nothing harms or benefits God, al-Ghazālī holds. Thus, given self-centered consequentialism, God has no constraint on how to create the universe. Al-Ghazālī also holds that God has no obligation to care for the well-being of His creatures, and He may bring suffering to innocent animals without ever being required to compensate it. For He would not be harmed by refraining from doing these actions (*al-Iqtisād*, 177–80). Similar results would hold if universal consequentialism is true. According to universal consequentialism, God's obligation is to create the maximum amount of goodness. This by itself imposes no restriction on His creation of heaven or hell, except for the fact that heaven and hell should be created in a way that the goodness (e.g., happiness) would be maximized. Consequentialism does not require God to care for the well-being of any particular individual, and it does not require God to compensate the suffering of any particular individual in the other world.

One might ask, at this point, whether there really is a significant difference between al-Juwainī's divine command theory and al-Ghazālī's consequentialism. The answer is both yes and no. From the point of view of metaphysics and semantics, al-Ghazālī's view is very different from al-Juwainī's. To appreciate the difference, think about standard objections to divine command theory. One might reject al-Juwainī's divine command theory because of its theological semantics of moral terms. Al-Ghazālī's semantics, however, is completely rationalist, and insofar as one finds consequentialism plausible, one might find al-Ghazālī's semantics more or less acceptable (at least if we modify al-Ghazālī view in terms of universal consequentialism). Another standard objection to divine command theory is that it implies that actions such as killing or rape in themselves are morally neutral. That is, they are wrong *solely* because God prohibited them; they would have been right had God commanded them. This implication is implausible. Al-Ghazālī's theological consequentialism is also less susceptible to this objection. Consider the act of killing. It is true that if God had created the world differently (i.e., if He had attached good consequences to killing), killing would have been permissible. But, if we understand al-Ghazālī's view in terms of universal consequentialism, it is necessarily true that there is something bad in killing a person; i.e., killing a person deprives her from future pleasures. In other words, contrary to divine command theory, al-Ghazālī's view does not entail that all actions are completely morally neutral in themselves and that there is no intrinsic value in the world. Pleasure and pain have intrinsic value, and actions, insofar as they entail pain and pleasure, are not morally neutral. Moreover, any modern consequentialist would accept that if the structure of the world had been different, the moral status of actions would have been different. This is just part of the consequentialism package that there is no absolute prohibition on any action. So the fact that God could have created a world in which killing is permissible (on balance) is consistent with any plausible version of consequentialism. What is particularly problematic about divine command theory is the implication that all actions are morally neutral "before" God's commands. However, al-Ghazālī's consequentialism has no such implication.

On the other hand, there is really no significant difference between al-Juwainī's divine command theory and al-Ghazālī's consequentialism in that they both give God *the absolute power to determine the moral status of actions*. They both hold that God is the author of morality, and He can write it in whatever way He wishes. This implies that there is no significant difference between al-Juwainī's moral epistemology and al-Ghazālī's. There are some *minor* differences, of course, since (in contrast with al-Juwainī) al-Ghazālī holds that we have some limited rational knowledge of the moral realm.[13] For instance, the intellect knows that pleasure is good and that pain is bad. But when it comes to the knowledge of what is right and wrong, al-Ghazālī's view

---

[13] In *Islamic Philosophy and Ethics of Belief*, Anthony Booth discusses al-Ghazālī's epistemology. Booth's view for the most part is similar to the view presented in this chapter. There are, however, some minor differences. For example, he writes: "Now, al-Ghazali wants of course to maintain that prophecy has a unique role, and yet maintain that the legitimacy of the Prophets has an evidential base. He attempts to do this, it seems, by holding that a good portion, *though not all* (e.g., not theoretical knowledge about what happens in the afterlife) of the *theoretical* claims of prophecy are available by consulting independent evidence. Further, *no* practical knowledge is available independent of knowledge of prophecy." While I think that Booth is basically right, I think he makes a mistake in saying that no practical knowledge is available to us by reason. As I explained, al-Ghazali holds that the general moral principle of self-centered consequentialism is known by reason. Moreover, that my pleasure is good for me is also known by reason. However, he thinks that those truths are true in virtue of the meaning of the terms 'obligation' and 'good', and thus are not *substantial* practical truths. See Anthony Robert Booth, *Islamic Philosophy and the Ethics of Belief* (London: Palgrave, 2016), 30.

accords with al-Juwainī's. They both hold that, independent of Scripture, we have no moral knowledge of what we should do. In sum, Al-Ghazālī's message to his fellow Ashʿarites is that they can maintain their theological epistemology without appealing to a theological semantics and an implausible metaphysics of morality. Moreover, the Ashʿarites do not need to reject any rational knowledge of morality; they just need to deny rational knowledge of deontic facts about rightness and wrongness.

4. The Argument for Strict Adherence to Scripture

Al-Ghazālī's view can be used to reconstruct a general argument from consequentialism for rejecting *the reliability of our independent moral judgments* when there is a clash between our independent moral judgments and Scripture. To illustrate, take any Qur'anic statement that seems to be in tension with our independent moral judgments. The case of wife-beating mentioned in the previous chapter can be an example. Let's assume, for the sake of argument, that the Qur'anic statement is something like this: "Those wives you fear may be rebellious, beat them."[14] Suppose that the literal meaning of the statement is clear and there is no linguistic reason not to take the statement at face value. Moreover, let's suppose that our independent moral judgments go against the literal meaning of the Qur'anic statement.

According to al-Ghazālī's view, the Prophet is informing us, via the Qur'anic passage, that God has issued certain commands and that obeying those commands has good consequences because God attached rewards to obeying the commands and punishments to violating them. Independent of Scripture, we have no knowledge of the total consequences of our actions, including their consequences in this world or the hereafter, which would raise doubts about the Prophet's claim. Therefore, there is no moral reason to interpret the statement in a nonliteral manner. We also assumed that there is no linguistic reason to reinterpret the text. Therefore, we have no reason, textual or moral, to depart from the literal meaning of the text, which, *ex hypothesi*, goes against our moral intuition. We can formulate

---

[14] Again, this is just one example. Any other example from morally controversial passages can be used here. Moreover, given Ephesians (5:22–25), which says wives should submit to their husbands in everything, this example has a Christian counterpart too.

this argument as follows (let's call this argument the *argument for strict adherence*):

(1) If the Qur'an states "φ-ing is obligatory" ("or φ-ing is permissible") and the Qur'an is God's words, God intends to convey that it is obligatory (or permitted) for us, or a certain group of people specified in the text or by the context, to do φ unless there are good reasons to think that the Qur'anic sentence "φ-ing is obligatory" (or "φ-ing is permissible") does not mean that it is obligatory (or permitted) to φ [truism about the nature of communication].

(2) There is no sufficient linguistic reason to think that the Qur'an's sentence "φ-ing is obligatory" (or "φ-ing is permissible") does not mean that it is obligatory (or permitted) to φ [assumption of the case].

(3) Given God's absolute power to determine the moral status of any action, God's moral nature provides us with no reason to think that the Qur'an sentence "φ-ing is obligatory" (or "φ-ing is permissible") does not mean that φ-ing is obligatory (or "φ-ing is permissible") [al-Ghazālī's main claim].

(4) Therefore, we have no good reason to think that the Qur'an sentence "φ-ing is obligatory" (or "φ-ing is permissible") does not mean that φ-ing is obligatory (or φ-ing is permissible) [from (1), (2), and (3)].

(5) Therefore, if the Qur'an states "φ-ing is obligatory" (or "φ-ing is permissible") and the Qur'an is God's words, God intends to convey that it is obligatory (or permitted) for us (or a certain group of people specified in the text or by the context) to do φ [from (1) and (4)].

(6) If God intends to convey that it is obligatory (or permitted) for us (or a certain group of people) to do φ, it is true that we (or those people) are morally obligated (or permitted) to do φ [God's Reliability].

(7) Therefore, if the Qur'an states "φ-ing is obligatory" (or "φ-ing is permissible") and the Qur'an is God's words, it is true that we (or a certain group of people specified in the text or by the context) are morally required (or permitted) to do φ [from (3), (5), and (6)].

(8) But according to our independent moral judgments, we (or a certain group of people specified in the text or by the context) are *not* morally required (or permitted) to do φ [assumption of the case].

(9) Therefore, our independent moral judgments do not accurately represent moral duties, and permissions; i.e., *the reliability of our independent moral judgments* (defined in the prologue) is false [from (7) and (8)].

We can apply this argument to the wife-beating example. Assuming that premise (2) is satisfied, the argument shows that those who believe that the Qur'an is God's words may reject their moral intuition and hold that they (or at least men at the time of the Prophet) are morally permitted to beat their wives when they fear they might be rebellious. In the prologue, I introduced the following two theses:

> *Existence of Seemingly Prescribed Evil.* There are some actions prescribed or permitted by the best interpretation of a Scriptural passage which seem immoral, according to our independent moral judgments.
>
> *Reliability of Our Independent Moral Judgments.* Our moral judgments reliably represent moral values, moral duties, and moral permissions

The conclusion of the argument for strict adherence is that the reliability of our independent moral judgments is false, and that seemingly prescribed evil is *not* in fact evil. This conclusion strikes many as implausible, and thus we might think that the argument is actually a reductio ad absurdum. The problem is that none of the premises of the argument can be easily rejected. Let's discuss the reasoning behind each premise of the argument.

Premise (1) of the argument is basically a truism about communication. It says that whenever someone says "P" and "P" literally means P, we should take the person to mean P unless there is a good reason to think that she does not mean that P. In other words, we should take people's words at their face value unless we have good reasons not to do so. Premise (2) is an assumption about the case. I assumed that this assumption applies to the wife-beating example. That is, there is no sufficient linguistic reason to think the Qur'anic statement should be read metaphorically or has indeed another meaning. (If premise (2) does not hold for the wife-beating example, there are other contentious statements in Scripture for which premise (2) does hold; see the prologue, sections 2 and 3). Premise (3) can be justified through al-Ghazālī's ethical view. I will get back to this premise shortly.

Regarding God's injunction in practical matters, barring linguistic reasons, the only relevant reason for a theist to interpret Scripture nonliterally is that it would be against God's moral nature to issue such commands or permissions. In other words, if theists believe that it is morally impermissible for God to intend the literal meaning of a Scriptural passage, then they have grounds to interpret the passage nonliterally. But when an action attributed to God by the literal understanding of Scripture is within God's moral power to perform, a theist has no moral reason not to impute that action to God. This reasoning explains why premise (4) follows from premises (2) and (3). Premise (5) is an inference from premises (1) and (4).

Premise (6) is justified on the grounds that if God is all knowing and all good, *we should rely on His testimony*. Premise (6) is just an application of a general principle which says if a very knowledgeable person who does not want to deceive you informs you about something that the person has knowledge about, you should believe it. Accordingly, if an omniscient and omnibenevolent God informs you about an obligation, you should believe Him and take yourself to have that obligation. Premise (7) is just the conclusion of premises (3), (5) and (6). Premise (8) is the assumption of the case, and the conclusion follows from premises (8) and (7).

The key premise of the argument is premise (3). Premise (3) is, in fact, a denial of Moral Justification, defined as follows:

> *Moral Justification*. There are moral reasons to interpret morally controversial passages nonliterally, as the literal understanding of the passages is inconsistent with a morally perfect God.

Al-Ghazālī would justify premise (3) by appealing to his self-centered consequentialism. If self-centered consequentialism is true, an action is right just in case it brings more benefit than harm to the agent, and God has the power of making an action right or wrong by attaching rewards or punishments to it. But would God be at liberty to give preponderance to any action He wishes through attaching rewards and punishments? On self-centered consequentialism, given that God has no benefit or harm, no action of God could be wrong or required, and thus nothing constrains God's act of giving a certain act preponderance over others. But note that premise (3) is not reliant on self-centered consequentialism. It can be justified even if universal consequentialism is the correct ethical theory.

If universal consequentialism is true, an act would be right just in case it brings about the best consequences for all sentient beings, and God has the power of making an action right by making it the case that the action would bring about the best consequences. In a similar vein, Philip Quinn argues that consequentialism can justify God to command someone to kill an innocent person:

> If God commands someone to kill an innocent person, then he ought to kill that person. Is this principle a manifestly repugnant one? The theist,

arguing on his own ground, need not be driven to agree that it is. From a consequentialist point of view, he can maintain that God, since he is omniscient, omnipotent and perfectly good, can appropriately compensate both the killer and his victim in the relevant felicific or beatific respects either here or hereafter.[15]

We might now ask whether God is at liberty to attach any consequences He wishes to actions. If universal consequentialism is true, it is the norm governing God's action as well. Al-Ghazālī held that in virtue of the meaning of 'obligation', we can see that consequentialism is true. Setting aside al-Ghazālī's semantical claim, modern consequentialists think that the principle of consequentialism specifies the metaphysical nature of obligation for any morally responsible being. So the principle of consequentialism, if true at all, is true of God, humans, and Martians (if there are any). According to universal consequentialism, an action is morally required if it brings about the best possible outcome. We can apply this principle of universal consequentialism to God's actions. That is, God's actions, including His act of determining rewards and punishments, are subject to consequentialist calculation. Therefore, God has a duty to attach rewards and punishments to actions in a way that his action brings about the most aggregate happiness in the universe (including this world and the other one). But there is no reason to think that any particular way of attaching rewards or punishment to action is required of God. It may well be the case that God has different ways of attaching rewards and punishments to actions to maximize the aggregate happiness. Moreover, for any action φ (e.g., wife-beating), we have no reason to think that God should attach punishments, rather than rewards, to it to maximize the aggregate happiness in both worlds. So for any action φ, we have no reason to think that God does not have power to make it obligatory or permissible through attaching rewards and punishments to it.

One might worry that God might not be subject to consequentialism because the moral standards for God's actions are different. But it would be strange to think that only humans, but not God, should bring about the best outcome. If the fact that humans can bring about the best outcome creates a moral obligation for them, why does the fact that God can bring about the

---

[15] Philip L. Quinn, "Religious Obedience and Moral Autonomy," *Religious Studies* 11.3 (1975): 275–76

best outcome does not create a moral obligation for Him? There is nothing in consequentialism that restricts its domain of application. But suppose, for the sake of argument, that we restrict consequentialism to nondivine beings. This, in fact, strengthens al-Ghazālī's point that we have no reason to think that God should attach rewards and punishments to actions in a specific manner. Even if God were subject to some kind of divine ethics, of which we have no idea, we would have no reason to think that God has some constraint to attach punishments to wife-beating.

Let me restate the strict adherence argument in simpler terms: in order to depart from the literal meaning of a particular Qur'anic passage, we should either have textual reasons or moral reasons. We *assume* that we don't have textual reasons, and al-Ghazālī's view, as stated in premise (3), implies that we have no moral reasons either. If the Qur'anic passage is intended in its literal meaning, given the reliability of God, we should believe what the Qur'anic passage says even when it goes against our independent moral judgments. Therefore, our independent moral judgments are not reliable when they are in conflict with the literal meaning of the Qur'an. While the strict adherence argument is a long argument, if we grant the assumptions of the case, and the truism about communication, there are only two substantial premises in the argument, i.e., premise (3) and premise (6). We can call the first one *al-Ghazālī's main claim*, and the second one God's Reliability. As I explained in previous paragraphs, there are strong reasons to support these premises, but there are also some important objections to them. Let me address them in turn.

We have a strong moral intuition that, say, wife-beating is wrong. Can this intuition provide us with a moral reason to not interpret Scripture literally? According to al-Ghazālī's main claim, the answer is no. For God has the power of making φ obligatory or permissible by attaching rewards or punishments to it, and we don't have epistemic access to God's decision; therefore, our moral intuitions are not reliable. Independent of revelation, we have no intuition about how God attaches rewards or punishments in this world or the hereafter. Nor do we have any intuition about the ways He could maximize happiness. In general, if consequentialism is right, given that the morality of actions is determined by their causal consequences, our moral intuition is, at best, about the causal mechanisms of the world. But if we can't in principle have access to the causal mechanism of this world or the other world, our moral intuitions do not track any truth. But one might worry that al-Ghazālī's main claim is too reliant on consequentialism. His rejection of the reliability of our moral intuitions is based entirely on consequentialism. But what if consequentialism is wrong? Al-Ghazālī provides us with no argument to the effect that moral intuitions in a deontological moral system are not tracking any truths. And if moral intuitions are reliable, then they provide us reason to think that God cannot make any action He wishes right or wrong. In other words, on a deontological account of ethics, al-Ghazālī's main claim might look very suspect. We will discuss this worry in the next chapter.

The other problem with the strict adherence argument is that there is a tension between God's Reliability and consequentialism. Let me restate God's Reliability:

> *God's Reliability.* If God intends to convey that it is obligatory (or permitted) for us (or a certain group of people) to do φ, it is true that we (or those people) are morally obligated (or permitted) to do φ.

God's Reliability is true on the assumption that God would neither lie to nor mislead us. However, consequentialism poses no general prohibition on lying or misleading. Lying and misleading are wrong only when they detract from the aggregate value of total consequences. There would be no moral objections to them if they contributed to the aggregate value of consequences. But now given that we have no reason to think that God would act in any particular way, we have no reason to think that God would not intend to mislead us by His Scripture. In other words, if consequentialism is true, and if the consequences of actions are determined by God in a cosmic scale and in way that is unknowable by us, we have *no reason* to believe that God's Reliability is true. Al-Ghazālī himself was very concerned with this objection, and he calls it "the strongest skeptical argument" (*al-Iqtisād*, 190). However, al-Ghazālī thinks that the objection has a response: The nature of God is such that He can't lie. He is constitutionally unable to lie.

> It might be said: What assures you that he did not mislead the messenger and those to whom he is sent, and did not say of the one who would be miserable [in the hereafter] that he would be happy and of the one who would be happy that he would be miserable? For this is not impossible, since you do not believe that the intellect can deem a thing bad.... [How] do we know that God is truthful? ... The response is that we can trust that God does not lie, since lying pertains to speech, and God's speech is

not sounds and letters, through which deceit could occur. It is, however, a meaning that subsists in the self of the Exalted. For each thing a man knows, there subsists in himself a tiding that represents what he knows in a manner appropriate to his knowledge. It is inconceivable that there should be lies in these things, similarly it is inconceivable with respect to God. (*al-Iqtisād*, 194)

Al-Ghazālī claims that a lie occurs when there is a mismatch between one's speech and one's thought. However, God's revelation is not verbal. There is no distance between God's thought and the revealed thoughts to the Prophet. Therefore, there is no possibility of lying for God.

It is clear that this argument fails. The question of whether or not God communicates through sounds and letters is a red herring. The relevant question is whether it is *possible* for God to be deceitful, and clearly it is. Nonverbal communication can be deceitful. One can deceive another person with one's actions. For example, if I pack my suitcase to pretend to my wife that I am leaving home, when I don't have this intention, I have deceived her. For God's *deception* to be possible, all that is needed is a possibility of a mismatch between God's *thoughts* and the *ideas communicated* to the Prophet, regardless of the form in which those ideas are communicated. God can deceive if He can imprint into the Prophet's mind ideas that He does not believe as His thoughts. God might have various ways to transfer thoughts to humans, including the Prophet.

Perhaps al-Ghazālī conceives revelation as a process in which the Prophet *sees* God's thoughts. That is, God becomes *transparent* to the Prophet. But this is quite an unusual view. It requires God not to be able to hide Himself from the Prophet. This restricts God's power in a radical way which is not acceptable, I suppose, to many believers.

To recap, the strict adherence argument is a powerful argument against the reliability of our independent judgments. It states that we have to follow the apparent meaning of Scripture and ignore our moral intuitions to the contrary. The argument is crucially dependent on al-Ghazālī's claim that for any particular action, independent of Scripture, we have no reason to think that the action is right or wrong; the argument also relies on the assumption that God is a reliable guide to morality. However, while al-Ghazālī's main claim is too much dependent on consequentialism, God's Reliability is in tension with consequentialism. Consequentialism is both a blessing and a curse for the argument.

5. *Taqlīd* and the Rule of Figurative Interpretation

It is well known that al-Ghazālī's opposed *taqlīd*, that is, uncritical acceptance. As Griffel puts it, "For al-Ghazālī, uncritical acceptance (*taqlīd*) is the root of all falsehood."[16] Is the conclusion of the strict adherence argument in tension with al-Ghazālī's very critical stance on *taqlīd*? The answer is no. But to see the reason, we have to see why al-Ghazālī is so critical of *taqlīd*, and what he means by it. Al-Ghazālī begins his intellectual autobiography, *Deliverance from Error*, in this way:

> You have asked me, my brother in religion, to communicate to you the aim and secrets of the sciences and the dangerous and intricate depths of the different doctrines and views. You want me to give you an account of my travail in disengaging the truth from amid the welter of the sects, despite the polarity of their means and methods. You also want to hear about my daring in mounting from the lowland of servile conformism [*taqlīd*] to the highland of independent investigation.[17]

Al-Ghazālī's main worry is that while there are many different conflicting views and religions, only one (or some) of them can be true, and it is a daring task to find the truth through independent investigations. The majority of people follow those views and religions by *taqlīd* (i.e., without independent investigations) and thus fall into error. The autobiography is written to show that (and how) he was rescued from error by his independent investigations. *Taqlīd* is the means by which various mistaken beliefs and religions are upheld, and renouncing it would be our way to deliverance from error. According to al-Ghazālī, if it was not for *taqlīd*, people would not follow the religion of their parents and would discover the true religion (which would be Islam according to him), and the correct understanding of it (which presumably would be something close to Ashʿarism).[18] *Taqlīd* is bad because it does not let us discriminate false religions from true ones on solid grounds. The opposite of *taqlīd* for al-Ghazālī would be to support one's view with

---

[16] Griffel, *Al-Ghazālī's Philosophical Theology*, 121. See also the excellent paper by Griffel on why Al-Ghazālī accuses philosophers of *taqlīd*: Frank Griffel, "*Taqlīd* of the Philosophers: Al-Ghazālī's Initial Accusation in His *Tahāfut*," in *Ideas, Images, and Methods of Portrayal: Insights into Classical Arabic Literature and Islam*, ed. Sebastian Günther (Leiden: Brill, 2005), 273–96.

[17] Al-Ghazālī, *Deliverance from Error (al-Munqidh min al-Dalāl)*, trans. Richard McCarthy (Louisville: Fons Vitae, 2004), 54

[18] Al-Ghazālī, *Deliverance from Error*, 54.

clear arguments and reasons. But this does not mean that following the literal meaning of the Qur'an, on al-Ghazālī's view, would count as a problematic case of *taqlīd*. Some Ashʿarite theologians would not even call the following of the literal meaning of the Qur'an a case of *taqlīd*. For it is not a case of uncritical acceptance.[19]

When we accept a belief after critical investigations, we might have reasons for the content of the belief. For example, we might have reasons to believe in God after being convinced by the arguments for God's existence. On the other hand, when we believe in the testimony of a reliable person, while we might not have independent reasons directly for the content of the testimony, the reliability of the person gives us a reason that the testimony is true. One might call one's acceptance of the testimony in such a case *taqlīd*. But this is not a problematic case of *taqlīd*. It is one's reason that leads one to accept the testimony. This is al-Ghazālī's position regarding strict adherence to Scripture. He uses the term *taqlīd* for adhering to Scripture, while he makes it clear that this *taqlīd* is not problematic. For instance, see the following passage from *Ihyā*.

> Regarding religious knowledge, it is acquired by *taqlīd* from the prophets.... And this knowledge is a result of learning from the Book of God and the tradition of the Prophet, and to understand the meaning of them after hearing them... For example, reason is not enough to maintain the health of the body, we need also to know about the effects and characteristics of medicines and drugs through learning from a physician, as reason alone cannot discover them. On the other hand, understanding something after hearing it would be impossible without reason. So, neither reason is independent of revelation, nor revelation is from reason.[20]

While *Ihyā* is a much later book than *al-Iqtisād*, the view expressed in *Ihyā* is similar to the one we discussed earlier. The role of reason, insofar as we are concerned about what we should do, is limited to (i) establishing that the prophet is a true prophet, (ii) understanding the (literal) meaning of Scripture, and (iii) understanding the meaning of moral terms (this

---

[19] See Richard M. Frank, "Knowledge and Taqlîd: The Foundations of Religious Belief in Classical Ashʿarism," *Journal of American Oriental Society* 109.1 (1989): 37–62.

[20] Al-Ghazālī, *Ihyā' 'ulūm ad-dīn*, vol. 3 (Beirut: Dār al-Maʿrifa, 1403/1982), 17. An English translation of volume 3, book 1, can be found here: *The Marvels of the Heart*, trans. Walter James Skellie (Louisville: Fons Vitae, 2010).

understanding helps us see that consequentialism is true). Apart from that, reason plays no role in critical moral evaluation of the content of revelation. A Scriptural injunction is like the prescriptions of physicians. Self-centered consequentialism implies that we have to follow them, without being able to justify their content.

Despite what I have said, on al-Ghazālī's view, there are cases in which reason may reject the apparent meaning of Scripture. Those cases, however, are limited to those in which we have a demonstration to the effect that it is *impossible* for the literal meaning of the text to be true. Al-Ghazālī addresses the issue in *al-Iqtisād* as follows.

> Whatever is claimed to be revealed must be examined. If reason deems it possible, then it must be believed conclusively if the testimonial evidence is conclusive.... Regarding what reason deems impossible, if it is reported in the revelation, it must be interpreted metaphorically. It is inconceivable that the revelation contains what is conclusively contrary to reason. (*al-Iqtisād*, 210)

Al-Ghazālī returns to this issue and discuss it in more details in his later work, *Faysal*.[21] Al-Ghazālī's main goal in *Faysal* is to give a criterion to determine whether a particular understanding of religion amounts to unbelief (*kufr*). Unbelief, on his view, "is to deem anything that Prophet brought to be a lie. Faith is to deem everything he brought to be true" (*Faysal*, 92). While some interpretations of the text are incorrect, al-Ghazālī acknowledges that one does not need to have a particular interpretation of the text to be included among believers. One is a believer just in case one has an interpretation of Scripture under which Scripture is deemed to be true. Al-Ghazālī also explains how we should understand "deeming a statement to be true." "The reality of deeming to be true is to acknowledge the existence of everything whose existence the Prophet informed us of" (*Faysal*, 94). Therefore, to deem a statement to be true, we have to provide an interpretation under which the statement's terms have some referents. He distinguishes between *five levels of existence* and notes that a true statement has referents which exist at least at one of these five levels.

---

[21] The complete title of the book is *Faysal al-Tafriqa bayna al-Islam wa al-zandaqa*. English translations are from *On the Boundaries of Theological Tolerance in Islam: Abū Ḥāmid al-Ghāzalī's "Faysal al-Tafriqa bayna al-Islam wa al-zandaqa,"* trans. Sherman A. Jackson (Oxford: Oxford University Press, 2002).

"Existence" (*wujud*), however, is of five levels. And it is only because of their obliviousness to this fact that all of the groups accuse their adversaries of deeming some or another aspect of what the Prophet taught to be a lie. Existence, meanwhile, can be: (1) ontological (*dhātī*); (2) sensory (*hissī*); (3) imaginative (*khayālī*); (4) noetic (*'aqlī*); or (5) analogous (*shabahī*). And no one who acknowledges the existence of what the Prophet informed us of *on any of these five levels* can be said to be categorically deeming what the Prophet taught to be a lie. (*Faysal*, 94)

While the details of how we should understand the five levels of existence is not important for our purpose, let me very briefly explain what they amount to.[22] We shouldn't understand al-Ghazālī as saying that there are five different *properties* of existence. There is only one property of existence, which some entities have and some don't. What he really means by "five levels of existence" is that there are five different categories of beings which can be the referent of a term. Things that have "ontological existence" are "*concrete things in the world external to both mind and senses*" (94). His examples of the beings of this kind are "the ottoman (*kursī*) and the seven heavens" (96). Things that have "sensory existence" "acquire form through the visual power of the eye. They are particular to the one whose senses grasp them." His nonreligious examples include illusion, hallucination, and things "seen" in a dream (94–95). In a religious context, his example is that the Prophet's statement that "Paradise was presented to me inside this wall" should be understood as "the image of Paradise being in the wall presented itself to the Prophet's senses" (97). Things that have "imaginative existence" are "images of things that are normally perceived through the senses in instances where these things themselves are removed from the reach of the senses." His example for this category is the image of an elephant when you imagine an elephant. His religious example is that when the Prophet said that he witnessed a past event involving Jonah, the son of Matthew, it was the image of Jonah which was presented to the Prophet.

Things that have "noetic existence" have a "functional nature." To use al-Ghazālī's example, we can understand "hand" as things that have "the ability to seize and to strike" (96). The last category is the things that have "analogous existence." "Analogous existence" is different from the other four levels, as it does not refer to a particular kind of beings. Rather, when you say that

---

[22] For a discussion of the levels, see Frank Griffel, *Al-Ghazālī's Philosophical Theology*, chapter 4.

the referent of a term has "analogous existence," you mean that the term does not refer to its semantical content. Rather, it refers to something "analogous to [its semantical content] that possesses some quality or attribute peculiar to [the semantical content]" (96). Al-Ghazālī's example of "analogous existence" is God's anger. Al-Ghazālī holds that the meaning of anger is "the boiling of blood in the heart engendered by a desire of vengeance." But God has no anger. So God's anger refers to "some other attribute [of God] which produces the same result as anger, such as the will to punish" (100).

Rending the Prophet's saying true under an interpretation that makes use of at least one of those kinds of beings is sufficient for one to be acquitted from the charge of unbelief (*kufr*), which is punishable by death according to the Islamic law. But, according to al-Ghazālī, being acquitted from the charge of *kufr* is not enough to make your interpretation *correct*. Rather, for your interpretation to be the correct religious interpretation, it has to satisfy the rule of figurative interpretation (*ta'wīl*).

> Listen now to the Rule of Figurative Interpretation [*ta'wīl*]. You already know that all of the parties agree on the aforementioned five levels of figurative interpretation, and that none of these levels falls within the scope of "deeming a statement to be a lie." They also agree, however, that the permissibility of engaging in figurative interpretation is contingent upon having established the logical impossibility of the apparent meaning (*zāhir*) of a text. The first level of apparent meaning corresponds to ontological (*dhātī*) existence. Whenever this is conceded, the remaining levels are entailed. If this proves (logically) impossible, however, one moves to the level of sensory existence (*hissī*), for it too embraces those levels below it. If this proves impossible, one moves to the level of imaginative (*khayālī*) or noetic (*'aqlī*) existence. And if this proves impossible, one moves to the level of analogous, allegorical existence (*al-wujud al shabahī al-majāzī*). Now, no one is permitted to move from one level (of interpretation) to a level beneath it without being compelled by logical proof (*burhān*). (*Faysal*, 104)

Nonliteral interpretation is permissible, on al-Ghazālī's view, only when we have a *logical proof* (*burhān*) that the literal interpretation of the text is *impossible*. Al-Ghazālī also holds that moving from each level to the next requires proof of impossibility in the higher level. The latter rule is not important for me, and I am not sure whether all his examples satisfy it. But the former is clear. Let's review how his examples meet the requirement imposed by the rule. It is logically impossible for Paradise to exist inside this wall, as "it is a logically proven fact that the smaller body cannot encompass the larger." Therefore, it is permissible for us to appeal to a sensory being to interpret the Prophet's saying that Paradise was presented to him inside this wall. Moreover, given that it is impossible for the Prophet to actually witness a past event involving Jonas, as "the actual existence of this event preceded the existence of the Prophet, and had long passed into non-existence," we may appeal to Prophet's imagination to understand his report of witnessing a past event. It is impossible for God to have physical hands. Therefore, "God's hand" in the Qur'an may be understood functionally, and, finally given that it is impossible for God to have anger, we are allowed to have an allegorical interpretation of "God's anger" mentioned in the Qur'an.

In sum, there are cases in which we are allowed to understand Scripture nonliterally. But what about practical injunctions of Scripture? Are we ever allowed, according to the rule of figurative interpretation, to interpret them nonliterally? Recall that a departure from the literal meaning is permissible only when we have a proof that the literal meaning is *impossible*. But what does it mean for a normative statement to be impossible? A state of affairs can be possible, actual, or impossible. A normative injunction does not make a claim about how the world is. It does not describe a state of affairs. However, one might say that a normative claim can be called impossible if it involves an impossibility. For example, one might think the normative claim that "the actual king of France should be just" is impossible because it is impossible for the actual king of France to exists. But regardless of whether or not this understanding of the impossibility of normative claims is correct, it is not applicable to our discussion, as none of the morally controversial passages involve any impossible entity.

The reason that al-Ghazālī allows one to interpret Scripture nonliterally when there is proof that the literal meaning is impossible is that, on his view, God does not make false claims. If we know that the literal meaning of a statement is impossible, there is no possibility for God to make that statement true. Given that this is the reasoning behind the rule of figurative interpretation, we might want to slightly weaken the rule to be more applicable to normative statements. Instead of a demonstrated impossibility, we can say that *a demonstration of falsity* is enough to give us a permission to depart from the literal meaning. While this more permissive version of the rule is applicable to injunctions of Scripture, it does not allow us to have a nonliteral understanding of moral injunctions. For, on al-Ghazālī's view, we have no reason, let alone logical proof, to conclude that the literal meaning of the normative statement is false. Reason, according to him, has no power to discover the consequences of actions, and thus in moral matters reason has no epistemic power whatsoever to discover the truth. He thinks that things such as "the resurrection and congregation, reward and punishment" are only known through revelation (*al-Iqtisād*, 210). Given that rewards and punishments determine the moral status of an action, we have no reason to think that the injunctions described by the literal meaning of Scripture are incorrect.

To sum up, neither the critical stance of al-Ghazālī toward *taqlīd* nor his permission to interpret revelation nonliterally in some cases warrant our questioning the conclusion of the argument for strict adherence. The argument for strict adherence presents a general al-Ghazālīan argument for the conclusion that when there is a clash between our moral intuitions and revelation, our moral intuitions are not reliable and we have to side with revelation. While this argument is too reliant on consequentialism for one of its premises, consequentialism generates a problem for another of its premises. The next chapter will discuss whether the strict adherence argument can be reconstructed within a deontological framework.

2
The Deontological Ethics of the Muʿtazilites

Summary of the Chapter

Section 1. This section briefly discusses the classical problem of evil, and the difference between the Ashʿarites' and the Muʿtazilites' approach to the problem.

Section 2. The section covers the metaethics of the Muʿtazilites theologian ʿAbd al-Jabbār. ʿAbd al-Jabbār holds that the fundamental moral concepts are concepts of blameworthiness and praiseworthiness. He also offers a theory of wrong- (and right-)making aspects. The section discusses two ways of understanding his aspect theory.

Section 3. This section overviews the normative ethics of ʿAbd al-Jabbār. His normative theory has some deontological elements: (i) it assigns intrinsic value to act-types; (ii) it recognizes deontological notions such as retribution and reparation; (iii) it does not require actions to have the goal of bringing about the highest good for everyone.

Section 4. ʿAbd al-Jabbār's moral epistemology is the subject of this section. In his view, while we have intuitive knowledge about pro tanto wrongness of actions, we don't have intuitive knowledge about actions' being wrong *everything considered*. Revelation helps us make judgments about everything-considered wrongness.

Section 5. This section explains how the argument for strict adherence can be defended against the objections presented in the previous chapter. ʿAbd al-Jabbār's moderate skepticism about the power of reason to make everything-considered moral judgments is in line with the skeptical theist's response to the classical problem of evil.[1]

---

[1] The reader who is not interested in *historical* discussions of ʿAbd al-Jabbār's ethical theory may skip sections 1, 2, 3, and 4. The main section that discusses the problem of prescribed evil is section 5. Section 4 works as an introduction to section 5.

1. The Ashʿarites and the Problem of Evil

In the previous chapter, we saw that the Ashʿarites hold that God has absolute power to determine morality. The divine command theory of the early Ashʿarites and the theological consequentialism of al-Ghazālī are two different attempts to specify how God is the author of morality. One of the main motivations of the Ashʿarites to give God the absolute power to determine morality is that they see no other way out of the classical problem of evil. We can formulate the classical problem of evil, roughly, as follows:

(1) An omnipotent, omniscience, and omnibenevolent God would not create a world which contains pointless evil.
(2) For all we know, there is pointless evil in the world.
(3) Therefore, for all we know, there is no God, or, if there is, He is not omnipotent, omniscience, or omnibenevolent.

Most modern theists accept premise (1) and seek a way to undermine premise (2). This is not true of the Ashʿarites. They believe that we have to reject the first premise to block the problem. Al-Ghazālī holds that we should not place any moral restriction on God's actions:

> *We claim that God is able to bring suffering upon an animal that is innocent of any crime, and that He is not required to reward it.* The Muʿtazilites say that this is impossible because it is bad. Hence, they are necessarily led to assert that if a bug or a flea is harmed by being smashed or swatted, then God (Exalted is He) is obligated to resurrect it and compensate for it. We, however, say that bringing suffering upon those who are innocent of crimes, such as animals, children and the insane is feasible, indeed it has witnessed and perceived.... *We claim that it is not obligatory for God to care for the well-being of His servants, but He may do whatever He wills and decree whatever He wants.* Thus we contradict the Muʿtazilites, who placed restrictions on the acts of God (Glorious is He), and made it obligatory for Him to care for the well-being [of his servants]. As previously stated, the same thing that proved that nothing is obligatory for God (Exalted is He) also proves [the] falsity of this view. (al-Ghazālī, *al-Iqtisād*, 177–79)

According to the Ashʿarites, God would not act wrongly in creating a world in which children suffer for no reason. Early Ashʿarites believed that there is no moral standard independent of His will with which we can morally evaluate God's actions. In the same vein, al-Ghazālī holds that self-centered consequentialism places no moral restriction on God because no action of God could benefit or harm Him. Therefore, God has no duty to care about animals and human beings. However, al-Ghazālī is aware that this implication is radical and hard to digest. To motivate his views, then, he notes that we have no way around the problem of evil if we place moral restrictions on the acts of God. Al-Ghazālī uses an example borrowed from Abu'l Hassan al-Ashʿarī to make this point.

> Observation and reality prove the falsity of the view [of placing restrictions on the acts of God] for we will show them acts of God (Glorious is He) that will force them to concede that they do not serve the interest of His servants. Let us suppose that there are three children: one of them dies a Muslim in his youth, another reached maturity, became a Muslim, and died a Muslim in his maturity, and the third became an infidel in his maturity and died while in the state of infidelity. Justice for them requires that the mature infidel reside forever in hellfire, and the mature Muslim have a higher rank in paradise than the Muslim youth. The Muslim youth might say: "O Lord, why did You give me a rank lower than his?" God might say "Because he reached maturity and obeyed me and you did not obey me by performing acts of worship, since you did not reach maturity." He might say "O Lord, You made me die before reaching maturity. My best interest would have been for my life to have been extended until I reached maturity, so that I might have obeyed you and attained his rank; why did You deny me this rank forever, where you were able to make me qualified for it?" God would have no answer but to say: "I knew that if you had reached maturity, you would have sinned rather than obeyed me, and then you would be subject to my punishment and wrath. The infidel might call from the abyss and say "O Lord, did You not know that if I reached maturity, I would be an infidel? Had you made me die in my youth and placed me at that low rank in paradise, I would have loved that and it would have been better for me than Your condemning me forever to hellfire; so why did You make me live when death was better for me?" There would be no answer available for God at all.[2]

---

[2] Abu Hamid M. b. M. al-Ghazālī, *Al-Ghazāli's "Moderation in Belief"*, trans. Aladdin M. Yaqub (Chicago: University of Chicago Press, 2013), 179.

According to al-Ghazālī, if we assume that moral standards are independent of God and are accessible to us, we should say that God's benevolence requires Him to let some children die because they would have been worse off had they lived longer. But then, if God can bring about someone's death to make him better off, justice requires Him to bring about an early death for all unbelievers to prevent them from going to hell and thus experience eternal suffering. But we know that many people die as unbelievers. So God fails to comply with the independent standards of morality.[3] Al-Ghazālī accepts premise (2) of the problem-of-evil argument. On his view, we should not seek any point in the death of innocent children. This is simply what God wills. Our best chance to answer the classical problem of evil is to deny that God is subject to (commonsensical) moral restrictions. But for the Mu'tazilites, that is, the rivals of the Ash'arites, denying the first premise of the argument is utterly unacceptable. A core element of the Mu'tazilite view is God's justice. Accepting premise (2) would be in conflict with their conception of God's justice.

2. The Metaethics of the Mu'tazilites

The Mu'tazilites are one of the earliest Muslim theological groups. They take God's justice as one of their main concerns, to the extent that they called themselves *ahl al-tuwhīd was-al-'adl* (i.e., the upholders of [God's] oneness and justice).[4] In this chapter, I will discuss the views of 'Abd al-Jabbār b. Ahmad b. 'Abd al-Jabbār al-Hamadhani (935–1025), who is certainly one of the most (if not the most) prominent Mu'tazilite theologians.[5]

---

[3] For a discussion of salvific luck and the case of three brothers from a Mu'tazilite perspective see my paper coauthored with Scott Davison, "Salvific Luck in Islamic Theology," *Journal of Analytic Theology* 8 (2020): 120–30.

[4] Due to political reasons, the influence of the Mu'tazilites declined rapidly. Many of their doctrines, however, especially on the matter of justice, are adopted by Imāmī theologians who represent theological Shi'i Islam. See Richard M. Frank, *Early Islamic Theology: The Mu'tazilites and al-Ash'arī* (Burlington, VT: Aldershot, 2007), for the history of early Islamic theology. For a general short introduction to the Mu'tazilites see Peter Adamson, *Philosophy in the Islamic World* (New York: Oxford University Press, 2016), chapter 2.

[5] See Gabriel Said Reynolds, "The Rise and Fall of Qadi 'Abd al-Jabbār," *International Journal of Middle East Studies* 37.1 (2005): 3–18, for a biography of 'Abd al-Jabbār. Unfortunately, none of his writings have been translated into English. Despite the importance of his works, they are largely neglected. For a good discussion of his moral philosophy see George F. Hourani, *Islamic Rationalism: The Ethics of 'Abd al-Jabbār* (New York: Oxford University Press, 1971). Also see Margaretha T. Heemskerk, *Suffering in the Mu'tazilite Theology: 'Abd Al-jabbār's Teaching on Pain and Divine Justice* (Leiden: Brill, 2000).

THE DEONTOLOGICAL ETHICS OF THE MUʿTAZILITES 71

The Muʿtazilites are the first group in the history of Islamic thought to undertake the development of a deontological moral theory, and although their moral theory was largely ignored by many later Islamic thinkers, they had a considerable impact on later Imāmī theologians. I will discuss in the long last section of this chapter how the al-Ghazālian argument reconstructed in the previous chapter, that is, the argument for strict adherence, would be affected if we deny consequentialism and adopt a deontological moral theory. But before getting to the strict-adherence argument, we need to have an understanding of the deontological theory of the Muʿtazilites. To this end, we need to know more about their metaethics, normative theory, and epistemology. This section explains the metaethics of ʿAbd al-Jabbār, which is closely connected to his epistemology.

Two central pieces of ʿAbd al-Jabbār's ethical theory are (i) that theological voluntarism (i.e., divine command theory) is wrong, that is, that the wrongness or rightness of actions is not constituted by God's prohibitions or commands, and (ii) that we have *intuitive* knowledge of morality. To argue for the former, he usually uses the latter claim. In other words, our intuitive knowledge of morality plays a central role in his metaethics. Let's review two of his interesting and convincing arguments against the theological voluntarism of the Ashʿarites.

> [1] If that were true [i.e., the wrongness were constituted by God's prohibition], it would be, then, the case that if God prohibited justice and fairness, they would be evil, and if He commanded injustice (*zulm*), and lies, they would be good ... and clearly this is false.... [2] If that were true, it would be the case that the one who does not know about commands or prohibitions, would not know that injustice and lie are evil, for knowledge of something's being evil is derived from knowledge of what makes that thing evil (directly or discursively). But it is clear that the infidels know that injustice is evil even when they do not know about prohibitions or the prohibitor.[6]

The *first* argument concerns the fact that intuitively it would be wrong of God to command acts, such as lying, that are generally acknowledged to be immoral. The moral status of these actions is known to be independent of God's commands and prohibitions. According to the *second* argument, if moral terms are defined in terms of God's commands, then atheists would have no

---

[6] ʿAbd al-Jabbār, *Sharh al-usul al-khamsah* (Cairo: Maktabat Wahbah, 1996), 11.

moral knowledge, but this implication is implausible too. Here 'Abd al-Jabbār not only claims that the infidels can use moral terms correctly (al-Ghazālī too accepts this claim), but also claims that they have ethical knowledge about what is wrong and right.[7] These arguments are particularly interesting for our purposes, because they rest on the assumption that all people, including theists and atheists, have intuitive moral knowledge. 'Abd al-Jabbār takes our moral intuitions much more seriously than al-Ghazālī does and uses them to argue against theological voluntarism.

'Abd al-Jabbār thinks that his arguments refute theological voluntarism of the early Ash'arites. As we noted in the previous chapter, later Ash'arites, such as al-Ghazālī, also reject theological voluntarism on the grounds that the semantics of moral terms should not be held hostage to theology. Yet the rejection of theological voluntarism would not preclude al-Ghazālī from maintaining that God's moral nature is consistent with His not caring for the well-being of any individual. What enabled al-Ghazālī to maintain such a view is his espousal of self-centered consequentialism, or ethical egoism. 'Abd al-Jabbār, however, thinks that ethical egoism can't be correct. For it too conflicts with our intuitions.

The different stances of al-Ghazālī and 'Abd al-Jabbār toward ethical egoism stem in part from their different understandings of the semantics of ethical terms such as 'obligation'. While al-Ghazālī thinks 'obligation' should be defined in terms of self-interest, for 'Abd al-Jabbār the most fundamental ethical notion is that of blameworthiness (and praiseworthiness), and 'obligation' is ultimately defined by reference to the notion of blameworthiness. In the following passages, 'Abd al-Jabbār seeks to provide the definitions of important ethical notions, such as the notions of evil and obligation, by using the concept of blameworthiness.

---

[7] But it should be noted that 'Abd al-Jabbār's claim that *the knowledge of something's being evil is derived from knowledge of what makes that thing evil* is clearly false. To give an example, it is false to claim that *the knowledge of something's being water is derived from knowledge of what makes that thing water* (i.e., *being composed of hydrogen and oxygen*). It may be the case that while the property of being good is identical with the property of, say, being commanded by God, infidels have access to moral properties under one mode of presentation but not under the other. In contrast with the semantical version of divine command theory, held by the early Ash'arites, Adams and Audi, among others, defend this metaphysical version of divine command theory, which is not susceptible to this objection by 'Abd al-Jabbār or that of al-Ghazālī. See Robert Merrihew Adams, "Moral Arguments for Theistic Belief," in *Rationality and Religious Belief*, ed. Cornelius F. Delaney (Notre Dame: University of Notre Dame Press, 1979), 116–40; Robert Merrihew Adams, "Divine Command Metaethics Modified Again," *Journal of Religious Ethics* 7.1 (Spring 1979): 66–79; Robert Audi, "Divine Command Morality and the Autonomy of Ethics," *Faith and Philosophy* 24.2 (2007): 121–43.

An act is obligatory when someone capable of doing it would deserve blame for refraining from it in certain respects. The proviso of 'in certain respects' is added to allow the cases of disjunctive obligation in which while the total disjunction is obligatory, the agent has an option. If the agent performs one of the disjuncts and omits the others, he would not deserve blame for omitting them because he has done his obligation. Nevertheless, he deserves blame [for the disjunct he did not perform] in certain respect *i.e.* he would be blameworthy if he had not done any of the disjuncts. If it were not for disjunctive obligation, I would not add the proviso. (*Sharh*, 39)

An act is evil when someone capable of doing it would deserve blame for doing it in certain respects.... The proviso of 'in certain respects' is added to allow the evil actions of children, the insane, and animals. Their action may be evil even though they are not blameworthy for it at all. Nevertheless, they are blameworthy for the action in certain respects *i.e.* they would be blameworthy if they knew that the action is evil, or could know that. I would not add this proviso if it were not for such cases. (*Sharh*, 41)

According to 'Abd al-Jabbār, then, roughly speaking, an action is evil if the agent is blameworthy for that action, and an action is obligatory if the agent is blameworthy for not doing it. 'Abd al-Jabbār thinks that his definitions need some proviso. In the case of obligation, he thinks that the short definition does not strictly apply to the case of disjunctive obligations, and so he adds a proviso to the definition to take care of cases of disjunctive obligations. I think we can ignore the proviso added for the definition of obligation.[8]

The proviso added for the definition of evil, however, is more interesting. If one defines evil in terms of blame, then one can't blamelessly do an evil action. Yet 'Abd al-Jabbār wants to make some room for this possibility. Evil might pull apart from blameworthiness in non-normal cases where some epistemic conditions are not met. A child's murder is evil even though he might not be blameworthy for it. He would be had he known that murder is evil.

On 'Abd al-Jabbār's way of thinking, our intuitions about an act's being blameworthy or praiseworthy would be our main guide to construct a plausible ethical theory. Given this way of understanding the moral concept of

---

[8] I am not sure why the proviso is needed. For if my obligation is *to do either A or B*, it is not that I have *an obligation to do A* or that I have *an obligation to do B*. The content of my obligation is the *disjunction*, and 'Abd al-Jabbār could easily say that I am not blameworthy if I satisfy the content of my obligation (i.e., the disjunction). But maybe this is what he has in mind. Imagine you have to save x or save y, but can't save both. Perhaps he thinks that if you save x, then 'in some sense', you are *still blameworthy* for not saving y, because you would normally be obligated to do so.

obligation, it is clear why he would disapprove of al-Ghazālī's ethical egoism. Acting egoistically is intuitively blameworthy. For example, as a matter of justice, it is obligatory to show gratitude to those who help us, and to pay our debts. Not paying one's debt is blameworthy even though it might be in our best interest. We have obligations to perform certain acts in virtue of the fact that it would be blameworthy for us to fail to perform them. These obligations cannot be explained by ethical egoism. I will get back to this issue later.

A terminological point is in order here. In contemporary ethics, axiological terms such as *'good'*, *'evil'*, or *'bad'* are distinguished from deontological terms such as *'wrong'*, *'right'*, or *'obligatory'*. An action might be *good* but *wrong*, if, say, there are better alternatives. An action can be *evil* but *right* if, say, the alternatives are much worse. No such distinction is drawn in 'Abd al-Jabbār's works. But it seems that 'Abd al-Jabbār's term *evil* (*qabīh*) is very close to the deontic concept of *wrongness*. This is supported by the fact that, on his definitions, obligations and evil can be inter-defined: they are both defined in terms of the notion of blameworthiness. If an action is obligatory, refraining from doing it would be blameworthy and thus *evil*. In the same vein, if an action is obligatory, it would be *wrong* not to do it. Accordingly, I will henceforth assume 'Abd al-Jabbār's term *evil* means wrong, and use those terms interchangeably.

A centerpiece of 'Abd al-Jabbār's ethical theory is that we have *intuitive moral knowledge*. 'Abd al-Jabbār seeks to explain intuitive moral knowledge by using his *theory of aspects* (or grounds). On his view, an action is evil in virtue of instantiating a wrong-making *aspect* (*wajh*). Wrong- or right-making aspects, or grounds, for which 'Abd al-Jabbār uses the term *wujūh*, are those properties of an action which ground their being wrong or right. Here is how he explains the issue.

> Know that although, as we said before, evil actions are subsumed under one single definition, the aspects (*wujūh*) for which they are evil are different. That [evil actions are all subsumed under one single definition] is not disputed, for this is what causes agreement about the essence of properties. But the things in virtue of which we apply a predicate [e.g., being evil] to a subject may vary.... If so, lying is evil because it is lying, wrongdoing is evil because it is wrongdoing, ingratitude is evil because it is ingratitude.[9]

---

[9] 'Abd al-Jabbār, *al-Mughnī fī abāb al-tawhīd wa'l-'adl*, 16 vols. (Cairo: Wizarat al-Thagafah wa-al-Irshad el-Qawmi, 1960–65), VI.i, 61.

According to 'Abd al-Jabbār, an act's being evil means by definition that the agent is blameworthy for performing the act (barring special cases). This definition is in common between all evil actions; it is in virtue of this definition that we call all evil things 'evil'. Nonetheless, blameworthiness is not *the ground* for which an act is evil. Rather, an act is evil *on the grounds* that it has instantiated some *wrong-making aspect*. As we will shortly see, the instantiation of a wrong-making aspect by an action *necessitates* the action's being evil. In this respect, wrong-making aspects are similar to truth-makers. Just as the truth-maker of a proposition necessitates its being true, the wrong-making aspect of an action necessitates its being wrong. 'Abd al-Jabbār's uses the example of causation to illustrate the issue. On his view, a wrong-making aspect necessitates the wrongness of an action in the same way that a cause necessitates its effect.[10]

> Know that what entails the evilness of an evil action, such as its being a lie, or being an unjust pain, functions in the same way that an efficient cause entails its effect. Just as it is impossible to have the cause, but not to necessitate the effect, it is impossible to instantiate the evil-making aspect (*wujūh*) but not to necessitate the action's being evil. (*al-Mughnī* VI.i, 122)

We can represent 'Abd al-Jabbār's aspect theory by the following proposition:

Necessitating Aspects. For any action φ and any wrong-making aspect w, necessarily, if φ instantiates the wrong-making aspect w, φ is evil.

Suppose we don't include the circumstance of an action in the individuation of the act-type. If we understand aspects as necessitating grounds of wrongness or rightness, we would be committed to either accepting absolutism about act-types (i.e., act-types necessitate the wrongness of act-tokens instantiating them), or holding that act-types can never be a wrong-making aspect. 'Abd al-Jabbār's adopts the latter option.

> It is not the case that what makes an evil action evil is its type. (*al-Mughnī* VI.i, 59)

---

[10] This example could be misleading if we have a modern notion of causation in mind. 'Abd al-Jabbār's notion of causation is not the modern notion of causation. It does not require time, as the causation, for him, is not a temporal notion. It also gives rise to metaphysical necessity.

If someone asks whether the evilness of an evil act is because of its character or nature, tell him that the same action may be evil one time—when it has an aspect that makes it evil, and good another time—when it has an opposite aspect. Don't you see that the act of entering a house could be evil when performed without permission, even though the same [type of] act would be good when it is done with permission? (*Sharh*, 310)

'Abd al-Jabbār denies absolutism. On his view, any act-type can be performed permissibly in one circumstance and impermissibly in another. In other words, for any act-type, there are tokens of that type which are evil, and tokens of that type which are not. We can express this nonabsolutist requirement as follows:

Nonabsolutism. Act-types would never necessitate the wrongness of act-tokens which instantiate them.

In addition to metaphysical role of grounding wrongness, aspects play an important epistemological role, too. According to 'Abd al-Jabbār, the foundation of our moral knowledge is our intuitive knowledge of the moral status of aspects. What is intuitively known is not that a particular action is wrong, but rather *the general claim that actions instantiating a certain wrong-making aspect are wrong*. But then the question is what are the necessitating grounds that are intuitively known. The main examples that 'Abd al-Jabbār mentions are the following: injustice (*zulm*), lying (*kadhb*), ignorance (*jahl*), ingratitude (*kufru n-nima*), commanding evil (*amru l-qabih*), uselessness (*abath*), imposing unattainable obligations (*taklif ma la yutaq*) (*al-Mughnī* VI.i, p. 61), and failing to repay your debt (*raddu l-vadieh*) (*al-Mughnī* XIV, 30). However, these examples are problematic, for they can't play the role that 'Abd al-Jabbār wants aspects to play in his epistemology. To illustrate the problem, we need an overall understanding of the distinction between *thick* and *thin moral concepts*.

The distinction between thick and thin moral concepts was first introduced by Bernard Williams. *Thin moral concepts* are purely evaluative, whereas *thick moral concepts* are partly evaluative and partly nonevaluative. According to Williams, thick concepts are both evaluative and "guided by the world [non-normatively described]."[11] The examples of thick concepts

---

[11] Bernard Williams, *Ethics and the Limits of Philosophy* (Cambridge, MA: Harvard University Press, 1985), 140.

include virtue, vice, injustice, cruelty, rudeness, generosity, gratitude, etc. Thin moral concepts, on the other hand, either have no nonevaluative content or their nonevaluative content is very thin. The main examples of thin concepts include good, evil, ought, obligation, permissible, right, etc.

'Abd al-Jabbār's uses mainly thick moral concepts to describe his examples of wrong-making aspects. Some examples, such as ingratitude and injustice, are clearly thick. Some explicitly involve evaluative and nonevaluative elements such as commanding evil, and imposing unattainable obligations. Some examples, such as lying and uselessness, are on the borderline. Whether they are thick might depend on how we understand them. If we take lying as asserting what one does not believe, then it is not a thick concept. However, this liberal understanding of lying implies that jokes and stories are all lies, for (arguably) a storyteller asserts what they do not believe. If we want to exclude story- and joke-telling from lying, we might need to incorporate some evaluative content into the concept of lying. For example, we might say lying is asserting something one does not believe in a context in which truth-telling should be assumed.[12] This more restricted understanding of lying makes it a thick concept.

'Abd al-Jabbār assumes that his wrong-making aspects, which are mainly described by thick descriptions, *necessitate* the instantiation of the thin property of evil or wrongness. This is not clear. I submit that all the wrong-making aspects he mentions necessitate *badness*.[13] But if we understand his term *evil* (*qabīh*) as 'wrong' (i.e., if want to say that we ought not to perform what is *qabīh*, as he wants to say), it is not clear that his aspects *necessitate* wrongness. Some cases of lying are justified. That is, in those cases our lying would not be wrong. Moreover, we can imagine cases in which ingratitude is justified (if the alternative is much worse). The same is true of ignorance, failing to return your debt and commanding evil. We can imagine cases in which one is justified to command a person to do something evil. For example, there might be a case in which by directing a person to do an evil thing one could save millions of lives. Therefore, lying, ingratitude, ignorance, failing to return your debt, and commanding evil may not necessitate wrongness.

---

[12] This is Shiffrin's account of lying. Seana Valentine Shiffrin, *Speech Matters: On Lying, Morality, and the Law* (Princeton, NJ: Princeton University Press, 2016).

[13] Some people even deny that thick concepts necessitate *any* evaluative judgments. On their views, the evaluative element of a thick concept is not in its content; rather it should be explained by the pragmatics of the usage of the term. See Pekka Väyrynen, *The Lewd, the Rude and the Nasty* (New York: Oxford University Press, 2013), chaps. 5–6.

In general, a thick moral concept is an indication of something's being good or bad in a certain manner. But something can be bad in a certain respect, and good in other respects. Moreover, the wrongness of an action is not fully determined by its goodness or badness; it also depends on the alternatives that are available. So, in general it is unlikely that most thick concepts necessitate wrongness. Some thick concepts, though, might be exceptions. For example, it might be the case that injustice is always wrong. But whether the instantiation of a thick concept necessitates wrongness is not the main problem for 'Abd al-Jabbār's theory of aspects; the main problem for him is that when we describe wrong-making aspects in terms of thick concepts, they can't play *the epistemological role* that 'Abd al-Jabbār wants them to play.

Aspects play an important epistemological role in 'Abd al-Jabbār's theory. According to him, our knowledge that an action instantiating a wrong-making aspect is wrong is *intuitive* moral knowledge. As I will explain shortly, if we supplement this intuitive knowledge with our observations, then on his view we can deduce almost *all* our moral knowledge. The problem with specifying wrong-making aspects in terms of thick concepts, however, is that (i) our intuitive knowledge that they are wrong would be *trivial*, and (ii) this knowledge can't be the foundation of our ethical knowledge.

There are two views about the relation between thick and thin moral concepts. On *the separability view*, the evaluative part of a thick concept is *separable* from its descriptive content; the evaluative and nonevaluative parts can be disentangled.[14] If the separability view is right, our knowledge that injustice or ingratitude is bad is just *analytic*. The thin content is a separable part of the meaning of a thick concept. On the other hand, according to the *inseparability view*, the evaluative and nonevaluative parts *can't* be disentangled.[15] On this view, 'cruel' does not mean being bad in a certain way, it is a sui generis concept, unanalyzable in terms of thin concepts and descriptive concepts. Yet this view is also committed to saying that the evaluative component contributes to the *semantical content* of a thick concept. That is, the evaluative component makes a difference

---

[14] See Michael Smith, "On the Nature and Significance of the Distinction between Thick and Thin Ethical Concepts," in *Thick Concepts* (Oxford: Oxford University Press, 2013), 97–120.

[15] See Williams, *Ethics*, 129–30; John McDowell, "Non-cognitivism and Rule-Following," in his *Mind, Value, and Reality* (Cambridge, MA: Harvard University Press, 1998), 198–219; Hilary Putnam, *The Collapse of the Fact/Value Dichotomy and Other Essays* (Cambridge, MA: Harvard University Press, 2002), chap. 2.

to the truth-condition of a thick moral term.[16] If so, there is a conceptual relation between thick and thin concepts. We see the conceptual connection when we understand the meaning of a thick term and the relevant thin term. Thus, even if the concept *cruel* can't be decomposed into evaluative and nonevaluative parts, cruelty conceptually entails badness, and thus our knowledge that cruelty is bad is *insubstantial*. If so, we cannot construct *all* our ethical knowledge solely on the basis of those *insubstantial* pieces of knowledge.

In our search for moral knowledge, what we want to know is what *normative predicates* apply to our actions described *in a non-normative way*. The sheer knowledge of relations between thick and thin moral concepts cannot justify the application of evaluative concepts to actions non-normatively described. The central question in moral epistemology is how we know that the world (non-normatively described) has normative properties. If we describe aspects in a normative way (by using thick concepts), the aspect theory would fail to answer this central question.

While ʿAbd al-Jabbār mainly uses thick concepts to describe his examples of aspects, we might think that a better way to identify aspects is to identify them non-normatively. For example, lying is a candidate for a wrong-making aspect, and, as I explained, we might define lying nonevaluatively (e.g., asserting a proposition one does not believe). However, wrong-making aspects, described purely descriptively, cannot play the role of *necessitating* wrong-making aspects for two reasons. *First*, intuitively the instantiation of an aspect such as lying by an action does not make the action necessarily wrong. One may justifiably lie (say, if doing so would save the lives of five persons). *Second*, when we specify wrong-making aspects in nonmoral terms, they clearly specify act-types. So if we say that purely descriptively specified wrong-making aspects necessitate the wrongness of an action, we are thereby committed to absolutism, which ʿAbd al-Jabbār vehemently denies.

Hourani convincingly argues that there are many passages in ʿAbd al-Jabbār's works in which he explicitly asserts an absolutist position about lying.[17] For example, lying to a murderer to save a prophet would be wrong

---

[16] Some (e.g., Väyrynen, *The Lewd*) deny that the evaluative component is part of the semantical content of the term. But those people deny that the instantiation of a thick property necessitates the instantiation of any thin property.

[17] Hourani, *Islamic Rationalism*, 76–81.

on his view. So 'Abd al-Jabbār violates *Nonabsolutism* when it comes to lying. But it does not matter whether he denies *Nonabsolutism* about the particular case of lying. For the problem is general: specifying necessitating wrong-making aspects in a purely descriptive manner commits one to absolutism about many act-types, and absolutism is not a plausible position. So 'Abd al-Jabbār faces a dilemma: either he should specify necessitating wrong-making aspects in terms of thick moral concepts (in which case necessitating wrong-making aspects are *epistemically useless*), or he should specify them in nonmoral terms (in which case he would be committed to *an implausible absolutist view* about many act-types).

One way to save 'Abd al-Jabbār's aspect theory is just to weaken the metaphysical role of aspects. 'Abd al-Jabbār requires wrong-making aspects to necessitate the wrongness of an action. Precisely because of this strong metaphysical requirement, either the knowledge of wrong-making aspects will be too insubstantial, or we should be committed to absolutism. But we might attribute a more modest role to wrong-making aspects by saying that they *contribute* to the wrongness of an action. On this weaker claim, a wrong-making aspect does not *necessitate* the wrongness of an action. There is a distinction between grounds that *necessitate* and grounds that only *contribute* to an action being wrong. Wrong-making aspects can be characterized as the latter type; that is, while the presence of a wrong-making aspect contributes to the wrongness of an action, the contribution of the wrong-making aspect can be overridden by the presence of some other right-making aspects. Let's express this weaker version of aspect theory as follows:

Contributory Aspects. For any action φ and any wrong-making aspect w, if φ instantiates the wrong-making aspect w, w contributes to (but does not necessitate) φ's being evil.

The distinction between contributory and necessitating aspects bears some similarity to the distinction between contributory deontic status and absolute deontic status. The latter distinction is often expressed as the distinction between *pro tanto* deontic status and deontic status *everything considered* (or *final* deontic status). *Pro tanto* literally means 'for so much' or 'to that extent'. An action is *pro tanto* wrong if there is an objection to, or reason against, it. However, an action which is pro tanto wrong might not be wrong *everything considered* because there might be overriding reasons in favor of the action.

For example, while killing is pro tanto wrong, a particular killing might not be wrong *everything considered* (for example, in a trolley case in which we can save five by killing one).

Now that we have weakened the metaphysical role of aspect, we can set aside thick concepts as candidates for wrong-making aspects. For simple non-normative properties, such as act-types, can play the role of wrong-making aspects. ʿAbd al-Jabbār did not want act-types to be wrong-making aspects because he did not want to be an absolutist about act-types. But now, given *Contributory Aspects*, we can say that an act-type such as killing plays the role of a wrong-making aspect without requiring a commitment to absolutism. Moreover, it would not be implausible to think that we have intuitive knowledge that killing is a contributory wrong-making aspect, and this would be a foundational knowledge on which our moral knowledge can be built up. Thus, there is no tension between *Contributory Aspects* and the epistemological role aspects are supposed to play.

ʿAbd al-Jabbār often describes his aspect theory in terms of necessitation. However, there are some other passages in which what ʿAbd al-Jabbār refers to using the term 'aspect' could be interpreted as a contributory wrong-making property. This is one representative example.

> [Inflicting] pains, just like other actions, may be evil one time, and good another time, when it is good, it is good due to an *aspect*—when performed with that aspect, it is good regardless of its agent; the same goes when it is evil. [Inflicting] pain is good when there are benefits in it or it prevents a greater evil, or it is deserved, or one believes that one of those *aspects* is present. (*Sharh*, 484)

In the passage, one can understand "aspect" as referring to things such as benefits, or prevention of greater evil. But, as ʿAbd al-Jabbār insists in many places, benefit in itself does not necessitate the rightness of an action and thus it is not a necessitating aspect. Benefit is only a contributory aspect. So, even though ʿAbd al-Jabbār does not show an explicit awareness of the distinction between *Necessitating Aspects* and *Contributory Aspects*, it would not be too heedless to attribute *Contributory Aspects* to him. *Contributory Aspects* is more suitable for playing the epistemological role that ʿAbd al-Jabbār wants the theory of aspects to play.

3. The Normative Theory of 'Abd al-Jabbār

In his presentation of 'Abd al-Jabbār's theory of aspects, Hourani says that 'Abd al-Jabbār's aspects are the same as Ross's prima facie duties.[18] Hourani discusses the following passage:

> Injustice is any harm that does not involve a benefit outbalancing it, and does not prevent a harm greater than it, and it is not deserved and it is not believed to have one of those aspects. (*al-Mughnī* XIII, p. 298)

Hourani states that "this is a way of saying that injury is *prima facie* wrong, therefore *prima facie* evil, and that an actual injury may be made right by the presence of compensating *prima facie* aspect."[19] But this interpretive move is too quick. For one thing, 'Abd al-Jabbār often characterizes aspects as necessitating grounds. There is no awareness of the distinction between necessitating aspects and contributory aspects, let alone the distinction between pro tanto (or prima facie) duties and everything-considered (or final) duties, in his works. For another thing, 'Abd al-Jabbār's view, *at best*, can be interpreted as a theory in which some aspects are contributory. It is a further claim to say 'Abd al-Jabbār actually believed in prima facie or pro tanto duties (these are, after all, modern technical concepts).

There are different ways to specify how contributory aspects can figure in our normative theory. For example, a consequentialist could also believe in contributory aspects.[20] A consequentialist, à la Moore, might say that we know intuitively that pain is intrinsically bad, and the right action is the one which promotes the most intrinsic value. On this view, the fact that an action brings about benefits, or that it prevents harm, contributes to an action's promoting the best. The consequentialist could then say that bringing about harms or injuring is a contributory wrong-making aspect. Ross, on the other hand, is not a consequentialist. On Ross's view, the notion of right (specified in terms of prima facie duties) takes precedence over the notion of good in

---

[18] Hourani, *Islamic Rationalism*, 32. This interpretation has been very influential, and many people followed Hourani in thinking that 'Abd al-Jabbār's theory of aspects is the same as Ross's theory of prima facie duties. For instance, see Maha Elkaisy-Friemuth, *God and Humans in Islamic Thought* (New York: Routledge, 2006).

[19] Hourani, *Islamic Rationalism*, 32. I have translated the Arabic term *darrar* as "harm." Hourani translates it as "injury."

[20] As noted in the previous chapter, when I refer to universal consequentialism throughout the book, I mean *agent-neutral* universal consequentialism, that is, a consequentialism whose value theory admits only agent-neutral values.

the sense that there can be cases in which I ought to do something which does not promote the best. For example, I ought not to kill even though my not killing would prevent two other killings.

It is difficult to clearly specify the normative theory that ʿAbd al-Jabbār favors. He seems to say that considerations such as promoting benefit, or preventing harms, play a contributory role in determining our obligation. However, the shape of a normative theory appears when one identifies the contributory aspects in the theory, and determines how contributory aspects interact with each other. While ʿAbd al-Jabbār's normative theory seems to be underdeveloped, there is evidence that he would not favor a consequentialist normative theory.

According to Hourani, ʿAbd al-Jabbār is a nonconsequentialist because on his view lying and repaying debts are the grounds of evil and good actions, respectively. When ʿAbd al-Jabbār says that lying and repaying debts are wrong-making or right-making aspects, he holds that those aspects necessitate the moral status of the action, and hence he fails to be a nonabsolutist with respect to lying and paying debts (despite his intention to be a thorough nonabsolutist). ʿAbd al-Jabbār seems to be absolutist with respect to his other aspects too. These are all nonconsequentialist constraints.

But we might think that ʿAbd al-Jabbār is wrong insofar as he endorses an absolutist position about such act-types. Those act-types are only pro tanto wrong. Suppose that this is true; that is, suppose that lying, failing to pay one's debt, ingratitude, ... are all only pro tanto wrong. Would our normative theory be a nonconsequentialist theory insofar as we identify some *act-types* such as lying, ingratitude, failing to pay one's debt as pro tanto wrong? The answer depends on how we formulate consequentialism. More specifically, it depends on how we understand "*the consequences*" in consequentialism.

According to a simple consequentialist view, consequences are just *states of affairs* that are *caused* by our action. Sophisticated consequentialism, however, holds that *act-types* that *constitute* our action have intrinsic value and are among the consequences of our actions.[21] According to sophisticated consequentialism, lying has negative intrinsic value. Accordingly, when we do our consequentialist calculation about, say, whether to lie, we have to take into account the fact that the act-type of lying in itself has some negative value. We could say the same about other act-types such as not paying one's

---

[21] See, for example, Stephen Darwall, "Agent-Centered Restrictions from the Inside Out," *Philosophical Studies* 50.3 (1986): 291–319.

debt, ingratitude, etc. Therefore, the mere fact that some act-types are contributory wrong-making aspects does not by itself favor a deontological view over a sophisticated consequentialist view.

There are two more convincing reasons that ʿAbd al-Jabbār's view is deontological in spirit. The first reason why ʿAbd al-Jabbār's view is deontological comes from his understanding of the notion of injustice (*zulm*). As we saw before, on his view, injustice is a necessitating wrong-making aspect. To make his view more substantial, he sometimes endeavors to give more content to his notion of injustice. The passage quoted at the beginning of this section specifies the content of the notion of injustice: "Injustice is any harm that does not involve a benefit outbalancing it, and does not prevent a harm greater than it, and it is not deserved and it is not believed to have one of those aspects" (*al-Mughnī* XIII, p. 298). Initially, one might think that this is just a consequentialist account of injustice: an act is unjust when it brings about more harm than benefit. But this is not accurate. A crucial element in the definition of the term is that in determining whether an act is unjust we have to look at only those harms that are not *deserved*.

According to ʿAbd al-Jabbār, the consideration that someone deserves punishment is a right-making aspect (or at least not a wrong-making aspect) for the act of punishing them; that is, it would be right to punish them because they deserve punishment. This contributory aspect is an aspect that would not be welcome in a consequentialist normative theory. On a consequentialist normative theory, whether punishing someone is right depends on whether the act of punishing them has good consequences. The retributive notion of justice is not a consequentialist notion. But for ʿAbd al-Jabbār, someone may deserve punishment for what they have done (and thus the act of punishing them would be just) regardless of what consequences the act of punishment would bring about.

One might, however, worry that the consideration that someone deserves punishment can't be a contributory right-making aspect. The function of contributory wrong-making or right-making aspects is to determine one's overall duty. But that someone deserves pain depends on one's overall duty toward that person; that is, someone deserves pain *just in case* there is a duty (or permission) to inflict pain on her, and thus deserving pain can't be a contributory aspect to determine one's overall duty.

ʿAbd al-Jabbār considers this objection and provides a response to it. Studying his response helps us see the nonconsequentialist element of his thinking.

> It might be asked how can we define being deserved to correctly be considered as a cause of goodness? Tell him that it is established by reason that the nature of blame is such that it corresponds to evil in such a way [that] it is a retribution for it. And it is in the nature of praise that it corresponds to good in the same way. When this establishes ([i.e., when someone's action is evil or good]), we express that the person deserves [retribution] and we consider this as the cause of an action's being good when it [i.e., the evil or good action] occurs before the person's being affected by the action; the reason for this is that the action belongs to the retribution [of the evil or good action]. (*al-Mughnī* XIII, 484)

In this passage, 'Abd al-Jabbār says that we should not understand the notion of *S's deserving X* as conceptually equivalent to the notion of *doing X to S is just*. Rather, deserving is like a moral residue that remains in us when we do something wrong or right. When we do something wrong, we are blameworthy (at least in normal cases), and thus the wrong action affects us in a way that we become *liable to future harms*. Doing a wrong action leaves a moral stain on us; that is, it makes us liable to future harms. This notion of being liable to harm because of one's past wrongdoing is a fundamentally nonconsequentialist element in his ethical theory. The distinction between being liable to harm and not being liable because of one's past actions is alien to consequentialism.

There is also a second reason that conclusively shows 'Abd al-Jabbār's view is not consequentialist. 'Abd al-Jabbār has a fundamentally nonconsequentialist stance toward benevolence; that is, he denies that we have a general duty of beneficence. According to him, "one has no duty of pure beneficence toward oneself or others. One has a duty to benefit others, as a matter of fairness, when there is a preceding cause" (XIV, p. 24). It seems that Abd al-Jabbār thinks that only in cases of *reparation* do we have a duty to benefit others.

In sum, to know whether or not a theory is deontological, we need to know about the interactions between contributory aspects. We have a deontological theory when a wrong-making aspect can override right-making aspects and make the action wrong, even though on balance the action would have better consequences than its alternatives. The normative theory of 'Abd al-Jabbār is underdeveloped in important respects. It does not tell us about the interactions between aspects. But it certainly has a nonconsequentialist flavor: (i) it assigns intrinsic value to act-types; (ii) it recognizes deontological notions such as retribution and reparation; (iii) it does not require actions to have the goal of bringing about the highest good for everyone. While one might have a sophisticated consequentialist theory to accommodate all those features, it is not implausible to think that there can be, on his view, contributory wrong-making aspects that are not subject to consequentialist calculations. Therefore, a deontological ethical theory with the following features would be an 'Abd al-Jabbārian ethical theory (if not precisely his own): (i) one's duty is determined by the contributory aspects that the action inherits; (ii) the balancing of contributory aspects is not calculated in a consequentialist manner; that is, some contributory wrong-making aspect can override the consideration that the action promotes the best; and (iii) we have intuitive knowledge that a contributory wrong-making aspect (e.g., killing or lying) is pro tanto wrong. The last element concerns moral epistemology, which we are to discuss in the next section.

4. The Moral Epistemology of 'Abd al-Jabbār

We noted that the metaethics of 'Abd al-Jabbār is built around the idea that we have intuitive moral knowledge. To specify our intuitive moral knowledge, 'Abd al-Jabbār claims that we have intuitive knowledge about moral aspects. What is intuitively known is not that a *particular* action is wrong, but rather the *general* claim that a certain wrong-making aspect makes an action wrong. We can know that a particular action is wrong by supplementing this intuitive knowledge with observation and reasoning.

> What we call immediate knowledge (*darūri*) is the knowledge that unjust harm is evil, this knowledge is direct (*mujmal*) and not discursive (*mufassal*). Disagreements can arises about the discursive knowledge of [what is] unjust [harm], when observations through which people come to believe what is unjust are different.... To have this discursive knowledge we need discovery, observation and reflection (*ta'ammol*).... When we know something about an object, sometimes our knowledge is immediate and non-discursive. In some cases, our knowledge is discursive and requires inquiry, observation and reflection. And in some cases [such as the case that this act is evil] we know something about an object by bringing these pieces of knowledge together. (*al-Mughnī* XIII, 305)

'Abd al-Jabbār distinguishes between *immediate* knowledge and *acquired* knowledge. Immediate knowledge is direct and is not the result of reasoning, whereas acquired knowledge is discursive. It requires observation and reasoning. According to 'Abd al-Jabbār, our knowledge that this act is wrong is the result of an inference from two other pieces of knowledge, a piece of *direct* knowledge (*mujmal*) and a piece of *discursive* knowledge (*mufassal*). The direct knowledge is the intuitive knowledge of the moral status of grounds. For example, we intuitively know that injustice is the ground of wrongness. On the other hand, for a particular action to be known to be wrong, we need to have some discursive knowledge as to whether this particular action instantiates a wrong-making aspect. We can bring our immediate direct knowledge of grounds, and our discursive knowledge of the instantiation of grounds by the action together to form an Aristotelian syllogism the conclusion of which is that this particular action is wrong (or not wrong). The conclusion of the syllogism is a piece of acquired knowledge, acquired from our direct and discursive knowledge of the matter. The first premise of the syllogism is our intuitive knowledge of aspects, for example, injustice is evil. The second premise is that this action is unjust. The conclusion is that this action is evil. We can state the epistemological element of wrong-making aspects in terms of the following proposition:

> *Knowledge of Aspects.* The intuitive part of our moral knowledge is the knowledge of the wrongness of wrong-making aspects. Substantial moral knowledge is either the knowledge of wrong-making aspects, or what is inferred from them.

Aspects, then, have a dual function, a metaphysical function expressed by *Necessitating Aspects* or *Contributory Aspects* and an epistemological function marked by *Knowledge of Aspects*. As discussed in the section on metaethics, the most plausible way to understand the metaphysics of aspects is to understand it in accordance with *Contributory Aspects*.

Would 'Abd al-Jabbār be willing to extend *Knowledge of Aspects* to contributory aspects? In other words, would he accept that we intuitively know that a contributory wrong-making aspect (say, inflicting pain) is pro tanto wrong? Given the lack of clear distinction between *Necessitating Aspects* and *Contributory Aspects*, there is little textual evidence to answer this question. We can say this, though: the intuitive knowledge of necessitating aspects presupposes the intuitive knowledge of contributory aspects. The only plausible way to specify a necessitating wrong-making aspect is to construct it out of all contributory aspects contributing to the moral status of the action. For example, a necessitating aspect can be constructed in this way: that this action is an act of killing, that there is no benefit to this killing, and that this killing is not deserved. These aspects together would necessitate the wrongness of the action. But if a necessitating moral aspect is just a combination of contributory moral aspects, *Knowledge of Aspects*—with regard to necessitating moral aspects—presupposes the intuitive knowledge of contributory moral aspects. So, it would be in spirit of 'Abd al-Jabbār's theory to answer yes to the question asked in the beginning of the paragraph.

'Abd al-Jabbār thinks that our knowledge of wrong-making aspects is *mujmal*: it is direct and intuitive. We know intuitively that injustice is evil. But this is not, on 'Abd al-Jabbār's view, enough for us to know whether any particular action is wrong. To know the moral status of a particular action, we require discursive knowledge about morally relevant properties of the action. As he puts, "all rational beings know that an unjust action is evil when they know that the act is unjust . . . there is no evil action unless its ground is known immediately; But we need acquired knowledge to correctly identify the ground [in an evil action]" (*al-Mughnī* VI.i, p. 64). If we understand our intuitive knowledge of aspects in terms of our intuitive knowledge of contributory aspects, we could say that *mujmal* judgments are judgments about pro tanto wrongness. For example, we know intuitively that lying is pro tanto wrong. But that does not mean that my lying is wrong everything considered. My lying might instantiate other right-making contributory aspects that override its wrong-making aspect. We could understand acquired knowledge as our knowledge of an action being wrong, *everything considered*.

While our knowledge of pro tanto judgment is intuitive, we don't have intuitive knowledge of wrongness, *everything considered*. According to 'Abd al-Jabbār, this knowledge can be acquired in two ways: by reason through experience and observation and by *revelation*. Revelation is an important epistemic source for our knowledge about the wrongness (or rightness) of actions, *everything considered*.

> What the prophet brings is only the discursive knowledge (*tafsil*) of what is established directly in reason. We already said that it is established in reason that promoting benefit is obligatory and bringing harm is evil. Given that it is impossible that we know by reason that this act is beneficial

and that one harmful, God the Exalted has sent us prophets to inform us about those features of actions. They should bring the detailed report of what God Exalted has already placed in our reason, that is, they provide the discursive knowledge of what is already established in reason. (*Sharh*, 565)

We have access to the intuitive grounds of morality, whereas we don't intuitively know the final moral status of our actions. Our intuitive moral knowledge, by itself, does not give us final moral knowledge about actions. If we supplement our intuitive moral knowledge by empirical knowledge acquired by reason and perception, we acquire substantial moral knowledge about the wrongness of an action, everything considered. 'Abd al-Jabbār thinks that in addition to reason and perception, revelation also provides us with discursive knowledge. Revelation can tell us that an action has benefits that we cannot discover by reason and perception. Discursive knowledge acquired through revelation can be used to yield substantial moral knowledge about particular actions. Knowledge acquired by revelation can play quite a decisive role in determining the moral status of an action to the extent that revelation can correct the mistakes or ignorance of reason. On 'Abd al-Jabbār's view, our moral judgments made by reason are sometimes mistaken. There are actions deemed impermissible by reason which are in fact obligatory, or permissible.

> There are different kind of cases in which revelation is used to discover the features of actions. In some cases, what is deemed obligatory by Revelation is found evil by reason, an example is the manner the prayer is performed. In some cases, what is recommended by Revelation is found evil by reason, an example is supplementary prayers. . . . In some cases, what is deemed permissible by Revelation is found prohibited by reason, an example is animal slaughtering. Revelation uncovers those features of an action which, if reason had known, reason would know its evilness or goodness. Had we known by reason that there are enormous benefits for us in prayer—which is, it helps us to perform our duties and thus become deserving for rewards—we would have known by reason that prayer is obligatory. And had we known that adultery leads us to corruption, we would have known by reason that it is evil. (*al-Mughnī* VI.i, 64)

It is curious that 'Abd al-Jabbār thinks that reason finds that the manner in which we perform Islamic prayer is evil. Probably, he thinks that reason in general disfavors prostrations. But the truth of this judgment does not matter for us. What matters is that on 'Abd al-Jabbār's view, we can't rely on judgments of reason about what is right or wrong when they are in tension with revelation. The power of reason in making final moral judgments is limited. We don't know what consequences prayer has, and thus we can't know all its contributory aspects. We might even have false beliefs about the morally relevant properties of prayers, and thus we have to rely on revelation to know the final moral status of prayers.

It is interesting that 'Abd al-Jabbār uses the example of animal killing, an example used by al-Juwainī in the previous chapter to prove that we have no intuitive moral knowledge. According to al-Juwainī, the fact that some people (e.g., Muslims) find this act to be permissible, while some other find it impermissible, shows that there is no universal intuitive moral knowledge. 'Abd al-Jabbār's response seems to be this: we have a genuine intuition that animal slaughtering is pro tanto wrong. This intuition is shared among everybody, Muslims and non-Muslims. But through revelation, we come to know that this act of killing is permissible, everything considered.

Even though the ethical view of 'Abd al-Jabbār is very different from that of al-Ghazālī, they have one common element: the claim that the epistemic power of reason in making everything-considered moral judgment, independent of revelation, is limited, and thus reason has no standing to question the ethical teachings of revelation. 'Abd al-Jabbār uses *the same example* as al-Ghazālī does (i.e., the example of a physician) to illustrate the relation between revelation and reason.

> The case is analogous to the case of physicians when they say that this medicine is beneficial and that one harmful. We already know that it is obligatory to prevent harm from oneself and that it is good to benefit oneself. In accordance with what we have said, physicians would not teach us something that opposes reason, and the same is true of the prophets. (*al-Mughnī* VI.i, 64)

What is in common between 'Abd al-Jabbār and al-Ghazālī is that we have the knowledge of fundamental moral principles. For al-Ghazālī, the fundamental principle would be self-centered consequentialism. For 'Abd al-Jabbār, the fundamental principles would be the rules about wrong-making aspects. But when it comes to the knowledge of wrongness, everything considered, both of them hold that our lack of knowledge about *all* the morally relevant properties of an action puts us in the same situation as we are in with regard to medicines. We don't know all the health-related properties of medicines and thus we have to follow the prescriptions of the physician. The same is true of actions. We don't know all the morally relevant properties of an action and thus we have to follow the prescriptions of the prophet.

5. Natural Evil, Prescribed Evil, and Skeptical Theism

The first section suggested that one of the main motivations of the Ash'arites for espousing theological voluntarism was to get around the classical problem of evil. The Mu'tazilites, on the other hand, did not see any urgency in denying the first premise of the argument. They rejected the second premise of the argument. On their view, there is no pointless evil in the world.

'Abd al-Jabbār thinks that there can be right-making aspects that make God's act of inflicting pain on others right. He specifies two general conditions that a justified act of inflicting pain should satisfy. The first condition is that pain must be compensated unproportionally. If benefit that comes as compensation ('awad) is much greater than the inflicted pain, any rational being would choose the benefit at the cost of pain (al-Mughnī XIII, 453–54). However, meeting this condition is not enough to make the act of inflicting pain justified. For it would be a vain action for God to randomly inflict pain on somebody and then compensate it disproportionally. God must have a *reason* in the first place to inflict pain. And this is the second condition. Some good must hinge on the infliction of pain. 'Abd al-Jabbār suggests that pain and suffering might be good to motivate people to fulfill their duties (al-Mughnī XIII, 390). These two elements, that is, the disproportional compensation in the hereafter and the benefits of inflicting pain, together justify God's act of inflicting pain.

A rather skeptical stance about the epistemic power of reason is common to 'Abd al-Jabbār's solution to the classical problem of evil, and his view on the role of revelation in our moral knowledge. Reason alone cannot discover all the morally relevant properties of, say, the killing of animals. Revelation aids us in knowing about the consequences of our actions. Similarly, some evil, say the illness of children, might look pointlessly evil when we look at it without taking into account the grand theological scheme of the universe. But theology helps us to see that these events are not in fact pointless evils.

The fact that God does not perform futile actions justifies us in thinking there are good consequences in God's allowing evil to occur.

The previous chapter discussed the argument for strict adherence. According to this argument, if the Qur'an states "φ-ing is permissible" (e.g., wife-beating is permissible) and the Qur'an is God's words, one is morally permitted to φ (e.g., to beat one's wife). That argument showed that our independent moral judgments are not reliable when they are in conflict with Scripture. There were only two substantial premises in the argument, and we called them *al-Ghazālī's main claim* and God's Reliability. According to *al-Ghazālī's main claim*, given God's absolute power to determine the moral status of any action, God's moral nature provides us with no reason to think that the Qur'an sentence "φ-ing is obligatory" (or "φ-ing is permissible") does not mean that φ-ing is obligatory (or φ-ing is permissible). And according to God's Reliability, if God intends to convey that it is obligatory (or permitted) for us (or a certain group of people) to do φ, it is true that we (or those people) are morally obligated (or permitted) to do φ. The function of *al-Ghazālī's main claim* in the strict-adherence argument is to show that Moral Justification is false. The argument needs the denial of Moral Justification to conclude that, in the absence of linguistic reasons, the Qur'anic passage should be taken at face value.[22] To recall, Moral Justification is the following thesis:

> *Moral Justification.* There are moral reasons to interpret morally controversial passages nonliterally, as the literal understanding of the passages is inconsistent with a morally perfect God.

Al-Ghazālī denies Moral Justification, on the ground that God has the power of making any action morally obligatory (or permissible) and He can inform us about it. As we discussed in the previous chapter, assuming consequentialism, God's power to attach rewards and punishments to actions gives Him the power to change the moral status of actions. Arguably, 'Abd al-Jabbār would not accept this consequentialist reasoning. On his view, God would not have absolute liberty to attach to actions whatever rewards and punishment He wishes. There are norms of justice that He should follow in determining reward and punishments for actions. Nevertheless, I will

---

[22] In fact, the first sub-conclusion of the strict-adherence argument (i.e., premise (4)) is derived from the truism about communication (premise (1)), the assumption of the case about the absence of linguistic reasons (premise (2)), and the denial of Moral Justification.

argue that 'Abd al-Jabbār denies Moral Justification on different grounds. The argument for strict adherence would not lose its force as long as we find independent reasons to reject Moral Justification. And if an independent justification, compatible with deontological ethics, can be found to reject Moral Justification, we can conclude that the strict-adherence argument is not dependent on Ash'arīsm or consequentialism. Even the Mu'tazilites, with their deontological ethics, should, and would, take the argument on board.

Given our discussion so far, it is not difficult to see why 'Abd al-Jabbār rejects Moral Justification. On 'Abd al-Jabbār's view, for any given act we need discursive knowledge to know whether the act is right or wrong, and reason alone has limited power in providing us with that knowledge. We are not in a position to claim that we know all of the morally relevant properties of an action. The morally relevant properties we discover by reason alone are not *representative* of all morally relevant properties of an action. For example, we would have had mistaken moral beliefs had we trusted reason alone about the morally relevant properties of the killing of animals or the manner in which prayer is performed. We cannot even form a justified *probabilistic* judgment about whether the killing of animals is wrong, everything considered, or whether prayer is wrong, everything considered. Given this, for any given seemingly immoral action we have no reason to think that the action could not turn out to be right. Thus, we have no reason to think that God would make a moral mistake in stating that a seemingly immoral action is in fact justified. If God would not make any mistake in stating that a seemingly immoral action is in fact justified, God's moral nature provides us with no reason to think that the Qur'an sentence "φ-ing is obligatory" (or "φ-ing is permissible") does not mean that φ-ing is obligatory (or φ-ing is permissible).

Another way to see why Moral Justification would be denied by even the Mu'tazilites is to consider the issue in light of the classical problem of evil. If we are skeptical about the epistemic power of reason in the moral realm, we would be skeptical about the second premise of the classical problem of evil as formulated in section 1 of the chapter. Philosophers rejecting the second premise might maintain that our moral intuition is not reliable enough to vindicate the existence of pointless evil. The following argument (let's call it *the parallel evil argument*) shows that why any theist who denies the second premise of the problem of evil argument has to reject Moral Justification.

The Parallel Evil Argument

(1) *Either* our intuition that a certain evil is pointless is a *reliable* guide for us to believe that there is no justifying reason for the occurrence of that evil, *or* not.

(2) *If* our intuition that a certain evil is pointless *is a reliable guide* for us to believe that there is no justifying reason for the occurrence of that evil, *then* the appearance of pointless evil would *undermine* the belief that there is an omniscient, omnipotent, and omnibenevolent God.

(3) *If* our intuition that a certain evil is *pointless is not a reliable guide* for us to believe that there is no justifying reason for the occurrence of the evil, *then* our intuition that a certain action commanded by Scripture (e.g., wife-beating) is immoral *is not a reliable guide* for us to believe that there is no justifying reason for the action.

(4) *If* our intuition that a certain action commanded by Scripture is immoral is *not a reliable* guide for us to believe that there is no justifying reason for the action, *then* our intuition that a certain action is immoral provides us *no reason to think* that it would be against God's nature to say that the action is morally right.

(5) Therefore, *either* the appearance of pointless evil would undermine the belief that there is an omniscient, omnipotent, and omnibenevolent God, *or* our intuition that a certain action is immoral provides us no reason to think that it would be against God's nature to say that the action is morally right.

The main idea of the argument is that either our moral intuitions about certain actions apparently prescribed by Scriptural passages go against God's commanding those actions—in which case, by parity of reasoning, our intuitions about natural evil also go against God's allowing it to happen, or we have no reason to believe that those actions are in fact morally questionable—in the same way that we have no reason to believe that natural evil is morally pointless. It is clear that the first disjunct is not acceptable to the theist. It undermines the belief in the traditional God. The theist, then, is forced to accept the second disjunct, and that implies that they should deny Moral Justification. But, given the strict-adherence argument, the denial of Moral Justification amounts to saying that we have to adhere strictly to the literal meaning of Scripture, even in the face of our strong moral intuition that a certain action is immoral. In other words, the second disjunct, together with some other plausible assumptions, specified in the argument for strict adherence, would lead to the conclusion that one may beat one's wife.[23] Of course, any *conscientious theist* would find this repugnant, but it is not easy to see how we can resist the parallel evil argument or the strict-adherence argument.

The parallel evil argument leads us to either skepticism about God or skepticism about commonsense morality. Let's discuss the premises of the argument briefly. The first premise of the parallel evil argument is trivial. Premise (2) is based on the idea that pointless evil goes against God's justice. Premise (3) also seems very plausible. If we humans are not in a position to see all the morally relevant properties of an event (say, the suffering of animals), why would we be in a position to see all the morally relevant properties of the act of, say, beating one's wife? 'Abd al-Jabbār would certainly take this premise on board. Premise (4) of the argument should not be controversial either. If our intuition that a certain action φ is immoral is not a reliable guide for us to believe that the action is immoral, then we have no reason to think that God would make a moral mistake in holding that there are justifying reasons for the action φ. Therefore, we should not take it to be against God's moral nature for Him to hold that the action φ is right.

In modern literature on philosophy of religion, those who reject the second premise of the problem-of-evil argument on the grounds that the epistemic power of reason in the moral realm is limited are called *skeptical theists*. Skeptical theism makes the following claims:

ST1. We have no good reason for thinking that the possible goods we know of are representative of the possible goods there are.
ST2. We have no good reason for thinking that the possible evils we know of are representative of the possible evils there are.
ST3. We have no good reason for thinking that the entailment relations we know of between the possible goods and the permission of possible evils are representative of the entailment relations there are between possible goods and the permission of possible evils.[24]

---

[23] If we use the example from the Bible's Ephesians (5:22–25), the conclusion of the Parallel Evil Argument for a Christian is that either their justification for theism is undermined or they should believe that a woman must submit to her husband in everything!

[24] Michael Bergmann, "Sceptical Theism and Rowe's New Evidential Argument from Evil," *Noûs* 35 (2001): 279.

ST1–ST3 provide grounds for us to deny our knowledge of the existence of pointless evil in the world. In other words, according to ST1–ST3, the things we know about morality are not *representative* of the moral realm, and so we can't make *everything-considered* judgments about morality. Using the terminology we used in this chapter, according to ST1–ST3, we have *no reason* to think that (i) the contributory wrong-making and right-making aspects we know of are *representative of all contributory wrong-making and right-making aspects*, (ii) the interactions we know of between different contributory aspects are *representative of all interactions*, and (iii) our knowledge of what aspects a particular action instantiates is *representative of all aspects that the action instantiates*. If so, for any particular action, we know some of its contributory wrong-making and right-making aspects, but the things that we know of, for all we know, might not be representative of all of its morally relevant properties. So based on the things we know, we cannot make even a *probabilistic* judgment about the moral status of action *everything considered*. This blocks the move from *judgments about pro tanto oughts* to a *judgment about the everything-considered ought*. Because we are basically in the dark about the moral realm, the little knowledge we have concerning some moral aspects does not enable us to make a reasonable probabilistic everything-considered judgment about morality.

It might be helpful here to slightly *digress* and talk about the *metaphysical relation* between pro tanto ought and everything-considered ought. Derek Baker has recently argued that there are metaphysical grounds to be skeptical about the move from pro tanto ought judgments to everything-considered ought judgments.[25] Baker thinks that we have different kinds of reasons: moral reasons, prudential reasons, epistemic reasons, legal reasons, reasons of etiquette, etc. Different kinds of reason generate different kinds of oughts: there are things we *morally* ought to do, there are things we *prudentially* ought to do, etc. But is there anything that we *simply* ought to do, when these different oughts tell us different things? Can we resolve the tension between different oughts by appealing to a *more authoritative* kind of ought, namely, the ought *simpliciter*? Baker is skeptical about whether there is any simple ought that has authority over all other oughts. He thinks that a simple ought is yet another kind of ought which is in competition with other oughts,

[25] Derek Baker, "Skepticism about Ought Simpliciter," *Oxford Studies in Metaethics* 13 (2018): 230–52.

and is doubtful that we can coherently specify a new kind of ought that has authority over all other oughts.

One can respond to Baker by saying the fundamental normative notion is the notion of *reasons*, and there is a *single class* of reasons.[26] Terms such as 'moral reasons' or 'prudential reasons' do not denote fundamentally different kinds of reasons. Rather, they specify only subclasses of reasons. Moral reasons are reasons concerned with the interests of other people; prudential reasons are reasons concerned with our own interests, etc. A pro tanto ought tells us what would be the case about what we ought to do, but only if a particular reason or a subclass of reasons *were in play*. An everything-considered ought tells us what we ought to do when all reasons are in play.

Baker does not find this response satisfying. He holds that reasons of etiquette or reasons of positive law are not a subclass of reasons; rather, they are different kinds of reasons. Yet they generate oughts of etiquette or legal oughts. There is then a tension between oughts of etiquette and the everything-considered ought, and to resolve it we need to appeal to a higher kind ought, so that the problem reappears.[27] I think that Baker is mistaken here. Legal reasons or reasons of etiquette, if genuine, can be reduced to *reasons*. But nothing that I say in the book hinges on the falsity of Baker's view. Baker's skepticism concerns whether we can resolve the tension between different kinds of pro tanto oughts (moral, prudential, legal, etc.) by appealing to the everything-considered ought. He does not think that we can find an everything-considered ought, standing above different kinds of ought. But throughout the book, in talking about 'reasons', 'pro tanto oughts', or 'everything-considered oughts', my applications of those terms are limited to *moral* reasons, pro tanto *moral* oughts, or everything-considered *moral* oughts. The problem of prescribed evil is a problem about the *morality* of God's actions and our actions. Even Baker could accept that an everything-considered *moral* ought can resolve the tension between different competing pro tanto *moral* oughts. His skepticism is about the supposedly unresolvable tension between oughts in different areas. However, within one single area,

---

[26] This view is defended by the main figures in contemporary moral philosophy. For instance, see John Broome, *Rationality through Reasoning* (New York: John Wiley & Sons, 2013); Thomas M. Scanlon, *Being Realistic about Reasons* (New York: Oxford University Press, 2014); Derek Parfit, "Normativity," in *Oxford Studies in Metaethics*, vol. 1, ed. R. Shafer-Landau (New York: Oxford University Press, 2006), 325–80.

[27] Reconstructed as such, Baker's argument against the authority of everything-considered oughts is reminiscent of Foot's (infamous) skepticism toward the practical authority of categorical imperatives. See Philippa Foot, "Morality as a System of Hypothetical Imperatives," *Philosophical Review* 81.3 (1972): 305–16.

namely the moral realm, he is not skeptical about the applicability of the notion of everything-considered ought.

We can now *turn back* to the skeptical theist's argument for the *epistemic illegitimacy* of moving from judgments about pro tanto ought to a judgment about the everything-considered ought. According to the skeptical theist, while it is in principle possible for us to form a judgment about the everything-considered moral ought on the basis of our knowledge of pro tanto moral oughts, given our lack of knowledge of all pro tanto oughts, and the unrepresentativeness of the pro tanto oughts we know of, we are not *epistemically justified* to form a (probabilistic) judgment about the everything-considered moral ought.

An atheist might respond, however, that this skepticism goes too far and makes us morally paralyzed. In other words, if we are in no position to know all morally relevant properties of an event, for example, the suffering of an animal—and if we can't even know the representative morally relevant properties of the event, we should be skeptical about moral knowledge in general. For example, suppose you see a terrorist attacking a child and you can easily save the child. According to the skeptical theist, you don't know all the morally relevant properties involved (with either the killing or the saving of the child), and so don't know that saving the child is the right thing to do. Thus you should not save her.

The worry just discussed is a well-known worry raised by some philosophers in response to skeptical theism, that is, the theistic view which says we don't know all morally relevant moral properties of seemingly pointless evil.[28] In fact, ʿAbd al-Jabbār did not want to be a thorough moral skeptic. He wants to espouse only *moderate* moral skepticism, according to which,

(a) When there is no revelation, reason alone can provide us with everything-considered moral judgments about particular actions.
(b) When there is revelation, reason should always defer to moral judgments acquired by revelation.

---

[28] See Michael J. Almeida and Graham Oppy, "Sceptical Theism and Evidential Arguments from Evil," *Australasian Journal of Philosophy* 81.4 (2003): 496–516; Stephen Maitzen, "Skeptical Theism and Moral Obligation," *International Journal for Philosophy of Religion* 65.2 (2009): 93–103; Bruce Russell, "Defenseless," in *The Evidential Argument from Evil*, ed. Daniel Howard-Snyder (Bloomington: Indiana University Press, 1996), 193–205.

THE DEONTOLOGICAL ETHICS OF THE MUʿTAZILITES 99

The problem is that there seems to be a tension between (a) and (b). If we accept skeptical theism, we can't accept (a), as we are never in a position to make an everything-considered moral judgment. But if we deny skeptical theism, how can we defend (b)? Why should reason *always* defer to revelation?

Despite initial appearances, there does not need to be a tension between (a) and (b) if we accept the *subjective* notion of obligation. According to the *objective* notion of obligation, our moral obligation is a function of *all* the moral reasons there are. The subjective notion of obligation, however, says that moral obligation is a function of all the moral reasons that are *epistemically accessible* to us.[29] If we accept the subjective notion of obligation as the primary notion of obligation, (a) and skeptical theism would be consistent. That is, even if our knowledge of the instantiation of different moral aspects by our actions is fairly limited, as skeptical theism maintains, our moral obligations are still determined by those aspects that we have epistemic access to. In fact, the proponents of skeptical theism have used the exact same strategy (i.e., adopting the subjective notion of obligation) to defend their view against the objection that skeptical theism is morally paralyzing. A skeptical theist might hold that when it comes to *my* actions, the permissibility (or impermissibility) of my action is determined by factors that I have *epistemic access* to. As a result, even though saving the child from the terrorist might have wrong-making features that I am not aware of, the impermissibility of my not saving the child is a function of morally relevant properties of the situation that I have access to.[30] In this sense, while I might be in the dark about my objective obligations, ethics is a matter of guiding our actions in light of reasons accessible to us.[31]

The subjective notion of obligation also can explain why (b) is true, if skeptical theism is. While it is true that the impermissibility of my act of, say, beating my wife is a function of morally relevant factors that I have access

---

[29] See Chapter 5 for a review of the contemporary literature in moral philosophy on these two notions.

[30] For this response, see Michael Bergmann and Michael Rea, "In Defence of Sceptical Theism: A Reply to Almeida and Oppy," *Australasian Journal of Philosophy* 83.2 (2005): 241–51

[31] Attributing a subjective notion of obligation to ʿAbd al-Jabbār's view allows him to be consistent with regard to (a) and (b). But we also have other reasons internal to his ethical theory for thinking that he espouses the subjective notion of obligation. According to ʿAbd al-Jabbār, the most fundamental ethical notion is that of blameworthiness (and praiseworthiness), and 'obligation' is ultimately defined by reference to the notion of blameworthiness. Blameworthiness is a subjective notion. It depends on agent's epistemic standpoint. We can't blame a subject for something which is completely outside of his epistemic perspective. Tying obligation to blameworthiness means that ʿAbd al-Jabbār does not recognize objective obligation as the primary ethical notion.

to, God might know that there are justifying reasons for this act which are inaccessible to me. God's informing me about the permissibility of the action would provide me with an *additional reason* that wife-beating is permissible, a reason I did not have access to prior to revelation. Independent of revelation, I am in the dark about the objective moral status of the action, and thus I can't rule out that there might be justifying reasons for wife-beating, and if God informs me about the existence of such a reason, through revelation, I will be in a new epistemic position with respect to the moral status of wife-beating.

In the case of wife-beating, the *revelation changes our epistemic standpoint altogether* and I acquire *new* subjective duties and permissions from my new epistemic standpoint. Evidence added by revelation informs me about the *overall* balance of reasons in the universe in favor of wife-beating. After receiving revelation, I get permission for wife-beating (everything considered), a permission that was not available before revelation. To repeat, revelation does not compete with my moral judgment before revelation. It does not say that I was wrong about my subjective duty before revelation, it changes the evidence, and thus my subjective duties.

Is this conclusion problematic for a theist? Yes, if the conscientious theist finds a permission to wife-beating repugnant. But the problem is that it is hard for the theist to know how they can avoid this repugnant conclusion. If we are in the dark about our objective duties, we can't say that it is against God's nature to say that wife-beating is wrong (i.e., we can't say that Moral Justification is false). Thus, the theist has no (nontextual) reason not to take the Qur'anic sentence at face value, and if the theist is justified in thinking that the Qur'anic sentence means that wife-beating is permissible, they would be in a new epistemic position with regard to wife-beating. The testimony of the Qur'an is a reason that they have access to. So, even though the moral status of the act of wife-beating is a function of morally relevant factors that we have access to, given God's testimony through Scripture, the theist should think that the act of wife-beating is permissible (assuming God's Reliability). In sum, while skeptical theism by itself does not imply that wife-beating is permissible, it does so when we supplement it with a few plausible assumptions.

The argument for strict adherence has two major premises: the denial of Moral Justification and God's Reliability. Skepticism about our knowledge of objective duty provides us with a justification to reject Moral Justification. In contrast to al-Ghazālī's reasons for rejecting Moral Justification, ʿAbd al-Jabbār's reasons for so doing are not reliant on consequentialism. No matter what ethical theory we adopt, ʿAbd al-Jabbār could reject Moral Justification as long as we adopt skepticism regarding our knowledge of objective duty.

Is this skepticism compatible with God's Reliability? In other words, if we don't have access to *all* moral reasons, how can we know that God does not lie justifiably? As noted, ʿAbd al-Jabbār was an absolutist with respect to lying. On his view, there is no justified lying. But we might find this position implausible. If so, how can we trust God's testimony?

Broadly speaking, there are two views with regard to our justification for accepting something based on testimony. According to *reductionism*, testimony is not a fundamental source of knowledge. Testimony needs justification from other sources of knowledge. On this view, when we hear someone's testimony, to be justified in accepting it, we need to establish that the source is morally and epistemically reliable.[32] On the other hand, *antireductionism* takes testimony as a fundamental source of knowledge. Tyler Burge, a major advocate of antireductionism, argues that "a person is entitled to accept as true something that is presented as true and that is intelligible to him unless there are stronger reasons not to do so."[33] With regard to moral reliability of the source of testimony, an antireductionist, such as Burge, would hold that one has a priori prima facie justification to accept what one is told, without considering whether the interlocutor is lying, lacking special reasons to think that they are (475). Burge justifies this claim on the grounds that the primary function of reason is to present truths. On his view, "lying occasions a disunity among functions of reason. It conflicts with one's reason's transpersonal function of presenting the truth, independently of special personal interests" (475). So, our default presumption toward the presentation of something as true by a rational being should be that we are rationally entitled to accept what is presented as true, unless there is reason to think that the rational source is rationally disunified (475).

If we accept *reductionism* with regard to testimony, skepticism about our knowledge of objective duty is in conflict with God's Reliability. We cannot establish that God is not lying, given our lack of knowledge of God's reasons for His actions. So our justification to reject Moral Justification undermines God's Reliability. However, skepticism about our knowledge of objective duty is consistent with God's Reliability providing that we accept

---

[32] There are many proponents of reductionism. The view historically traces back to Hume. A notable contemporary advocate of the view is Elizabeth Fricker; see, for instance, "The Epistemology of Testimony," *Proceedings of the Aristotelian Society Supplementary* 61 (1987): 57–83.

[33] Tyler Burge, "Content Preservation," *Philosophical Review* 102 (1993): 467.

antireductionism with regard to testimony. In other words, the acceptance of antireductionism in testimony allows us to reject Moral Justification and to accept God's Reliability. It is also important to note that antireductionism is reliant on the existence of prima facie rational norms about reason and practical reason. If we think that the *only* norm governing practical reason is self-centered or universal consequentialism, we can't accept antireductionism. Therefore, while al-Ghazālī can't appeal to antireductionism to preserve God's Reliability, 'Abd al-Jabbār can.

The argument for strict adherence presented in the previous chapter had two major flaws. First, it was too reliant on consequentialism for the rejection of Moral Justification. Second, God's Reliability could not be justified if consequentialism were true. In this chapter, I have argued that *both* of those problems can be fixed in 'Abd al-Jabbār's ethical theory. We don't need consequentialism to deny Moral Justification, and if we reject consequentialism, we can adopt antireductionism in testimony and accept God's Reliability. If we do that, the strict-adherence argument would show that our independent moral judgments are not reliable. Therefore, prescribed evil would not be genuinely evil, thus providing a solution to the problem of prescribed evil. That is, the tension between *the divinity of Scripture, the existence of seemingly prescribed evil*, and *the reliability of our independent moral judgments* can be resolved by renouncing the reliability of our independent moral judgments. This solution, while coherent, comes at a cost, however, since it is not acceptable to a progressive, conscientious Muslim. For it requires them to take *all* morally controversial passages at face value, believing that *all* morally counterintuitive actions are in fact moral, and acting in accordance with them.

I believe that rejecting the reliability of our independent moral judgments is a mistake. I believe that Muslims should trust their modern moral sensibilities according to which discriminations against women and other minorities are wrong. But the question is how a progressive conscientious Muslim can resist the strict-adherence argument. Part II of the book explores two different paths that a conscientious Muslim (and theists in general) could take to get out of this conundrum. But before getting to Part II, there is still one more topic to discuss. How do Islamic *philosophers* view the relations between ethics and revelation? Islamic philosophers are descendants of Plato and Aristotle, and, like them, they espouse virtue ethics. What do Islamic virtue ethicists think about the problem of prescribed evil, and the strict-adherence argument? This is the topic of our next chapter.

3
The Virtue Ethics of Islamic Philosophers

Summary of the Chapter

Section 1. The section explains the project of Islamic philosophers to reconcile philosophy with religion. The project involves adopting a highly intellectual epistemology as well as developing theological virtue ethics.

Section 2. Al-Fārābī's epistemological view of reason and religion is described. On his view, while knowledge requires demonstration, religion does not use the demonstrative method. Composed of metaphorical truths which imitate the universal demonstrative truths, religious truths are most helpful for those without access to demonstrations. Al-Fārābī holds that religious truths should be understood in light of demonstrative truths discovered by reason.

Section 3. This section discusses Averroës's solution for the conflict between philosophy and religion. Averroës argues that the departure from the literal interpretation of Scripture is permissible only if we have a demonstrative proof that the apparent meaning is not true. But, on this al-Fārābian view, a departure from the literal meaning of practical injunctions is not permissible since demonstrative proofs in moral matters are scarce.

Section 4. This section overviews al-Fārābī's theological virtue ethics and its differences from Aristotelian virtue ethics. Contrary to Aristotle, al-Fārābī does not hold that happiness is constitutively dependent on virtue. He offers an otherworldly conception of happiness. On his view, the rightness or wrongness of an action is determined by its instrumental contribution to something to which practical reason has no access. Therefore, we should rely on the views of the *theoretically* wise person (i.e., the prophet) to know what we should do; our moral judgment has no standing vis-à-vis the prophet's.[1]

---

[1] The reader who is not interested in a *historical* discussion of the relationship between ethics, religion, and philosophy in Islamic philosophy may skip the entire chapter. However, section 4 shows how the Scripture-first view can be defended by adopting theological virtue ethics.

1. The Project of the Reconciliation of Reason and Religion

It is very well known that when there is a conflict between reason and religion, Islamic philosophers, including al-Fārābī (872–950), Avicenna (980–1037), and Averroës (1126–1198) side with reason over religion. The problem is that this well-known truth is not true, at least when it comes to morality. The goal of this chapter is to show that, contrary to conventional wisdom, Islamic philosophers are committed to a view in which Scripture takes precedence over moral reason. I will argue that, despite their love of reason, Islamic philosophers' way of reconciling reason with religion is yet another version of the Scripture-first view.

Let's begin our story with the Arabic translation movement. That movement made it possible for Muslim scholars to study the texts of ancient Greek philosophers. Muslim philosophers were fascinated by the discovery of this new source of knowledge. They found ancient Greek philosophers, especially Aristotle, an important avenue to the acquisition of knowledge. Muslim philosophers, however, were part of the Islamic culture; as Mahdi puts, "If there is a single attitude to characterize [this culture], it is gratitude for revelation and the divine law, . . . adherence to the way of life of the Prophet and his companions as the correct way, . . . and the conviction that deviation from the way of these pious ancestors is wrong."[2] While Aristotelian philosophy, on the face of it, looks very different from religion, Muslim philosophers, in general, were not ready to give up on one for the sake of the other (al-Rāzī, as we will discuss in the next chapter, was perhaps an exception). They wanted to maintain both sources of knowledge at the same time, and thus they had to find a way to reconcile them. To this end, the first step for Islamic philosophers such as al-Fārābī and Averroës was to make Aristotelian philosophy more religion friendly. This could be done by adding Neoplatonic elements to Aristotelian philosophy (and from this perspective, it should not be very surprising that the attribution of the *Theology of Aristotle*, which is in fact a Neoplatonic text, to Aristotle was not critically scrutinized).[3]

Having made Aristotelian philosophy more transcendental, Islamic philosophers then announced that although there is only one truth, there are

---

[2] Muhsin Mahdi, *Alfarabi and the Foundation of Islamic Political Philosophy* (Chicago: University of Chicago Press, 2001), 17.

[3] See Mahdi, *Alfarabi*, on this.

different ways of getting at that truth. Aristotelian philosophy provides a *demonstrative method* to get at the truth, whereas religion expresses the truth in a nondemonstrative way. Hence, Aristotelian philosophy accords with, and in fact supports, religion. In his well-known treatise *Fasl al-Maqāl*, Averroës states,

> Since this religion [i.e., Islam] is true and summons to the study which leads to knowledge of the Truth, we the Muslim community know definitely that demonstrative study does not lead to [conclusions] conflicting with what Scripture has given us; for truth does not oppose truth but accords with it and bears witness to it.[4]

We might think that the unavoidable implication of this way of reconciling philosophy to religion is that philosophy should take precedence over religion. For it is philosophy that provides us with a more reliable route to truth; philosophy uses demonstration, that is, the most reliable path to truth. As a result, when there is an apparent conflict between philosophy and revelation, revelation must be reinterpreted to become consistent with philosophy. Butterworth characterizes this conclusion as follows: "To say that philosophy and religion express the same truth, albeit in different ways, does not mean that each arrives at the truth by equally legitimate paths. Such a contention would mean that truth is twofold. Rather, the point is that the figurative speech used in religion is to be judged and interpreted according to the rules for rational speech. This and this alone is the reasoning that guides al-Fārābī in his writings and that Averroes sets forth so clearly in his *Decisive Treatise* [i.e., *Fasl al-Maqāl*]."[5]

The reconciliation project *might* be promising for anyone interested in making *science* and religion consistent. But, regardless of whether the project can fulfill the promise of making religion consistent with *theoretical* knowledge, I will argue that the project is conceived in such a way that it makes it very difficult for our independent *practical* judgments to have a say in the reconciliation project. There are two reasons for this:

> First, al-Fārābī, and his successors such as Averroës, prioritize philosophy over religion by taking a very *intellectualized* epistemological view.

---

[4] Jon McGinnis and David C. Reisman, trans., *Classical Arabic Philosophy: An Anthology of Sources* (Indianapolis: Hackett, 2007), chap. 2, p. 313. I use this translation for all passages in *Fasl al-Maqāl*.

[5] Charles Butterworth, "Al-Fārābī's Goal: Political Philosophy, Not Political Theology," in *Islam, the State, and Political Authority: Medieval Issues and Modern Concerns*, ed. Asma Afsaruddin (New York: Palgrave Macmillan US, 2011), 53–74.

They set the epistemic standard for knowledge so high that religion can never meet it. Only philosophy can meet such a high standard, and thus only philosophy can yield real knowledge. But the problem for this al-Fārābīan reconciliatory project is that the epistemic standards are set so high that it cannot be met by our independent moral judgments. Therefore, the al-Fārābīan solution for adjudicating the conflict between reason and Scripture is of no use when it comes to moral matters.

Second, the kind of philosophy that takes precedence over religion is not, as it were, secular philosophy. Rather, al-Fārābī makes Aristotle's philosophy more religion friendly by incorporating Neoplatonic elements into it. But the Neoplatonic revisions to Aristotelian philosophy come at a significant cost for practical reason. Al-Fārābī's moral theory is essentially a *theological virtue ethics*. His moral theory becomes very influential for later Islamic philosophers, as later Islamic philosophers adopt a variant of al-Fārābī's moral theory. Al-Fārābī's theological virtue theory, precisely because of its Neoplatonic elements, differs from Aristotelian virtue ethics in crucial ways which are significant for moral epistemology. As we will see, the theological virtue ethics of al-Fārābī does not support the reliability of our independent moral judgments. Therefore, the theological virtue ethics of al-Fārābī faces the now-familiar problem of skepticism regarding the epistemic power of reason in the moral realm.

In this chapter, I will mainly discuss the ideas of al-Fārābī. Al-Fārābī is among the very first Islamic philosophers to argue for the priority of reason over revelation. His views become very influential and are, more or less, incorporated by later philosophers such as Avicenna and Averroës. I will also discuss Averroës's *Fasl al-Maqāl*, which explicitly addresses the question of the clash between philosophy and religion from an al-Fārābīan standpoint.

2. Al-Fārābī's View on Epistemology and Religion

In *Posterior Analytics*, Aristotle specifies a set of requirements for (scientific) knowledge (i.e., *epistēmē*). Scientific knowledge must be acquired through *demonstrations*, and there are demonstrations only for necessary propositions. Therefore, the object of scientific knowledge is only necessary propositions. Scientific knowledge is of necessary propositions, according to Aristotle, because knowledge is about that which cannot be otherwise, and contingent propositions could be otherwise. Aristotle's view on the nature of *epistēmē* is adopted by al-Fārābī (as well as many other Islamic philosophers, including Avicenna, and Averroës).[6] Al-Fārābī states his view on the nature of knowledge as follows:

> Knowledge in truth is what is accurate and certain for all time, not for some [particular time] but not some other, nor existing at one moment and possibly becoming nonexistent afterwards. For if we are cognizant of something existing now and when time passes it is possible for it to be abolished, we are not aware of whether it exists or not. So our certainty comes back as doubt and falsehood, and what can possibly be false is neither knowledge nor certainty. Therefore, the Ancients did not set down as knowledge the perception of what can possibly change from condition to condition, such as our knowing that this human being is sitting now.[7]

The passage says that knowledge requires *certainty*. It also seems to suggests that knowledge is only of necessary and eternal propositions.[8] In *The Condition of Certainty*, al-Fārābī provides an account of what certainty amounts to.[9] For example, on his view, for one's belief to be certain, one needs to be infallibly aware of its epistemic grounds.[10] Only demonstration can help us to produce such certainty. A demonstrative proof, on an Aristotelian understanding of it, could produce the (infallible) knowledge of the ground of the conclusion via its middle term. No matter how we construe the details of al-Fārābī's view on knowledge and certainty, the received view is that al-Fārābī's goal in giving the conditions of certainty is "to differentiate

---

[6] On the influence of Aristotle's account of episteme on Islamic philosophers see Peter Adamson, "XI—On Knowledge of Particulars," *Proceedings of the Aristotelian Society* 105.1 (2005): 257–78.

[7] Selected Aphorism, Section 36, in *Al-Fārābī: The Political Writings: Selected Aphorisms and Other Texts*, trans. Charles Butterworth (Ithaca, NY: Cornell University Press 2001), 29.

[8] Some reservations toward this claim are in order. See Anthony Robert Booth, *Islamic Philosophy and the Ethics of Belief* (London: Palgrave Macmillan, 2016), 46–47, and D. Black, "Knowledge ('ilm) and Certitude (yaqīn) in al-Fārābī's Epistemology," *Arabic Sciences and Philosophy* 16.1 (2006): 24.

[9] For excellent discussion of this work, see Deborah Black, "Knowledge ('ilm) and Certitude (yaqīn)"; Booth, *Islamic Philosophy*.

[10] Booth, *Islamic Philosophy*, 46.

philosophically demonstrative certitude from dialectical and rhetorical conviction."[11]

It is not hard to see why, for al-Fārābī, reason takes precedence over revelation. Reason, due to its demonstrative method, yields knowledge, whereas religion does not. One might wonder, however, why religion can't produce knowledge through some nondemonstrative methods. Al-Fārābī thinks that religion only uses dialectical and rhetorical methods which can't yield knowledge. But can't religion produce knowledge through another method? Al-Fārābī does not consider this possibility. But in *Epitome of the Parva Naturalia*, Averroës considers this possibility and argues against it.

> Scientific knowledge in its nature is one single thing regardless of whether it is learnt by study or without study.... Now we have two options: Either we take it that "scientific knowledge" is a common predicate for different kinds of human knowledge or we take it there is one single thing as scientific knowledge but it has different causes [i.e., study and revelation] in which case the relation of a thing to the cause by which it exists would not be necessary, which would be impossible.[12]

Averroës's argument is based on the assumption that every class of effect can only have one class of necessitating cause. Based on this assumption, scientific knowledge can only have one class of necessitating cause, that is, study. Knowledge learned by revelation either is not knowledge at all or has a completely different nature than scientific knowledge. Averroës never discusses any different kind of human knowledge. Thus, it is safe to assume that on his view knowledge cannot be acquired by revelation.[13]

---

[11] Black, "Knowledge ('ilm) and Certitude (yaqīn)," 30. It is worth noting that Booth argues that for al-Fārābī, it requires more than demonstrative proofs to reach to the level of *absolute* certainty. Only "a person with the correct prophetic psychological makeup will necessarily come to be in an epistemic situation where they have absolute certainty towards those propositions about which there can be absolute certainty—necessary, eternal truths." But even on Booth's view, demonstration is necessary for certainty. Moreover, Booth also holds that philosophers without prophetic makeup could reach a lesser degree of certainty by using demonstrations. Whether "absolute" certainty is accessible to nonprophet philosophers is tangential to the point I am making here.

[12] Averroes, *Epitome of Parva Naturalia*, Arabic text, trans. Harry Blumberg (Cambridge, MA: Medieval Academy of America, 1972), 90.

[13] For a helpful discussion of *Epitome of Parva Naturalia*, and Averroës's account of prophecy in general see Herbert A. Davidson, *Al-Fārābīi, Avicenna, and Averroes on Intellect: Their Cosmologies, Theories of the Active Intellect, and Theories of Human Intellect* (Oxford: Oxford University Press, 1992), 340–51.

Al-Fārābī holds that religion, both in its practical doctrines and in its theoretical doctrines, is subordinate to philosophy because it is only philosophy that provides demonstrations. In the following passage, he says that religious practical doctrines are just determinate applications of universal truths learned in philosophy. Religious doctrines, moreover, require philosophy for their justification.

> Virtuous religion is similar to philosophy. Just as philosophy is partly theoretical and partly practical, so it is with religion: . . . The practical things in religion are those whose universals are in practical philosophy. That is because the practical things in religion are those universals made determinate by stipulations restricting them, and what is restricted by stipulations is more particular than what is pronounced unqualifiedly without stipulations. . . . The theoretical opinions that are in religion have their demonstrative proofs in theoretical philosophy and are taken in religion without demonstrative proofs. Therefore, the two parts of which religion consists are subordinate to philosophy. . . . Further, if to know something is to know it demonstratively, then [the practical] part of philosophy is the one that gives the demonstrative proof for the determined actions that are in virtuous religion. And since it is the theoretical part of philosophy that gives demonstrative proofs for the theoretical part of religion, it is philosophy, then, that gives the demonstrative proofs of what virtuous religion encompasses. Therefore, the kingly craft responsible for what the virtuous religion consists of is subordinate to philosophy.[14]

Religion does not add anything to either practical or theoretical philosophy. At best, it incorporates the truths of philosophy. But given that it is only philosophy that explains why those truths hold, only philosophy yields real knowledge. Therefore, while religion is in harmony with philosophy, it is religion that must be interpreted in light of philosophy (and not the other way around).

What is religion in al-Fārābī's view? He defines religion as follows: "Religion is opinions and actions, determined and restricted with stipulations and prescribed for a community by their first ruler."[15] It is noticeable that

---

[14] *Book of Religion*, 97–98, in *Al-Fārābī: The Political Writings: Selected Aphorisms and Other Texts*, trans. Charles Butterworth (Ithaca, NY: Cornell University Press 2001),
[15] *Book of Religion*, 93.

al-Fārābī defines religion in terms of the *ruler*, and not in terms of revelation. On this definition, we can have good religions and bad religions: "If the first ruler is virtuous and his rulership truly virtuous, then ... that religion will be virtuous religion" (*Book of Religion*, 93). But who is a virtuous first ruler? To understand al-Fārābī's characterization of the virtuous first ruler, we need to understand his view on different types of intellect.

The virtuous first ruler is the rational soul who possesses an *acquired intellect*. Al-Fārābī distinguishes at least four kinds of intellect: *passive* (or *purely potential*) *intellect, actual intellect, acquired intellect*, and *active intellect*. Potential intellect is a disposition to learn forms. Using al-Fārābī's analogy, potential intellect is like a piece of wax on which forms (or intelligibles) are stamped. Passive intellect is purely potential (and thus it is sometimes called purely potential intellect). A potential intellect becomes actual intellect when it apprehends some intelligibles. But what is actually intellect may be the actual intellect with respect to one form, and the potential intellect with respect to another form which has not yet come to be in it. So being actually intellect comes in degrees. An intellect can become more actually intellect.

When the actual intellect apprehends all the intelligibles, and thus reaches its perfection, it becomes acquired intellect. When an intellect reaches this stage, that is, when it becomes actual with regards to all intelligibles, it does not intellect anything outside of itself; rather, it intellects its very own self. The fourth kind of intellect is the active intellect. While every human being has a passive intellect, becomes actual intellect, and can in principle become acquired intellect, there is only *one* active intellect in the universe. The active intellect is an incorporeal transcendent cosmic being which has a precise place in the hierarchy of incorporeal things. On al-Fārābī's cosmology, the first cause (i.e., God) eternally emanates the first intelligence, the first intelligence eternally emanates the second intelligence, and so on. The tenth intelligence is the active intellect. It is the last link in the chain of celestial intelligences. It parallels the sublunary world which would be the last cosmic body. The main task of the active intellect is to cause the human intellect to pass from potentiality to actuality. With this preliminary explanation of different types of intellect, we can proceed to al-Fārābī's description of the true first ruler (i.e., "the ruler of the excellent city") in *al-Madina al-Fadila* (translated as *The Perfect State*):

> That man is a person over whom nobody has any sovereignty whatsoever. He is a man who has reached his perfection and has become actually

intellect and actually being thought (intelligized), his representative faculty having by nature reached its utmost perfection in the way stated by us; this faculty of his is predisposed by nature to receive, either in waking life or in sleep, from the Active Intellect the particulars, either as they are, or by imitating them, and also the intelligibles, by imitating them. His Passive Intellect will have reached its perfection by [having apprehended] all the intelligibles.... Indeed any man whose Passive Intellect has thus being perfected by [having apprehended] all the intelligibles and has become actually intellect and actually being thought, so that the intelligible in him has become identical with that which thinks in him, acquires an actual intellect which is superior to the Passive Intellect and more perfect and more separate from matter than the Passive Intellect. It is called the "Acquired Intellect" and comes to occupy a middle position between the Passive Intellect and the Active Intellect, nothing else between it and the Active Intellect.[16]

The true first ruler is then someone who possess the acquired intellect and also a representative faculty which has reached its utmost perfection. The first ruler possesses the acquired intellect in the sense that the ruler has all the intelligibles in the intellect, that is, has learned all universal principles. But what does al-Fārābī mean by a *representative* faculty which has reached its *perfection*?

The faculty of representation is intermediate between the faculty of sense and rational faculty ... when the faculties of sense and representation and reason are in the state of their first perfection and thus do not perform their actions, as happens during sleep, the faculty of representation is on its own, free from the fresh imprint of sensibles ... and is relived of the service of the rational and appetitive faculties. Thus it will turn to those imprints of sensibles which are preserved in it and have remained.... But in addition to the preservation of the imprints of the sensibles and their association with one another it displays a third activity, namely "reproductive imitation" [mimesis].... The faculty of representation also imitates the rational faculty by imitating those intelligibles which are present in it with things suitable for imitating them. It thus imitates the intelligibles

---

[16] Al-Fārābī, *Al-Madina al-Fadila*, trans. R. Walzer in *Al-Fārābī on the Perfect State* (New York: Oxford University Press, 1985), 241–43.

of utmost perfection, like the First Cause, the immaterial things, the heavens.... The Active Intellect acts in some way upon the faculty of representation as well by providing it sometimes with the intelligible whose proper place is in theoretical reason, and sometimes with particulars in the form of sensibles whose proper place is in practical reason. It receives the intelligibles by imitating them with those sensibles which it puts together and receive the particulars, which are usually produced by practical reason though deliberation, sometimes by representing them as they are and sometimes by imitating them with other sensibles.... It is not impossible, then, that when a man's faculty of representation reaches its utmost perfection, he will receive in his waking life from the Active Intellect present and future particulars of their imitations in the form of sensibles, and receive the imitations of the transcendent intelligibles and other glorious existents and see them. This man will obtain through the particulars which he receives "prophecy" (supernatural awareness) of present and future events, and through the intelligibles which he receives prophecy of divine things.[17]

The representative faculty (*al-quwwa al mutakhayyila*), which could also be translated as the *imaginative* faculty, usually gets its inputs from the sensory faculty. It manipulates and reconfigures sensations into new sensible representations, which may or may not correspond to things in the external world. The representative faculty provides input for the rational and appetitive faculties for deliberation and action. It is also responsible for retention of sensible representations and dreams. The representative faculty can also create metaphorical images through mimesis (*muhākāt*). They are sensible representations that symbolize intelligibles and truths. Besides the rational faculty, the representative faculty can be also a recipient for the emanations of the active intellect. The emanation of the active intellect to the representative faculty takes the shape of sensible presentations that metaphorically represent intelligibles and universal truths. It can also take the shape of the metaphorical truths about particular events as well as predictions about future events. The first ruler's representative faculty reaches its utmost perfection, and that means the representative faculty's primary function is not to serve practical and theoretical intellect. It can work on its own

---

[17] Al-Fārābī, *Al-Madina al-Fadila*, 211–25.

and thus receives metaphorical truths from the active intellect in waking life. These metaphorical truths received from the active intellect are called revelation.[18]

To sum up, then, religion does not provide us with demonstrative truths. Yet the prophet, through revelation, receives metaphorical truths, which imitate the universal truths. All universal truths can be acquired by reason alone, and the human with acquired intellect does in fact acquire all universal truths. But for those people who don't have access to truths through demonstration, religion can be very helpful. For it represents those truths in a way that they can understand. But religion can never oppose reason, in the same way that a metaphorical statement cannot undermine the truth it metaphorically represents. Religion must be understood in light of reason because the truths it expresses are just the truths of reason represented in an imaginative way.

3. Averroës's View on the Harmony of Religion and Philosophy

Averroës's philosophy is very much under influence of al-Fārābī. On the main question we are interested in, that is, the epistemological relation between reason and revelation, there is almost no difference between the two thinkers.[19] In his well-known treatise *Fasl al-Maqāl*, Averroës adopts an al-Fārābīan framework and seeks to explain in a systematic way how we should respond to the disagreement between philosophy and religion. The major premise of Averroës is that religion and philosophy are both true and that truth agrees with truth. Let me restate the passage we saw in the introduction of the chapter:

> Since this religion [i.e., Islam] is true and summons to the study which leads to knowledge of the Truth, we the Muslim community know definitely that demonstrative study does not lead to [conclusions] conflicting with what Scripture has given us; for truth does not oppose truth but accords with it and bears witness to it.

---

[18] In the passage quoted, al-Fārābī only uses the term "prophecy." But in a*l-Siyasa al-Madaniyya*, he uses the term "revelation" for the metaphorical truths received by the acquired intellect.
[19] See Davidson, *Al-Fārābīi, Avicenna, and Averroes*, 340–51.

If truth accords with and bears witness to truth, any conflict between religion and philosophy is just apparent and will be removed in our final judgment. The assumption that religion and philosophy must ultimately agree with each other is not peculiar to al-Fārābī or Averroës. All rationalist Islamic theologians and philosophers would accept this. After all, if God is all good and all-knowing, what he says must be true. The reasoning behind al-Ghazālī's rule of figurative interpretation (discussed in Chapter 1) is the same. But if so, why are there apparent conflicts between religion and Scripture? Like al-Fārābī, Averroës makes a distinction between three different ways to know the truth (or, as he puts it, to assent to the truth): the demonstrative way, the dialectical way, and the rhetorical way.

> For the natures of men are on different levels with respect to [their paths to] assent. One of them comes to assent through demonstration; another comes to assent through dialectical arguments, just as firmly as the demonstrative man through demonstration, since his nature does not contain any greater capacity; while another comes to assent through rhetorical arguments, again just as firmly as the demonstrative man through demonstrative arguments. Thus since this divine religion of ours has summoned people by these three methods, assent to it has extended to everyone, except him who stubbornly denies it with his tongue or him for whom no method of summons to God the Exalted has been appointed in religion owing to his own neglect of such matters.[20]

Different people have different intellectual capacities. Not everyone can come to know the truth in a demonstrative way. Most people are, indeed, incapable of demonstration. So God cannot use demonstration very often. As a result, religion mostly consists in nondemonstrative truths:

> Not everyone has the natural ability to take in demonstrations, or [even] dialectical arguments, let alone demonstrative arguments which are so hard to learn and need so much time [even] for those who are qualified to learn them. Therefore, since it is the purpose of Scripture simply to teach everyone, Scripture has to contain every method of [bringing about] judgments of assent and every method of forming concepts. Now some of the methods of assent comprehend the majority of people, i.e., the occurrence of assent

---

[20] Averroës, *Fasl al-Maqāl*, chap. 1, p. 313.

as a result of them [is comprehensive]: these are the rhetorical and the dialectical [methods], and the rhetorical is more comprehensive than the dialectical. Another method is peculiar to a smaller number of people: this is the demonstrative. Therefore, since the primary purpose of Scripture is to take care of the majority (without neglecting to arouse the elite), the prevailing methods of expression in religion are the common methods by which the majority comes to form concepts and judgments.[21]

Religion, to have a broad appeal, must use a variety of methods to communicate the truth. It cannot always rely on demonstration. But this comes at a cost. In order to make the truths of religion accessible to everyone, God uses methods that are not ideal at capturing the truth. If everyone were capable of using demonstration, everyone could understand the truth as it is. But in order to communicate the truth in a nondemonstrative way, God uses pictures and images that represent abstract truths in a pictorial or metaphoric way. The pictorial or metaphorical representations do not represent truths accurately—in the sense that they are literally false. But they are the second-best way to communicate important truths to those who are not capable of grasping them in an abstract way.

> With regard to things which by reason of their recondite character are only knowable by demonstration, God has been gracious to those of His servants who have no access to demonstration, on account of their natures, habits or lack of facilities for education: He has coined for them images and likenesses of these things, and summoned them to assent to those images, since it is possible for assent to those images to come about through the indications common to all men, i.e. the dialectical and rhetorical indications. This is the reason why Scripture is divided into apparent and inner meanings: the apparent meaning consists of those images which are coined to stand for those ideas, while the inner meaning is those ideas [themselves], which are clear only to the demonstrative class. These are the four or five classes of beings mentioned by Abu Hamid in *The Book of Distinction* [*Faysal*].[22]

The real reason that Scripture is divided into apparent and inner meaning is that inner meaning is not accessible to most people. Consider a Scriptural

---

[21] Averroës, *Fasl al-Maqāl*, chap. 3, p. 324.
[22] Averroës, *Fasl al-Maqāl*, chap. 2, p. 320.

passage which is in conflict with truths discovered by demonstration. This is a case in which the demonstrative truth is not accessible to people with no demonstrative power. In such a case, God (through Active Intellect) produces some images in the sensory or imaginative faculty of the prophet, or He uses objects that everybody knows to communicate those truths to them in a nonliteral way. The apparent meaning does not represent the truth accurately. But this is the best that God could achieve if He wants religion to be accessible to everyone.

Averroës confirms al-Ghazālī's rule of figurative interpretation in *Faysal* (see Chapter 1, section 4). According to this rule, a departure from the literal meaning is allowed only if we have a demonstrative proof that the literal interpretation is *impossible*. Averroës, however, construes the rule in a more permissive way. In his view, one may depart from the literal meaning only if one has a demonstrative proof that the literal meaning is *not true*. In the following passage, Averroës explains his method of interpretation when there is a conflict between religion and reason:

> Whenever demonstrative study leads to any manner of knowledge about any being, that being is inevitably either unmentioned or mentioned in Scripture. If it is unmentioned there is no contradiction. . . . If Scripture speaks about it, the apparent meaning of the words inevitably either accords or conflicts with the conclusions of demonstration about it. If this [apparent meaning] accords there is no argument. If it conflicts, there is a call for allegorical interpretation of it. The meaning of "allegorical interpretation" is: extension of the significance of an expression from real to metaphorical significance, without forsaking therein the standard metaphorical practices of Arabic, such as calling a thing by the name of something resembling it or a cause or consequence or accompaniment of it, or other things such as are enumerated in accounts of the kinds of metaphorical speech.[23]

There are three possibilities. (1) The apparent meaning of Scripture accords with demonstration. There is no conflict in this case. We can follow reason and Scripture simultaneously. (2) The conclusion of a demonstration is not mentioned in Scripture. There is no conflict in this case either. We can follow reason without being worried that it contradicts Scripture. (3) A demonstration's conclusion does not accord with the apparent meaning

---

[23] Averroës, *Fasl al-Maqāl*, chap. 2, p. 292.

of Scripture. The conflict arises only in this case. On Averroës's view, "There is a call for allegorical interpretation" of Scripture only in this case. So, if we have a demonstrative argument to the effect that the apparent reading of a Scriptural passage is false, we may to interpret the passage metaphorically.

Averroës believes that there is nothing suspect in the fact that different scholars have different views about which Scriptural passages should be interpreted nonliterally. Different scholars have different arguments about abstract theoretical matters such as the nature of reality, time, and free will. They all take their arguments to be demonstrative, and when they find their demonstrative arguments in tension with the apparent meaning of Scripture, they depart from the apparent meaning. The situation with practical passages is different, though. According to Averroës, contrary to theoretical matters, there is unanimity among different scholars about how to understand practical passages of Scripture.[24] On Averroës's view, there would not be unanimity among scholars about moral passages had some of them believed that they could show demonstratively that the apparent meaning of a moral passage in Scripture is false. So the fact that Averroës believes that there is unanimity among different scholars about how to understand moral passages shows that he believes that Islamic scholars, for the most part, have not claimed that they could show demonstratively that the apparent meanings of moral passages are false.

In moral matters, demonstrative proofs are, in fact, scarce. It is very hard, at least for most of us, to *demonstratively prove* that a particular instance of a killing, rape, or torture is wrong. For one thing, only universal principles, according to Aristotle, can be proved demonstratively, and many moral claims are about particular actions. But more importantly, for many moral propositions, it is very hard for us to show that they are true beyond any reasonable doubt. We do *believe* that a certain killing is wrong, and we might be able to provide *good reasons* in support of that judgment. But can we show that this judgment *logically* follows from some principles that are *epistemically certain*? For many of us, our moral judgments ultimately boil down to our basic moral intuitions. Moral intuitions, however, hardly enjoy epistemic certainty.[25] If so, given Averroës's method of interpretation, a departure from the literal meaning of Scripture in moral matters is rarely permissible.

---

[24] Averroës, *Fasl al-Maqāl*, chap. 2, p. 315.
[25] In "Moral Faith," *Journal of Philosophy* 92.2 (1995): 75–95, , Robert Adams argues that we can't be certain about various important ethical matters.

In general, the al-Fārābīan reconciliation between reason and revelation is impotent in the moral realm. For, on al-Fārābī's view, the bar for knowledge is set so high that moral judgments can hardly meet them. If knowledge is only limited to beliefs supported by demonstration, most of us can seldom have knowledge in moral matters. Moral intuitions do not yield demonstrative moral knowledge, and thus we should ignore our moral intuitions when they are in conflict with Scripture.

But even if moral demonstration *were* more accessible to *scholars*, al-Fārābīan solution would not give us everything we want. For *most people* lack demonstrative capacities. Only very few people have demonstrative powers. Even if it were possible for scholars to show demonstratively that it is wrong to beat one's wife, few people would know this by demonstration. Moreover, Averroës argues that demonstrative people should keep their interpretations to themselves.

> When something of these allegorical interpretations is expressed to anyone unfit to receive them, especially demonstrative interpretations because of their remoteness from common knowledge—both he who expresses it and he to whom it is expressed are led into unbelief. The reason for that [in the case of the latter] is that allegorical interpretation comprises two things, rejection of the apparent meaning and affirmation of the allegorical one; so that if the apparent meaning is rejected in the mind of someone who can only grasp apparent meanings, without the allegorical meaning being affirmed in his mind, the result is unbelief, if it [the text in question] concerns the principles of religion. Allegorical interpretations, then, ought not to be expressed to the masses nor set down in rhetorical or dialectical books.[26]

According to Averroës, even in cases in which inner meaning and apparent meaning are in conflict, people who are not capable of understanding demonstrative truths should stick to the apparent meaning. Moreover, people who know the inner meaning should keep it to themselves. For revealing it to nondemonstrative people who have no knowledge of it only results in denying Scripture altogether. In sum, the al-Fārābīan way of removing the tension between reason and Scripture has two main problems. First, we have few demonstrations in practical matters. Second, regardless of the possibility

---

[26] Averroës, *Fasl al-Maqāl*, chap. 3, pp. 325–26.

of finding demonstration in ethics, on this view most people should stick to the literal meaning. Therefore, in cases of the conflict between moral judgments and Scripture, it is not clear if we could ever side with moral intuitions, and even if a minority of people could, the majority of people should side with Scripture.

Al-Fārābī's rejection of the reliability of our independent moral judgments, when they are in conflict with Scripture, is thus grounded in *his intellectualized epistemology*. Given his very demanding conception of knowledge, it is no surprise that most of us can have little moral knowledge. It can be argued that on this intellectualized epistemology, we have also very few pieces of theoretical knowledge.

But if we had a more modest epistemology, we could perhaps use the al-Fārābīan framework to approach the problem of prescribed evil. There are some hints in Averroës's text that suggests that the basis of nonliteral interpretation is not the fact that we have demonstrative proofs. Rather, it is that we should side with reason in cases of the conflict between reason and Scripture because we can't *freely* choose to go against our reasoning. Consider the following passage, for example:

> It seems that those who disagree on the interpretation of these difficult questions earn merit if they are in the right and will be excused [by God] if they are in error. For assent to a thing as a result of an indication [of it] arising in the soul is something compulsory, not voluntary: *i.e.* it is not for us [to choose] not to assent or to assent, as it is to stand up or not to stand up. And since free choice is a condition of obligation, a man who assents to an error as a result of a consideration that has occurred to him is excused, if he is a scholar. This is why the Prophet, peace on him, said, "If the judge after exerting his mind makes a right decision, he will have a double reward; and if he makes a wrong decision he will [still] have a single reward." And what judge is more important than he who makes judgments about being, that it is thus or not thus? These judges are the scholars, specially chosen by God for [the task of] allegorical interpretation, and this error which is forgivable according to the Law is only such error as proceeds from scholars when they study the difficult matters which the Law obliges them to study.[27]

---

[27] Averroës, *Fasl al-Maqāl*, chap. 2, p. 319.

The suggestion is that the acceptance of a good argument for a scholar is not *optional*. The good scholar has no option but to believe in the conclusion of a good argument. If he gets it right, he gets a "double reward" (for both following the good argument and getting at truth); if he does not, he still has a "single reward" (for following the good argument). We can apply the same reasoning to moral matters. If we have a good argument against the apparent meaning of Scripture in a certain moral matter, regardless of whether this argument is demonstrative or not, we might have no option but to depart from the apparent meaning.

This *modest al-Fārābīan solution* is empty, however, for two reasons. *First*, according to this "solution," *if* we have good arguments for the reliability of our independent moral judgments, we can rely on our independent moral judgments. But the question at issue is *whether we have good arguments* for the reliability of our independent moral judgments, given our ignorance of all moral reasons. In the previous chapter, we noted that reason might not be able to make an *everything-considered* moral judgment (even probabilistically), given its ignorance of the total distribution of reasons. The question of the justification for relying on our moral judgments, when our knowledge of moral reasons is limited, is left unanswered by this solution.

Moreover, suppose for the sake of the argument that reason alone can justify an everything-considered moral judgment. There is a reason why al-Fārābī and Averroës think that we need demonstrations to depart from the apparent meaning of Scripture. Demonstrations *guarantee* the truth of the judgment of reason, and revelation, to remain true, must make itself consistent with this truth. But a nondemonstrative argument does not *guarantee* the truth of our independent judgment about an everything-considered ought. If that is the case, a clash between our independent moral judgment and revelation is a clash between two pieces of evidence. The stronger evidence wins. But, *ex hypothesi*, we have strong reasons for the authority of Scripture. Whenever there is a clash between our independent reasons and reasons provided by revelation, then, the reasons of revelation override our independent reasons. Add the reasons provided by revelation to the pile of our evidence, and the good scholar will see that the balance of evidence is in favor of revelation. In other words, if our independent argument is nondemonstrative, it might not be able to defeat revelation. Therefore, the real question is whether on an al-Fārābīan view we have reasons to support an everything considered moral judgment, and how strong those reasons are.

The next section reviews the virtue ethics of al-Fārābī and the epistemology that comes with it. We will see that, according to al-Fārābī's virtue ethics, as most people are unable to discover moral truths, their best epistemic path to the moral realm is through the judgments of the prophet.

4. The Virtue Ethics of al-Fārābī

Al-Fārābī's ethical view is Aristotelian and essentially teleological. The human telos is to achieve felicity, eudemonia, or final happiness (sa'ada); actions and character traits are evaluated in terms of the roles they play in enabling the soul to achieve its telos. There is no surprise that al-Fārābī's ethics is influenced by Aristotle. He studied Aristotle's *Nicomachean Ethics* (*NE* henceforth) closely and wrote a commentary on it (which is unfortunately lost). Nevertheless, I will argue in this section that there is an important difference between al-Fārābī and Aristotle. The difference stems from the fact that Aristotle's eudemonia is this-worldly, while al-Fārābī's felicity is completely otherworldly. This difference, as we will see, makes al-Fārābī's virtue ethics significantly different from Aristotelian virtue ethics (as understood in contemporary ethics).

In order to highlight the difference, I am going to explain briefly the main elements of Aristotelian virtue ethics. But first let me make an interpretive remark from the outset. It is a well-known fact that there is an apparent disparity between *NE* I–IX and *NE* X. Aristotle characterizes human happiness in *NE* I–IX as a life of practical and moral activities. However, in *NE* X, Aristotle says that real happiness consists in a life of contemplation. This disparity raises many questions. Why is a practical life a good life, if the contemplative life defines true human happiness? Why shouldn't one abandon the practical life in favor of the contemplative life? If the ultimate happiness is to study, why we should act kindly, courageously, justly, and so forth?

Contemporary virtue ethicists are more inclined to reconstruct Aristotle's view mainly based on *NE* I–IX. While these theorists remain optimistic about finding a way to reconcile *NE* X with the rest of the book, they hold that *NE* X is not the cornerstone of Aristotelian virtue ethics. I will follow this strategy because the character of al-Fārābīan theological virtue ethics can be better revealed when we contrast it with Aristotelian virtue ethics reconstructed based on *NE* I–IX. As I will explain shortly, I think there is a way to reconcile *NE* X with my interpretation of Aristotelian virtue ethics. But whether or not this reconciliatory project succeeds is of no importance for the purpose of understanding al-Fārābī's theological virtue ethics.

Aristotle begins *NE* by noting that happiness is the final point, or the telos, of all rational actions (*NE* 1094a). We can understand Aristotle as saying that happiness provides a success norm for actions; that is, successful actions are conducive to happiness.[28] Aristotelian virtue ethics is teleological in this sense:

(A1) A right human action is that which is conducive to human happiness.

We should not be misled, however, by (A1) into thinking that it provides us with an Archimedean point from which we can determine what one ought to do based on what is conducive to happiness; for it is an important aspect of Aristotle's view that human happiness, that is, *eudaimonia*, cannot be characterized in a morally neutral way. The conclusion of the celebrated function argument, which Aristotle presents to specify the content of *eudaimonia*, is that *eudaimonia* consists in engaging in reason-involving activities in accordance with human *virtues* (*NE* 1098a). Let's state this upshot of the function argument in terms of the following propositions:

(A2) Human happiness is constituted by morally virtuous activities.
(A3) The content of happiness cannot be specified without reference to the agent's moral life.

Assuming that "moral activities" in (A2) and "moral life" in (A3) are understood in terms of an agent's practical activity, one might think that (A2) and (A3) are inconsistent with *NE* X. For in *NE* X, contrary to (A3), Aristotle characterizes happiness in terms of theoretical virtues which enable the person to contemplate. And so, the objection goes, the view I attribute to Aristotle in (A2) and (A3), which is based on *NE* I–IX, is inconsistent with *NE* X.

(A2) and (A3) are clearly endorsed by *NE* I–IX. If Aristotle does not characterize happiness in terms of practical life in *NE* X, we may say that Aristotle has two inconsistent conceptions of happiness, and thus there is an unresolvable tension between *NE* I–IX and *NE* X. Nevertheless, one can interpret *NE*

---

[28] See Amir Saemi, "Aiming at the Good." *Canadian Journal of Philosophy* 45 (2) (2015): 197–219, for an elaborate defense of the idea.

X in a way that it is consistent with *NE* I–IX. Lawrence reconciles *NE* X with the rest of the book by saying that while the contemplative life is the best life in *the ideal condition*, the best life we can lead given our *nonideal* circumstance in the actual world is the life of ethically virtuous activity.[29] In actual life, we might be able to occasionally engage in the contemplative life if the situation arises, for example, when we have no moral obligation, say, to help others.

As Moss notes, Aristotle is very explicit that *moral virtue makes the goal right*.[30] As a result, the contemplator and the one who leads a practical life must have the same goal; otherwise, the virtuous person would not have the right goal (that is, moral virtues do not make the goal right). The virtuous person, in virtue of having moral virtues, pursues noble activities. In ideal circumstances, when virtuous people do not need to combat injustice any longer, they know that the noblest activity for them, under that condition, is contemplation, and they will engage in contemplative activities. On this way of understanding *NE* X, as long as we live under the nonideal condition, happiness should be understood in terms of the agent's practical life, and this is what (A2) and (A3) state.

Putting (A1) and (A2) together, one might think that we can define *moral rightness* in terms of moral virtues. That is,

(A4) The right action is what a morally virtuous person would do.

While (A4) may well be correct, it cannot be used to determine what one ought to do when one has an Aristotelian understanding of virtue. For on Aristotle's view, the notion of moral virtue is itself dependent on the notion of right action. Let me explain.

On Aristotle's view, moral virtues, which represent excellent conditions of the nonrational part of the soul (*NE* 1103a), are dependent on *phronesis* (i.e., practical wisdom). Phronesis, roughly speaking, is the virtue of the practical intellect, which is responsible for making judgments about what one ought to do. Given the way that Aristotle defines moral virtues, there can be no moral virtue without phronesis. Aristotle defines virtue as "a state involving rational choice, consisting in a mean ... determined by reason—the reason,

---

[29] Gavin Lawrence, "Aristotle and the Ideal Life," *Philosophical Review* 102.1 (1993): 1–34.
[30] Jessica Moss, "'Virtue Makes the Goal Right': Virtue and Phronesis in Aristotle's Ethics," *Phronesis* 56.3 (2011): 204–61.

that is, by reference to which the practically wise person [*phronismos*] would determine it" (*NE* 1107a).

While it is clear that Aristotle thinks that one cannot exercise virtue without employing phronesis, it is less clear what role phronesis would play in one's exercising virtues, given that Aristotle says, "Virtue makes the aim right, and practical wisdom the things towards it" (*NE* 1144a). On an influential interpretation, virtue provides one with an *indeterminate* goal which serves as the starting point of practical reasoning. The practically wise person then employs phronesis to make the indeterminate goal determinate. Practical reasoning is *constitutive reasoning* through which the agent determines what specific goals constitute the general end identified by virtue.[31] Irwin characterizes the role of phronesis as follows: "The practical intellect is not concerned with means as opposed to ends. Insofar as it is concerned with constituent "means," it is also concerned with ends."[32] Let's state the function of phronesis in the following way:

(A5) The virtuous agent employs phronesis to determine what particular action constitutes indefinite goals supplied by moral virtues.

Given (A5), (A4) is not very helpful in identifying the right action. So it is no surprise that Aristotelian virtue ethics faces the concern that it does not provide us with general principles to identify right actions. Some people, for example, McDowell and Wiggins, have suggested that virtuous agents have a kind of moral perception by which they can see what the right action is in each particular circumstance.[33] This brief introduction to Aristotelian ethics helps us see how and why al-Fārābī's view diverges from Aristotle's in crucial aspects.

As I noted earlier, al-Fārābī's ethics is, like Aristotle's, teleological. The telos for human beings is ultimate perfection, which is the ultimate happiness or felicity. On al-Fārābī's view, "The voluntary actions which help in attaining felicity are the good actions . . . But the actions which are an obstacle to felicity are the bad things, namely the evil actions."[34] The same goes

---

[31] Moss, "Virtue," has a detailed and plausible discussion of Aristotelian notion of phronesis; see also John McDowell, "Some Issues in Aristotle's Moral Psychology," in McDowell, *Mind, Value and Reality* (Cambridge, MA: Harvard University Press, 1998), 23–40; Terence Irwin, "Aristotle on Reason, Desire and Virtue," *Journal of Philosophy* 73 (1975): 567–78.

[32] Irwin, "Aristotle on Wisdom," 571.

[33] David Wiggins, "Deliberation and Practical Reason," in *Essays on Aristotle's Ethics*, ed. Amélie Oksenberg Rorty (Berkeley: University of California Press, 1980), 221–40; McDowell, "Some Issues."

[34] Al-Fārābī, *The Perfect State*, section 13, p. 207.

for virtues and vices: "The dispositions and habits from which these actions proceed are the virtues, these being goods not for their own sake but good for the sake of felicity ... and the dispositions and habits from which these actions arise are defects, vices and bad qualities."[35] But what is ultimate happiness for al-Fārābī? Al-Fārābī's conception of ultimate happiness is different from Aristotle's in two respects. First, unlike Aristotelian happiness, which is earthly, al-Fārābī's ultimate happiness is associated with the afterlife, that is, it is achieved only when the soul is separated from the body:

> The presence of the first intelligibles in man is his first perfection, but these intelligibles are supplied to him only in order to be used by him to reach his ultimate perfection i.e., felicity. Felicity means that the human soul reaches a degree of perfection in [its] existence where it is no need of matter for support, since it becomes one of the incorporeal things and the immaterial substances that remains in that state continuously for ever. But its rank is beneath the rank of the Active Intellect.[36]

The ultimate perfection of the human being is determined by the place of humans in the Neoplatonic cosmic order he envisages. Humans are in the sublunary world, and thus inferior to the ten intellects. When human intellect actualizes all its potentials (by acquiring all intelligibles), it achieves its highest place, which is very close (if not identical) to the rank of the active intellect. This characterization of ultimate happiness gives rise to the second difference between al-Fārābī's account of happiness and Aristotle's. The ultimate perfection of the human, on al-Fārābī's view, is a *theoretical* achievement through and through. A human achieves its ultimate perfection when its intellect becomes fully actualized.

> When the rational faculty attains to being an intellect in actuality, that intellect ... becomes similar to the separate things and it intellects its essence that is [now] intellect in actuality.... Through this, it becomes such as to be in the rank of the active intellect. And when a human being obtains this rank, his happiness is perfected.[37]

---

[35] Al-Fārābī, *The Perfect State*, section 13, p. 207.
[36] Al-Fārābī, *The Perfect State*, section 13, pp. 206–7.
[37] Al-Fārābī, "Political Regime," in *The Political Writings: "Political Regime" and "Summary of Plato's Laws,"* trans. Charles Butterworth (Ithaca, NY: Cornell University Press, 2015), 33.

As noted before, the human intellect has three stages: the potential intellect, the actual intellect, and the acquired intellect. When a human's intellect becomes fully actual, it acquires all intelligibles and it intellects itself; such an intellect reaches the stage of the acquired intellect. This is the ultimate perfection (and thus the ultimate happiness) of a human. While the acquired intellect is in rank slightly lower than the active intellect, it is almost united with it: "This man [i.e., the acquired intellect] has the most perfect rank of humanity and has reached the highest degree of felicity. His soul is united as it were with the Active Intellect in the way stated by us."

Conceiving ultimate happiness as a theoretical achievement has the implication that ultimate happiness is not constituted by practical virtues. According to al-Fārābī, virtues are only *instrumentally* necessary for happiness; they are good "not for their own sake but good for the sake of felicity." So, while al-Fārābī would accept (A1) and (A4), he would deny (A2), (A3), and (A5). Ultimate perfection is a matter of acquiring all universal principles and intelligibles and learning all theoretical sciences, and thus can be specified without reference to the agent's moral life.

There is nevertheless a debate among scholars of al-Fārābī as to whether human perfection is purely theoretical. While many scholars hold that it is purely theoretical, some hold that for al-Fārābī perfection is at least partly practical.[38] Holding that perfection is not purely theoretical, Booth writes,

> The central trouble with theoretical perfection is that it seems at odds with what can be called al-Farabi's motivational externalism—the view that knowing one "all things considered" ought to φ (and there are no excusing conditions with respect to φ-ing) does not guarantee that one will be motivated to φ. Following Aristotle, al-Farabi clearly held that weakness of the will (akrasia) is possible. As such, it appears that al-Farabi held that one could know what happiness is, and yet fail to be motivated to pursue it, such that knowledge of happiness does not entail being happy.[39]

---

[38] See M. Fakhry, A History of Islamic Philosophy (New York: Columbia University Press, 2004), and T. J. De Boer, *The History of Philosophy in Islam*, trans. Edward R. Jones (New York: Dover, 1967), for the former view. See M. Galston, *Politics and Excellence: The Political Philosophy of Alfarabi* (Princeton, NJ: Princeton University Press, 1990); M. Galston, "The Theoretical and Practical Dimensions of Happiness as Portrayed in the Political Treatises of Al-Farabi," in *The Political Aspects of Islamic Philosophy*, ed. Charles E. Butterworth (Cambridge, MA: Harvard University Press, 1992; and Booth, *Islamic Philosophy*, for the latter view.

[39] Booth, *Islamic Philosophy*, 68.

Booth uses his account of al-Fārābī's certainty to show how perfection for al-Fārābī is partly practical. According to Booth, the prophet's perfect power of *imagination* contributes to his having *absolute* certainty. For, the prophet's power of *imagination* helps him to have the superior *understanding* of the world which is necessary for absolute certainty. "What gives someone the property of superior understanding, the particular imaginative powers, perforce also gives that person superior practical wisdom. This means that all theoretical knowledge, insofar as it admits of absolute certainty, is a composite of theoretical and practical virtue."[40] Given this understanding of theoretical knowledge, on Booth's view, because of his theoretical knowledge, derived partly from his power of imagination, the prophet does not succumb to the weakness of the will, and thus a perfect life, at least on earth, is the life of the prophet, which is a composite of theoretical and practical perfection.

For one thing, I am not sure if I quite understand the objection to theoretical account of perfection based on al-Farabi's acceptance of *motivational externalism* (i.e., the view that one's knowledge that one ought to do an action does not guarantee that one will be motivated to do that action). It is true that al-Farabi holds that "one could know what happiness is, and yet fail to be motivated to pursue it." But happiness for him is not *the knowledge of happiness* (or the knowledge of what one ought to do to achieve happiness); it is the knowledge of all theoretical truths. One does not attain perfection when one knows what perfection is. One attains perfection when one acquires all intelligibles. Motivational externalism does not seem to be relevant to whether perfection is a purely theoretical matter.

The worry might be that it is possible that one acquires all intelligibles without being happy. But this possibility is different from the possibility of akrasia. Moreover, it is quite likely that al-Fārābī would deny this possibility. He could deny it by holding that knowledge of all theoretical truths is associated with significant intellectual pleasure. This is in fact what Avicenna holds, and Avicenna's practical philosophy is greatly influenced by al-Fārābī.[41]

---

[40] Booth, *Islamic Philosophy*, 70–71.
[41] "If the rational faculty had brought the soul to a degree of perfection by which it is enabled, when it separates from the body, to achieve that complete perfection that is [appropriate] for it to attain, its example would then be that of the benumbed person made to taste the most delicious taste and exposed to the most appetizing state but [who] does not feel this, but [who thereafter] has the numbness removed, experiencing [as a result] momentous pleasure all at once. This pleasure would not be of the same genus as sensory and animal pleasure, but a pleasure that is similar to the good state that belongs to the pure living [celestial] substances. It is more elevated than every [other] pleasure and more noble. This, then is happiness." Avicenna, *Metaphysics of Healing*, trans. M. Marmura (Chicago: University of Chicago Press, 2005), 9.7.17, p. 352.

Al-Fārābī could accept motivational externalism while denying that the person who achieves theoretical perfection could be unhappy.

The more important point is that even if Booth and others are right that for al-Fārābī perfection is partly practical, my main point that al-Fārābī's morality is defined in terms of theoretical perfection still stands. In other words, their view of al-Fārābian perfection does not entail that al-Fārābī accepts (A5). Let's grant, for the sake of argument, that Booth is right that absolute certainty requires imagination, and that the imaginative faculty is necessarily coextensive with the practical faculty. Let's also grant for the sake of argument that the prophet needs appropriate practical power not to succumb to the weakness of will. That still does not imply that practical virtues or phronesis do not have instrumental roles. The view of the opponents of purely theoretical perfection is consistent with saying that the goal of the practical faculty is to figure out the best way to achieve theoretical perfection and to produce the appropriate motivational attitudes to make this goal possible. Motivational externalism has no implication about whether virtuous agents have a kind of moral perception by which they can see what the right action is in each particular circumstance. So even if the perfect life partly consists of having appropriate motivational attitudes, the perfect life could still be a life of *pursuing* theoretical truths. Therefore, the current debate about whether al-Fārābī's conception of perfection is partly practical does not bear on the issue of whether practical wisdom has autonomy in figuring out what the right action is.

According to al-Fārābī, practical reason is subservient to theoretical reason. On his view, "Practical reason is made to serve theoretical reason. Theoretical reason, however, is not to serve anything but has as its purpose to bring man to felicity."[42] Practical reason does not discover practical truths independent of theoretical reason. On al-Fārābī's view, *phronesis* (or as he calls it, prudence) does not play an autonomous role in discovering which action is right. While al-Fārābī is certainly familiar with *NE* VI, in which Aristotle discusses the role of phronesis in discovering moral truths, he gives a secondary role to phronesis to the extent that it does not even deserve to be called wisdom.[43] It isn't wisdom since it is only for humans, and divine beings don't need it.

---

[42] Al-Fārābī, *The Perfect State*, section 13, p. 209.

[43] In differentiating different meanings of 'intellect', al-Fārābī explicitly addresses NE VI, and says that the practical intellect discussed by Aristotle is a very different from theoretical intellect discussed in metaphysical works of Aristotle. See "On the Intellect," in McGinnis and Reisman, *Classical Arabic Philosophy*, 70.

> Prudence is the ability for excellent deliberation and inference concerning the things that are better and more appropriate for a human being to do to attain a truly major good. A group of people calls the prudent wise. Wisdom is the most excellent knowledge of the most excellent beings. Yet since only human things are perceived by means of prudence, it ought not to be wisdom unless human beings are the most excellent of what is in the world and the most excellent of the beings. Since human beings are not like that, prudence is wisdom only metaphorically and as a simile.[44]

On al-Fārābī's view, this human "wisdom" is only a servant of the real wisdom, which is theoretical wisdom. It is the job of the theoretical wisdom to discover what happiness consists in. Once this is done, practical wisdom's duty is to figure out what human actions are *instrumentally* necessary for achieving happiness.

> It is particularly characteristic of [theoretical] wisdom that it knows the ultimate reasons for every ultimate being.... Wisdom, therefore, is what seizes upon happiness in truth, whereas prudence is what seizes upon what ought to be done so that happiness is attained. These two, therefore, are the two mutual assistants in perfecting the human being-wisdom being what gives the ultimate goal, and prudence being what gives the *means* by which that goal is gained.[45]

Theoretical wisdom, then, "seizes upon happiness in truth," whereas practical wisdom is "what seizes upon what ought to be done so that happiness is attained." Practical wisdom plays only an instrumental role in al-Fārābī's view. If Booth and others are right that al-Fārābī's perfection, at least on earth, is partly practical, then al-Fārābī might accept (A2) and (A3). That is, it might be the case that in characterizing the prophet's perfect life, we have to mention his motivational makeup and his power of imagination. Yet, given the denial of the autonomy of practical wisdom by al-Fārābī (which entails the denial of (A5)), we could say that al-Fārābī's ethical theory is inconsistent with the following revised versions of (A2) and (A3).

(A2*) Human happiness is constituted by morally virtuous activities *the goals of which are not to achieve theoretical wisdom*.

---

[44] Selected Aphorism, in al-Fārābī, *The Political Writings*, section 52, pp. 34–35.
[45] Selected Aphorism, in al-Fārābī, *the Political Writings*, section 53, p. 35.

(A3*) The content of happiness cannot be specified without reference to the agent's moral life, *when the agent's moral life has no goal beyond itself.*

According to (A2*) and (A3*), human happiness is essentially practical in the sense that practical life has no goal beyond itself. Denial of (A3*) by al-Fārābī is a clear departure from Aristotle virtue ethics developed in *NE* I–IX. Yet one might think that al-Fārābī's view on the human good is similar to Aristotle's conception of happiness in *NE* X. That is, the afterlife presents the ideal condition for human beings, and so it is very much under the influence of *NE* X that al-Fārābī holds that happiness is to contemplate the world in the afterlife.

There is, however, an important difference between *NE* X and al-Fārābī's view of felicity. As I noted before, for Aristotle, our nonideal condition is not a stage that *temporally* precedes the ideal condition. It is likely that we can never live under the ideal circumstance, and given our nonideal condition in the actual world, happiness is constituted by a life of morally virtuous activity. For al-Fārābī, however, the ideal condition, that is, the afterlife, in which we can attain perfection, can come to us all. In other words, while Aristotle's contemplative life is just a utopian ideal, contemplation in heaven, for al-Fārābī, is a *temporal stage* in human life. As a result, al-Fārābī thinks that we have to lead an ethical life on earth *in order to* be able to attain perfection in the afterlife. Our earthly life is a step toward attainment of felicity, whereas Aristotle's contemplative life is just a utopian ideal which does not obtain for the most part in the actual world. On Aristotle's view, happiness, in the actual world, is constituted by the moral life of the agent, whereas for al-Fārābī moral life is instrumentally necessary for other worldly happiness.

In sum, according to al-Fārābī, moral virtues do not set the goal, nor does phronesis play a constitutive role in determining it. On al-Fārābī's view, the human telos is completely determined by theoretical wisdom. Practical intellect comes into play only in order to deduce universal and particular judgments as to which actions will bring happiness to humans. This is a radical departure from (A5). On Aristotle's view, as specified in (A1)–(A5), notions of happiness, virtue, and right action are interdependent and form a large circle. As a result, it is very hard to have a first principle by which we can determine what we ought to do in each circumstance. Ultimately, the virtuous person uses phronesis as a kind of moral perceptual power, to determine the right action in each particular case. But, on al-Fārābī's view, given the superiority of the notion of the theoretical life and the fact that practical wisdom has no autonomy in determining the goals, no circle is formed. Theoretical perfection provides an Archimedean point for al-Fārābī's virtue ethics. It is theoretical perfection that determines what virtues are and what actions are correct.

The denial of (A5) is not an accidental feature of al-Fārābī's view; it is central to his overall position. In fact, any theological virtue ethics that espouses the following two elements should necessarily reject (A5). The first element is the teleological conception of basic moral concepts. According to the eudaimonist teleological view, the values of actions should be understood in terms of their contributions to final happiness. Actions have no intrinsic value; their values are derived from the role they play in the life of the agent. The second element is to understand eudaimonia in terms of otherworldly success. Putting together these two elements, we have to draw the conclusion that intuitively moral actions are not constitutive of happiness, and that the practical faculty has no epistemic access to the nature of happiness. As a result, the rightness or wrongness of an action is determined by its instrumental contribution to something to which practical wisdom has no access.[46]

Theological virtue ethics, of the sort I specified in this section, leads to an intellectualized moral epistemology. Al-Fārābī does not shy away from this implication. He thinks that one needs to have a fairly serious theoretical education in order to be able to determine what action is right or wrong. To be truly virtuous, one needs to have extensive theoretical training:

> Practice is virtuous and correct only when a human being has (a) become truly cognizant of the virtues that are truly virtues, (b) become truly cognizant of the virtues that are presumed to be virtues yet are not like that. . . . This is a state that is not attained or perfected except after becoming sophisticated; perfecting cognizance by means of demonstration; and becoming

---

[46] Any ethical theory of this type must face the worry that it may not fully capture the extension of commonsense morality. On al-Fārābī's view, just actions in a society are required because they enable agents to achieve felicity. It may well be possible, however, that an intuitively unjust action is instrumentally necessary to bring about happiness, in which case intuitively unjust actions are judged to be obligatory by al-Fārābī's theory. To give an example, suppose φ is an *intuitively* morally wrong action, say a failure to perform one's duty in an easy rescue case, for example, not saving the little girl in the pond in Singer's famous example (Peter Singer, *Famine, Affluence, and Morality* [New York: Oxford University Press, 2016]). Doing φ (i.e., failing to fulfill one's duty in an easy rescue case) can bring about, or at least not hinder, acquiring theoretical wisdom. Therefore, on al-Fārābī's view, doing φ can be right.

perfect in the natural sciences, what follows upon them, and what is after them according to rank and order, so that he finally comes to knowledge of the happiness that is truly happiness.[47]

Immediately after the passage quoted, al-Fārābī goes on to explain in more detail just the sort of training the virtuous person needs to have: it starts with logic, math, and quantitative subjects such as optics, mechanics, astronomy, and music, and it ends with the natural sciences and metaphysics. Of course, al-Fārābī knows that this extensive training is not possible for the majority of people. That's why every society needs some sort of king or virtuous leader (or leaders) to help people to know what is right and what is wrong. In other words, if your theoretical faculty is not advanced enough to perform the job it is supposed to do, you may delegate this job to some sort of philosopher king who is able to figure out what happiness is; only by relying on such a philosopher king you can become happy (and even then only to some extent).

> The king in truth is the one whose purpose and intention concerning the art by which he governs cities are to provide himself and the rest of the inhabitants of the city true happiness. This is the goal and the purpose of the kingly craft. It necessarily follows that the king of the virtuous city be the most perfect among the inhabitants of the city in happiness since he is the reason for their being happy.[48]

Notice, again, that this sort of elitist moral epistemology is not an accidental feature of al-Fārābī's view. As soon as one denies (A5) in one's virtue theory, and as soon as one establishes that theoretical achievement is the foundation of ethics, one is led into the position that one must rely on the theoretically wise person to know the right course of the action.

Suppose that the theoretically wise person says that you ought to φ. On al-Fārābī's view, you have no grounds to reject what the theoretically wise persons says. Now suppose that the theoretically wise person writes a book in which he says you ought to φ. The same conclusion follows. The book of the theoretically wise person, the prophet, is Scripture. According to al-Fārābī's moral philosophy, then, so long as we are theoretically inferior to the prophet, our practical wisdom has no standing to question his sayings. In

---

[47] Selected Aphorism, in al-Fārābī, *The Political Writings*, 61.
[48] Selected Aphorism, in al-Fārābī, *The Political Writings*, 27.

al-Fārābī's theological virtue ethics, our epistemic path to the ethical realm is mainly through the judgments of the theoretically wise person (i.e., the prophet). If we are not theoretically wise ourselves, we would not know the universal truths that specify the nature of happiness, and thus we would lack moral knowledge. If we lack moral knowledge, how can we question the prescription of Scripture, taken at its apparent meaning?

In conclusion, while al-Fārābī's philosophy promised to make religion subordinate to philosophy, in his view our independent moral judgments are subordinate to religion. But one might wonder what would happen if we rejected al-Fārābī's theological virtue ethics altogether and went back to Aristotelian virtue ethics, according to which phronesis is autonomous and provides us with independent access to moral grounds. Can a modest al-Fārābīan solution, discussed in the previous section, helps us tackle the problem of prescribed evil if we accept an Aristotelian view in accordance with (A1)–(A5)? I don't think so.

Suppose that you have excellent arguments that S is practically wiser than you. Suppose that S states "P." Furthermore, suppose that you have some arguments that P is false. Should you interpret P in a nonliteral way? Not necessarily. Suppose your arguments for S's being practically wiser than you are stronger than your argument against P. If so, it would be rational for you to believe that your argument against P is overridden by your testimonial argument in favor of P. The same holds for Scripture; as long as our argument for the infallibility of Scripture is stronger than our argument against a certain injunction of Scripture, the argument against the injunction might not override the testimonial evidence for it.

There is also a second, and more important, problem for the combination of Aristotelian virtue ethics and the modest al-Fārābīan solution. According to Aristotelian virtue ethics, we have perceptual moral knowledge. However, we can't have perceptual knowledge about things that are epistemically *inaccessible* to us. Suppose my φ-ing is in fact, everything considered, wrong because it causes a large group of *angels* to die. It is implausible to think that I can have perceptual knowledge about the wrongness of my action, given that I have no epistemic access to the consequences of my action. So if a practically wise person who knows all descriptive truths about the universe asks me not to φ, it would be quite implausible to think that my perceptual moral knowledge can justify me in rejecting what he asks me to do. In the previous chapter, I explained that the theist might plausibly hold that we might not have epistemic access to all moral reasons in the universe. Moreover, the moral reasons we have access to might not be representative of all reasons there are. If so, it is quite mysterious how we can have perceptual knowledge about wrongness, everything considered. It is also implausible to think that our judgments can undermine the judgment of someone who has access to all reasons in the universe. Aristotelian virtue ethics by itself does not say anything about how the argument for strict adherence can be avoided.

In order to avoid the Scripture-first view, we need to answer two questions: (i) How we can have knowledge about everything considered wrongness? (ii) May we resist deferring to the testimony of the prophet? These are the issues we are going to discuss in the next two chapters.

PART II
ETHICS FIRST

"The world is all grown strange.... How shall a man judge what to do in such times?"

"As he ever has judged. Good and ill have not changed since yesterday; nor are they one thing among Elves and Dwarves and another among Men. It is a man's part to discern them, as much in the Golden Wood as in his own house."

—J. R. R Tolkien, *Lord of the Rings* (*The Two Towers*)

4
The Impermissibility of Moral Deference

Summary of the Chapter

Section 1. Many find moral testimony off-putting. Overviewing the contemporary literature on moral testimony, the section describes and categorizes recent attempts to explain the problematic nature of moral testimony.

Section 2. The section describes the ethical view of al-Rāzī, who is a pessimist about moral testimony. In his view, our goal is to liberate our souls from the body by performing intellectual activities, but in so doing, we should not impose unnecessary harms on other sentient beings.

Section 3. This section presents al-Rāzī's objection to moral deference. He thinks that the point of morality is the redemption of the soul, and this can be achieved only through understanding, which is lacking in the case of moral deference. Despite his view, some cases are presented in which we would not be wrong to act on the basis of moral testimony.

Section 4. The main argument for the permissibility of moral deference is that moral deference makes it more likely that we act morally. I argue that this argument does not show that it is *rationally* permissible to defer to Scripture. Using the Qur'anic story of Moses and Khidr, I defend the Moses principle, according to which one should not act on the basis of moral testimony when the stakes are asymmetrically high.

Section 5. If the argument in section 4 is correct, we might suspend judgment about the objective reliability of our independent moral judgments, while holding that our independent moral judgments are rationally reliable. This constitutes an ethics-first solution to the problem of prescribed evil.[1]

---

[1] The reader who is not interested in a historical discussion of the moral theory of al-Rāzī may skip section 2.

1. Moral Deference in Contemporary Philosophy

A major premise of the argument for strict adherence, discussed in Part I, is God's Reliability. God's Reliability is defined as follows:

> *God's Reliability.* For any action φ, if God intends to convey that it is obligatory (or permitted) for us (or a certain group of people) to do φ, it is true that we (or those people) are morally obligated (or permitted) to do φ.

In Part I, we discussed God's Reliability vis-à-vis whether we can assume the *truthfulness* of God. I *assume* in this chapter that God is truthful. God's Reliability seems to imply the *rational necessity of moral deference* to God in all cases, and this is what I am going to argue against in this chapter.

I assume that the divine command theory is false.[2] Moreover, in line with al-Ghazālī, the Muʿtazilites, and the Islamic philosophers, I assume that some version of moral objectivism is true. By this, I mean that (1) moral judgments can be true or false, and (2) the truth-makers of moral judgments are not, in general, God's (or our) intentional attitudes.[3] If morality is not generally determined by God's commands and prohibitions, why, then, should we rely on God's moral teachings? The assumption behind God's Reliability is that God is morally perfect and that He is truthful. Thus, if God intends to convey to us that an action is obligatory or permissible, that action is in fact obligatory or permissible. By deferring to God, we can live morally.

Moral deference to God is an instance of the general phenomenon of deference to *moral experts.* A moral expert, by definition, is an individual who has considerable moral knowledge and does not deceive those people whom they inform about moral truths. The main goal of this chapter is to argue that God's Reliability does not imply that it is rational to defer to God in all cases, especially in the cases with morally controversial injunctions. If so, the argument for strict adherence does not imply that we should act in accordance with morally controversial passages in Scripture. I will explain later in the

---

[2] I argued for this claim in Part I, Chapter 1, section 1.

[3] While some passages of Avicenna in *Remarks and Admonitions* seem to suggest that he espoused subjectivism, most scholars of Avicenna believe that those passages do not support a subjectivist reading. Moreover, other parts of Avicenna's work clearly show that he was not a subjectivist. See Deborah Black, "Practical Wisdom, Moral Virtue, and Theoretical Knowledge: The Problem of the Autonomy of the Practical Realm in Arabic Philosophy," in *Moral and Political Philosophies in the Middle Ages: Proceedings of the Ninth International Congress of Medieval Philosophy,* ed. B. Carlos Bazán, Eduardo Andújar, and Leonard G. Sbrocchi, 3 vols. (New York: Legas, 1995), 1:451–65. See also Michael E. Marmura, "Ghazali on Ethical Premises," *Philosophical Forum* 4 (1968–69): 393–403.

chapter how the denial of the permissibility of moral deference to Scripture will help us to find a new solution to the problem of prescribed evil.

In science, history, and everyday life, we frequently defer to experts. We defer to the views of scientists, historians, physicians, lawyers, and so on to learn about the world. We defer also to total strangers when we ask them about trivial things, like addresses. But many contemporary philosophers have noticed that there is something *off-putting* about *moral deference*. Robert Howell's example involving Google Morals illustrates this phenomenon:

> Although I don't know the streets and subways of New York very well, I get around with little difficulty. And if I'm suddenly struck by a desire for tofu bahn mi, no sweat. Like many of you I have an application on my phone, Google Maps, which gives me directions and directs me to restaurants at the push of a few buttons. I am therefore somewhat dependent on my phone, but so what: it's a perfectly reasonable way to get around.
>
> Suppose those wizards at Google come out with a new app: Google Morals. No longer will we find ourselves lost in the moral metropolis. When faced with a moral quandary or deep ethical question we can type a query and the answer comes forthwith. Next time I am weighing the value of a tasty steak against the disvalue of animal suffering, I'll know what to do. Never again will I be paralyzed by the prospect of pushing that fat man onto the trolley tracks to prevent five innocents from being killed. I'll just Google it. Again I find myself dependent on Google for my beliefs, but in this case it seems to many, myself included, that this is not a good way to go. There seems to be something wrong with using Google Morals.[4]

The kind of moral deference that looks particularly off-putting is *direct* and *pure* deference about an assertion whose content includes a normative *thin* concept.[5] One's deference is *direct* when it is *solely* based upon the testimony of someone else. One's deference is *pure* when the content of testimony does not include any explanation of why the normative judgment is true. *Thin moral concepts* are purely evaluative, whereas *thick moral concepts* are partly evaluative and partly nonevaluative (see Chapter 2, section 2). The main

---

[4] Robert J. Howell, "Google Morals, Virtue, and the Asymmetry of Deference," *Noûs* 48.3 (2014): 389–415.

[5] Fletcher and Lord use this terminology. See Guy Fletcher, "Moral Testimony: Once More with Feeling," *Oxford Studies in Metaethics* 11 (2016): 45–73, and Errol Lord, "How to Learn about Aesthetics and Morality through Acquaintance and Deference," *Oxford Studies in Metaethics* 13 (2018): 71–97.

examples of thin concepts include good, evil, ought, obligation, permissible, right, and so on. In Howell's example, our deference to Google Morals is pure and direct, and it concerns the instantiation of thin properties by actions. Suppose, for example, Google Morals says that meat-eating is *wrong*. It does not say *why* it is wrong, and I form my judgment *solely* based on its verdict. Henceforth, I focus only on direct pure moral deference about thin moral properties, and I will call it *pure moral deference*.

There is an intuition that there is something off-putting about deferring to Google Morals. Sarah McGrath thinks that the attitude that pure moral deference is more problematic than nonmoral deference is a *datum* that needs to be explained.[6] Some calls this "the puzzle of moral deference."[7] Recent empirical studies also confirm an asymmetry in our attitude toward testimony about moral and descriptive matters.[8] While there is a large agreement about the off-puttingness of pure moral deference, there are different views about what is particularly problematic about it. It will be useful for my purposes in this chapter to provide a broad categorization of different views from the recent literature concerning moral testimony.

To get around the philosophically complex problem of attributing beliefs and judgments to mobile apps, let's suppose that Google Morals just expresses the views of the Google Guru, a moral expert with considerable moral knowledge in various areas. Suppose that Google Morals says that one ought to φ. This means that the Google Guru believes that one ought to φ. Let's assume that this belief has a positive *epistemic* status. It might be *knowledge* or *justified* belief. One question is whether my belief that one ought to φ, formed through pure moral deference, inherits the same (or similar) positive epistemic status if I pick it up through moral deference to the Google Guru. *Epistemic optimists* would say that the answer is yes. Moral deference preserves knowledge or justification. The method of forming belief, based on pure moral testimony, is a knowledge- or justification-preserving method of belief formation. *Epistemic pessimists*, on the other hand, deny that I can acquire knowledge or justification through pure moral deference. There are some reasons to be an epistemic pessimist. With a dose of antirealism, one might think that moral knowledge requires appropriate moral sentiments,

---

[6] Sarah McGrath, "The Puzzle of Pure Moral Deference," *Philosophical Perspectives* 23 (2009): 321–44.

[7] There are different formulations of the puzzle. McGrath and Lewis describe the puzzle as the mere fact that moral deference, in contrast with nonmoral deference, is off-putting. Max Lewis, "The New Puzzle of Moral Deference," *Canadian Journal of Philosophy* 50.4 (2020): 460–76.

[8] James Andow, "Why Don't We Trust Moral Testimony?," *Mind & Language* 35.4 (2020): 456–74.

and it is difficult to form moral sentiments on the basis of pure testimony.[9] One might also think that to acquire knowledge by moral testimony, one needs to establish that the testifier is a moral expert, and it is difficult to do this.[10]

Most contemporary philosophers are *epistemic* optimists. Epistemic optimists, however, need to explain the off-puttingness of pure moral deference in some other way. We can divide epistemic optimists into two groups. The first group thinks that the act of moral deference is *morally defective* in some way. The second group, however, thinks that the act of pure moral deference in itself is not morally defective. We might call the first group *moral pessimists*, and the second group *moral optimists*.[11] We should be cautious about these terms, though. Some philosophers define the term *moral pessimism* in a more restrictive way. They define it as the view that says moral deference is (at least pro tanto) *wrong*.[12] My definition of moral pessimism is broader. For example, Lord thinks that while pure moral deference is morally *suboptimal*, the defective nature of pure moral deference does not constitute pro tanto wrongness.[13] Under my definition, moral pessimism includes his view.[14] With this broad definition of moral pessimism, most contemporary moral philosophers writing on the subject fall in this category.

Moral pessimists seek to explain the puzzle of moral deference by explaining the defective nature of pure moral deference. When you form a moral belief on the basis of pure moral deference, you don't know *why* your belief is true. You don't know *the relevant moral properties* that make that belief true. You might not acquire the set of *abilities* that enable you to draw similar conclusions in similar cases.[15] You might not have a full *understanding* of the content of that belief.[16] You might not be able to form appropriate

---

[9] Fletcher, "Moral Testimony."

[10] McGrath, "Puzzle"; J. Driver, "Autonomy and the Asymmetry Problem for Moral Expertise," *Philosophical Studies* 128.3 (2006): 619–44. It is worth noting that neither Driver nor McGrath is an epistemic pessimist. They just think that it is *difficult* to meet the conditions for moral expertise and know that those conditions are met.

[11] If one is epistemically a pessimist, it seems one should be morally a pessimist as well. For if moral deference is not justification preserving, one should not act on the basis of an *unjustified* moral belief acquired by pure moral testimony.

[12] For example, Howell, "Google Morals"; Robert Hopkins, "What Is Wrong with Moral Testimony?," *Philosophy and Phenomenological Research* 74.3 (2007): 611–34.

[13] Lord, "How to Learn."

[14] Lord calls himself a moral optimist because he thinks that moral deference is not pro tanto wrong.

[15] Alison Hills, "Moral Testimony and Moral Epistemology," *Ethics* 120.1 (2009): 94–127.

[16] Hills, "Moral Testimony"; Laura Frances Callahan, "Moral Testimony: A Re-conceived Understanding Explanation," *Philosophical Quarterly* 68.272 (2018): 437–59.

moral sentiments on the basis of pure moral testimony.[17] You might not be *motivated* to act in accordance with the belief formed on the basis of moral testimony alone.[18] These negative features of pure moral deference may constitute various moral problems for moral deference. Because you don't respond to morally relevant features of the case, moral deference is not *a moral achievement*.[19] Because you don't have the full set of appropriate affective and conative reactions to the case, you can't acquire *appreciative* knowledge by pure moral deference.[20] Because you don't act for the right moral reasons, your action might not have *moral worth*.[21] Because you have not grasped the grounds of your belief, you might not have *the right to use* the belief acquired by moral deference.[22] Because of the lack of understanding, or appreciation, or affective attitudes, moral deference might not cultivate *virtues* for you.[23] A central question in the literature on moral testimony is whether these accounts correctly identify the morally problematic features of pure moral deference, and whether they adequately explain the supposedly puzzling nature of pure moral deference. For example, Lewis argues that other methods of belief formation might exhibit features similar to those mentioned by moral pessimists without being considered equally off-putting.[24]

Moral optimists, on the other hand, either deny the datum altogether,[25] or seek to explain it away. For example, Sliwa chooses the latter option, arguing that while moral deference is not in itself morally problematic, agents who use pure moral testimony to know the basic truths of morality might have some moral defects.[26] Their moral ignorance is off-putting. They should know better. Moreover, they might rely on moral testimony because they are trying to avoid taking responsibility for their actions, and this explains, in part, why we regard pure moral deference as off-putting.

An important point for our purposes in this chapter is that few people hold that moral deference is *always* wrong. Moral pessimists in general are

---

[17] Fletcher, "Moral Testimony"; David Enoch, "A Defense of Moral Deference," *Journal of Philosophy* 111.5 (2014): 229–58; Lord, "How to Learn."
[18] Lord, "How to Learn"; Callahan, "Moral Testimony."
[19] Enoch, "Defense of Moral Deference."
[20] Lord, "How to Learn."
[21] Hills, "Moral Testimony."
[22] Hopkins, "What Is Wrong."
[23] Lord, "How to Learn"; Hills, "Moral Testimony"; Callahan, "Moral Testimony"; Howell, "Google Morals."
[24] Lewis, "New Puzzle."
[25] For example, Peter Singer, "Moral Experts," *Analysis* 32.4 (1972): 115–17.
[26] Paulina Sliwa, "In Defense of Moral Testimony," *Philosophical Studies* 158.2 (2012): 175–95.

willing to accept that sometimes moral deference is morally permissible or even morally required. Lewis expresses the point as follows:

> Both Hopkins (2007) and Hills (2009) make it explicit that if one cannot gain moral understanding about why the claim under consideration is true, then it shouldn't be off-putting or impermissible for one to defer. In fact, Hills (2009) argues that if you cannot acquire moral understanding of why p, but you can come to acquire knowledge that p via deference, then you should defer. This is because knowing that p will help you do the right thing.[27]

I will argue, however, that moral deference to Scripture (at least in high-stake situations) is impermissible. In the Islamic tradition, Abū Bakr Muhammad ibn Zakariyyā al-Rāzī (854–925) argues for pessimism about pure moral deference. On his view, we may never defer to Scripture. Al-Rāzī's argument is similar to the arguments of some contemporary moral pessimists. In the next two sections, I will discuss al-Rāzī's ethical view and his pessimism about moral deference. I will argue that his argument against the permissibility of moral deference fails. But this does not show that pure moral difference is always permissible. In section 4, I will argue that the main argument for the permissibility of pure moral deference, offered by both moral optimists and moral pessimists, is not convincing in the case of moral deference to Scripture. There are reasons to hold that pure deference to Scripture (at least in high-stake situations) is impermissible. At the end of section 4, I will show that my argument for the impermissibility of moral deference to Scripture may be in line with the views of some medieval Islamic Shi'a jurists. The last section discusses where my argument for the impermissibility of moral deference to Scripture situates us vis-à-vis the problem of prescribed evil.

2. Al-Rāzī's Ethical Theory

Al-Rāzī is one of the earliest Islamic philosophers who practiced *falsafa* under the influence of Greek philosophers.[28] While al-Rāzī believed in God,

---

[27] Lewis, "New Puzzle," 462.

[28] For an excellent review of al-Rāzī ethical works, see T. A. Druart, "The Ethics of Al-Rāzī," *Medieval Philosophy and Theology* 6 (1997): 47–71. See also Peter Adamson, "Abu-Bakr al-Rāzī (d. 925), *The Spiritual Medicine*," in *The Oxford Handbook of Islamic Philosophy*, ed. Khaled El-Rouayheb and Sabine Schmidtke (New York: Oxford University Press, 2016), 63–82, for a clear review of *The*

he was skeptical that there was any need for the prophets. His criticism of prophecy gained him a reputation as a heretic, and perhaps because of this reputation, very few of his philosophical works have survived. Before getting to al-Rāzī's view on moral deference, it would be good if we had a general understanding of his ethical theory, which is the subject of this section. His view on moral testimony will be discussed in the next section.

Al-Rāzī is well known for holding that there are five eternal elements: God, absolute space, absolute time, matter, and soul. We see orderly forms in the universe; therefore, there must be *God* to create them. God's actions happen in time, hence there should be *absolute time*. God makes the universe out of something (and not from nothing), therefore there should be *eternal matter*. God needs to place the universe somewhere, so there should be *absolute space*. But why does he believe that there is an eternal soul? Soul is posited to explain the existence of evil in the universe. Fakhr Dīn al-Rāzī, a late Ash'arite theologian, reports al-Rāzī's view on the matter as follows:

> Then [there are] those who maintain that the source of the world is not a body. There are two such groups. One is the Harranians [followed by al-Rāzī], who established five eternals: the Creator, Soul, Prime Matter, eternity, and void. They said that the Creator (exalted is He!) is the perfection of knowledge and wisdom to Whom neither neglect nor oversight happens and from Whom the intellect emanates like the light from the orb; He (may He be exalted!) knows things perfectly. Next, from the Soul life emanates like light from the orb, but it is ignorant, not knowing things as long as it has not applied itself to them. The Creator (may He be exalted!) knew that the Soul is inclined toward cleaving to matter, to desiring it passionately, to seeking bodily pleasures, to loathing separation from bodies, and to forgetting its true self. Since perfect wisdom is characteristic of the Creator (may He be exalted!), He directed Himself to Prime Matter after the Soul had cleaved to it, and He combined it in a variety of combinations, like the heavens and the elements, and combined the bodies of the animals in the most perfect way, though the corruption that remains in them cannot be eliminated. Next, He (sublime and exalted is He!) caused intellect and perception to flow down on the Soul, which became the reason for the

---

Spiritual Medicine. Adamson's "The Arabic Tradition," in *The Routledge Companion to Ethics*, ed. John Skoruspki (New York: Routledge, 2010), 63–75, also is a good introduction to al-Rāzī's ethics. For a general introduction to al-Rāzī metaphysics see Adamson's recent book, *Al-Rāzī* (New York: Oxford University Press, 2021), which provides a comprehensive study of al-Rāzī's views.

Soul's recollection of its world and for its understanding that as long as it remained in the material world, it would never be unfettered from pain. When the Soul realizes that and understands that in its own world it would have pleasures free from pain, it will yearn for that world, and rise up after its separation [from its world] and remain there forever and ever in utmost joy and happiness.[29]

The soul, which is a foolish and ignorant element, seeks bodily pleasure and is thus inclined toward cleaving to matter. This is in part why the world, as we know it, exists. But the soul is also a source of chaos and evil in the world. God's plan is to help the soul lose this desire and get back to its original place. God accomplishes this plan by creating the world in the most perfect way that is possible (despite the chaos that the soul brings with itself into the world), and by causing intellect to flow down upon the soul. With intellect, the soul gains the power to reflect on the world and its structure. This helps the soul to gain the necessary knowledge it needs to redeem itself from matter. This grand metaphysical story helps us better understand al-Rāzī's ethical view, which is designed to show how to get rid of the material world.

A main goal of al-Rāzī's remaining ethical books, *The Philosophical Way of Life* and *The Spiritual Medicine*, is to discuss what the human telos is, or what a good human life should look like. Al-Rāzī presents our final goal in different terms in his two books. In *The Spiritual Medicine*, he says:

> Failure in the rational soul is recognized when it does not occur to it to wonder, and marvel at this world of ours, then mediate upon it with interest, curiosity and a passionate desire to discover all that it contains, and above all to investigate the body in which it dwells, and its form and fate after death. Truly, if a man does not wonder and marvel at our world, if he is not moved to astonishment at its form, if his soul does not gaze after the knowledge of all that it contains, if he is not concerned or interested to discover what his state will be after death, his portion of reason is that of beasts—nay, of bats, and fishes, and worthless things that never think or reflect.[30]

---

[29] The translation is from Jon McGinnis and David C. Reisman, trans., *Classical Arabic Philosophy: An Anthology of Sources* (Indianapolis: Hackett, 2007), 47.
[30] Translation of *The Spiritual Medicine* from *The Spiritual Physick of Rhazes*, trans. Arthur J. Arberry (London: John Murray, 1950), 31.

The final goal of human beings is to contemplate the world and themselves. Eternal bliss and suffering, on al-Rāzī's view, should be understood with regards to the fulfillment of this goal. If one progresses toward the fulfillment of this goal in the present life, one will experience eternal bliss when one's soul is detached from one's body. On the other hand, if one's passions hinder one's development of intellectual capacities, one will face eternal suffering.

> [Plato correctly] believed that when the time comes for the sentient soul to leave the body in which it is lodged, if it has acquired and believed firmly in these ideas it will pass immediately into its own world, and will not desire to be attached to any particle of the body thereafter; it will remain living and reasoning eternally, free from pain, and rejoicing its place of abode. . . . But if the soul leaves the body without having acquired these ideas and without having recognized the true nature of the physical world, but rather still yearning after it and eager to exists therein, . . . it will not cease to suffer continual and reduplicated pains. (*Spiritual Medicine*, chap. 2, 32–33)

If our goal is to acquire and to actualize intellectual capacities, what kind of bodily actions we ought to do? If the final telos is contemplation, our bodily actions should be such that they enable and cultivate our intellectual capacities. That is, we ought to take care of our bodies, since health is required for intellectual life. We should not let pleasure get in the way or distract us from performing intellectual activities.

In *The Philosophical Way of Life*, al-Rāzī characterizes the human telos in slightly different terms. Using Platonic language again, he says that our telos is to imitate God.

> Creator is the Knower Who is not ignorant, the Just Who does no wrong; since knowledge, justice, and compassion exist absolutely; since we do have a Creator and Lord; since we are to Him servants to be ruled; and since the servants most beloved of their masters are those who carry out their way of living and pursue their code of behavior, then the servant closest to God (mighty and exalted is He!) is the most learned, most just, most compassionate and merciful. The whole of this statement is what is meant by the philosophers' saying, "Philosophy is imitating God (mighty and exalted is He!) to the degree that humans are able." This is a summary

statement of the way of philosophy, the details of which are found in *On Spiritual Medicine*.[31]

While *The Spiritual Medicine* and *The Philosophical Way of Life* both present the intellectual life as the human telos, the difference between the two characterizations of the human telos in these books has a rather important implication. In *The Spiritual Medicine*, the telos is just contemplation. Accordingly, the right action should be defined in terms of whatever is conducive to this aim. In *The Philosophical Way of Life*, however, the telos is the *imitation of God*, of which contemplation would be an important part. But God is also described as acting justly.[32] Accordingly, acting justly would be part of our imitation of God. It is not clear whether, on al-Rāzī's view, just conduct is constitutive of human happiness or merely an instrumentally necessary condition for it. He thinks that since God watches over us, and since He abhors injustice, our unjust actions will lead us to suffer. On this reading, we should act justly in order to attain eternal bliss.

> Since the principle that we set down—that is, that our Lord and Master takes a concern in us, watches over us, and has compassion for us—also entails that He abhors any harm that befalls us, ... then, on that account, we must not harm any sentient creature whatsoever unless it is absolutely necessary to inflict that harm or by doing so we avert a greater harm.[33]

This passage highlights a rather important difference between the normative theory in *The Spiritual Medicine* and that of *The Philosophical Way of Life*. The normative theory in *The Spiritual Medicine* is very clear (though implausible). An action is permissible just in case it does not hinder contemplation. But the normative theory in *The Philosophical Way of Life* is slightly different. It specifies a general normative principle: we should not harm other sentient beings unless it is absolutely necessary in order to prevent greater harm.

What is the justification of this principle? Al-Rāzī is not very clear on this point. Maybe we should not harm other sentient beings because we should

---

[31] The translations of *The Philosophical Way of Life* are from McGinnis and Reisman, *Classical Arabic Philosophy*, section 20, 42.

[32] Al-Rāzī seems to think that there are intrinsic moral properties. On the other hand, he is well known for holding that there are only five eternal elements: God, soul, matter, space, and place. What about moral properties? Are they eternal, as his realism suggests? Or they are created, as the theory of five elements might suggest? If they are not eternal, how are they created?

[33] *The Philosophical Way*, section 13, 39–40.

imitate God, and God would not do this (it is not clear why He would not). Maybe we should not harm other sentient beings because God watches over us and will punish us if we do. Or maybe it is just bad to create unnecessary evil (as a good God would not do that either). No matter how we understand the rationale behind this principle, it introduces another element into al-Rāzī's normative system: although the final goal is contemplation, there is a secondary goal of avoiding the causing of unnecessary harm.

Should we understand this new element in a utilitarian way? Al-Rāzī's example of two men stranded in a waterless wasteland supports this approach. In this example, one of the men has just enough water to save a single person, but not both of them. Al-Rāzī thinks that the right thing to do here is to use the water to save the man who would be most beneficial to society as a whole. Another example of al-Rāzī's, which is also consistent with a utilitarian picture, is that we should not overload domestic animals unless it is necessary for one's survival. "Spurring on a horse to arrive at safety from an enemy" would be just, because it would be necessary for a greater good (namely, one's survival).

Al-Rāzī's example about hunting carnivorous animals, however, makes it clear that even in the realm of animal ethics, pain and pleasure are not the only values we need to be concerned about. Instead, the metaphysical truth about the nature of happiness (i.e., that ultimate happiness lies in the contemplation of the soul liberated from the body) is also relevant to determining the right action. According to al-Rāzī, hunting for fun is not in general permissible because it is not necessary to prevent greater harm. However, he thinks that hunting carnivorous animals is permissible because they eat other animals, and also because "liberating souls from animal bodies is akin to paving the way to and facilitating [the] liberation" of their souls, as "souls are liberated only from human bodies."[34] Hunting is morally permitted in part because of the fact that these souls would not achieve salvation in animal bodies.

In sum, in al-Rāzī's view, the final aim or telos of human life is to cultivate our intellectual capacities and to liberate our souls from our bodies; this is our true happiness. But in this world, we are imprisoned in our bodies, and because of that, we experience pain and suffering. We can liberate our souls from our bodies by performing intellectual activities, but in so doing, we should not cause unnecessary harm for other sentient beings.

---

[34] *The Philosophical Way*, section 14, 40.

Whether one can develop a plausible detailed normative theory from these two books of al-Rāzī is not really important for us here, since we are mainly interested in his skeptical stance toward moral deference. But from this brief discussion about his normative theory, it should be apparent that al-Rāzī is quite confident that reason can find out what one should do. He thinks that reason alone is always in position to know which action is necessary to prevent greater harm and which action is not. He does not find moral epistemology to be problematic at all. Reason alone can find out all truths about morality.

3. Al-Rāzī on Moral Deference

Al-Rāzī takes a very skeptical stance toward moral deference. As noted, because of his criticism of prophecy, he was called a heretic by his critics. Al-Rāzī does not deny the existence of God; he does not deny the afterlife, nor does he deny eternal rewards and punishments in the afterlife.[35] In this sense, he endorses the basic tenets of Islam. There is also evidence that he engaged contemporary theologians with the aim of showing them that his metaphysical doctrine of five eternal elements is consistent with the Qur'an.[36] Moreover, Rashed argues that al-Rāzī's critical remarks about prophecy are consistent with his acceptance of the existence of genuine prophets.[37] So there is some room for thinking that al-Rāzī's critical remarks about prophecy do not imply that he denies prophecy altogether. Nevertheless, al-Rāzī's thinks that when there is a conflict between reason and revelation, reason should take precedence. In general, reason should be one's guide in acting. Even if there are genuine prophets, their job is not to tell us what to do, and we should not defer to them.

Al-Rāzī begins *The Spiritual Medicine* by talking about the fact that our reason makes us different from other animals. We are true to human nature as long as we don't let anything control or govern our reason.

> In short, Reason is the thing without which our state would be the state of wild beats, of children and lunatics; it is the thing whereby we picture

---

[35] *The Philosophical Way*, section 10, 38.
[36] Marwan Rashed, "Abu Bakr al-Rāzī et le Kalam," *Mideo* 24 (2000): 39–54.
[37] Marwan Rashed, "Abu Bakr al-Rāzī et le Prophetie," *Mideo* 27, 169–82 (2008).

our intellectual acts before they become manifest to the senses, so that we see them exactly as though we had sensed them, then we represent these pictures in our sensual acts so that they correspond exactly with what we have represented and imagined. Since this is its worth and place, its value and significance, it behooves us not to bring it down from its high rank or in any way to degrade it, neither to make it the governed seeing that it is the governor, or the controlled seeing that it is the controller, or the subject seeing that it is the sovereign. (*Spiritual Medicine*, chap. 1, 21)

Reason is what makes us different from other animals. Nonhuman animals do not have the capacity to reflect on their actions "before [their actions] become manifest to the senses." We have the capacity to reflect on our actions before performing them, and this sets us aside from other animals. The human way of life is to reflect upon one's actions and to investigate consequences and moral implications before one acts. Because of this capacity, we should not permit our reason to be controlled or governed by any other faculty.

Proofs of Prophecy is a book written by the theologian Abu-Hātim al-Rāzī (d. 993) containing Abu-Hātim's reports of his debates with al-Rāzī on the nature of prophecy. Abu-Hātim wrote the book to defend prophecy against al-Rāzī's criticism of prophecy. We should, however, be cautious in attributing any considered view to al-Rāzī based on the reports of his bitter critic. For example, in his new book on al-Rāzī, Peter Adamson suggests that the debate between al-Rāzī and Abu-Hātim was actually about the existence of imams, who, according to Shia tradition, are the rightful successors of the Prophet, rather than the prophets themselves. It's just that Abu-Hātim misrepresented the debate as being about the nature of prophecy. Adamson justifies this position in part by arguing, in line with Rashed, that al-Rāzī believed that there could be genuine prophets, and in part by appealing to the following passage by Abu-Hātim:

> This is what the heretic said, though I have cut out a lot of it to avoid prolixity; but I've mentioned the main points. By saying "making some to be imāms for others," he means precisely that [God] chooses some as prophets and messengers, and makes them to be imāms of others.[38]

---

[38] Abu Hātim al-Rāzī, *The Proofs of Prophecy*, trans. T. Khalidi (Chicago: University of Chicago Press, 2012), 132.

Adamson writes, "The first thing I want to point out about the passage is that Razi is not actually speaking about prophets. This is unintentionally underscored by Abu-Hātim's closing remark, where he feels the need to stress that when Rāzī spoke of imāms, he actually meant 'prophets and messengers.'"[39] The passage, however, fails to indicate what Adamson claims it does. In Arabic, the term *imām* primarily means "leader" and "example." The Shia community also uses this term to refer to a person who they believe is the rightful successor to the Prophet. It is highly likely that Abu-Hātim uses *imām* in its general sense in this passage. What Abu-Hātim really means here is that al-Rāzī, in his criticism of prophecy, refers to prophets as people whom God makes the leaders of others.

And this brings us to the second point. I am not concerned, contra Rashed or Adamson, whether al-Rāzī believed there could be genuine prophets. He may well have held such a belief. The question I am interested in is whether God made prophets imams (i.e., moral leaders) for others. The view I attribute to al-Rāzī is that pure moral deference to others, including the prophets, is inconsistent with salvation, and thus the prophets (whether or not genuine) cannot be *imāms*. While I use Abu-Hātim's work to construct al-Rāzī's argument, the arguments I discuss here align with and complement al-Rāzī's ethical theory and metaphysical view (and appear to be consistent with Adamson's interpretation of al-Rāzī's).

Abu-Hātim reports the heretic's (i.e., al-Rāzī') skeptical argument about prophecy as follows:

> The heretic debated with me the question of prophecy.... He said "why do you hold it to be necessary that God singled out one particular people for prophecy rather than another, preferred them above all other people, made them to be guides for mankind and caused mankind to need them? Why do you hold it to be possible for the Wise One in His wisdom to have chosen this fate for them, setting some people against others, establishing enmities among them, and multiplying the causes of aggression, thus leading mankind to destruction.... It would have been more worthy of the wisdom of the Wise One—more worthy also of the wisdom of the Merciful—for Him to have inspired all His creatures with the knowledge of what is to their benefit as well as to their harm in this world and the next. He would not have privileged some over others; and there would be no cause for

---

[39] Adamson, *Al-Rāzī*, 132.

quarrel and no dispute among them, leading to their destruction." (*Proofs of Prophecy*, 1)

Al-Rāzī holds that it would be wiser for God to create all human beings with the knowledge of what to do. He thinks that God in fact made morality available to reason. One might, then, explain the problematic nature of moral deference by the universal availability of moral knowledge. If moral knowledge is already available to all human beings, the prophet has no new knowledge with which to inform humans. This would explain al-Rāzī's pessimism about moral deference. But the problem for this argument is that while moral truths might be *in principle* accessible to everyone, they might not be actually present in everyone's mind. For al-Rāzī, morality is part of philosophy. Philosophical truths may be in principle accessible to everyone. But it is not that everybody actually knows all philosophical truths. The difference in knowledge of morality between different people makes room for the possibility of moral deference. Abu-Hātim makes the same point. He says that people have different intellectual capacities, and because of this variation in intellectual power, intellectually inferior people must submit to the judgment of intellectually superior people.

> I said "How can you maintain this view and deny self-evident truth? We see and experience the fact that human beings are diverse ranks and classes. You cannot deny what all people have agreed upon when they say that one person is more intelligent than another . . . that one person is smarter than another, that one person is sharp while the another is slow-witted. . . . In every class of people, there is superior and inferior, master and pupil. We don't see anyone capable of attaining anything at all entirely through his own intelligence, quick wits or reason, but only if there is a teacher to guide him and a rule by which he abides, and which he then emulates and bases himself upon." (*Proofs of Prophecy*, 3)

Abu-Hātim sees the variation in intellectual capacities as a justifying reason for the permissibility of deference. Abu-Hātim also presents another objection to al-Rāzī's view. He understands al-Rāzī as saying that if moral knowledge is not equally distributed, then we might have disagreements at different levels, including disagreements among different prophets, and this makes the world less perfect. Abu-Hātim, on the other hand, knows that the philosophers, in al-Rāzī's view, are our role models because they occupy themselves exclusively with independent investigations to find the truth. Abu-Hātim's objection is that if disagreement is problematic for prophecy, it should be equally problematic for philosophers, since philosophers disagree on many things. So al-Rāzī's ideal of independent investigation fares no better than relying on prophets. What is very interesting for our purpose is al-Rāzī's answer to Abu-Hātim's point:

> Know that every later philosopher applies his full energy to philosophical inquiry, does so diligently, uses independent reasoning, and investigates those issues over which philosophers' views diverge because of their complexity and difficulty; he would acquire the knowledge of predecessors, digest it, and arrive through his intelligence, intensive inquiry, and investigations at different conclusions. This is because he would have mastered the knowledge of his predecessors, become aware of other valid conclusions, and preferred them.... If a person ... occupies himself with reasoning and investigation, then *he has embarked on the road to truth*. For *the human soul cannot purify itself entirely from the pollution of this world*, and cannot make its way to the other world except through philosophical investigation. If a person looks into philosophy and attains of it something, even if this is the smallest part, his soul will purify itself from this pollution and be saved.... *I do not consider this to be false and erroneous*. For he who investigates and uses independent reasoning is *a follower of the truth, even if he does not attain the ultimate goal*. For *the soul cannot become pure except through examination and investigation*. This is the sum total of my argument. (*Proofs of Prophecy*, 8–10, italics added)

Al-Rāzī thinks that what distinguishes philosophers from others is that they use independent reasoning. Given al-Rāzī's view on the telos of human beings, there is no clear distinction for him between philosophy and morality. Morality and philosophy are very close to each other, and they both function to redeem us from the material world. The point of morality is to purify the soul so that it learns that it should go back to its original place. For the human soul to purify itself from the pollution of this world, it should embark on the road to truth. The road to truth is not just to learn what propositions are true and false. "A follower of truth" should gain knowledge by reasoning. For the soul cannot become pure except through independent investigation. Even if this method of forming beliefs does not attain the ultimate goal of discovering the truth, it is still the only way for us to achieve salvation. By relying on prophecy, on the other hand, we are not on the road to truth (even if we learn true propositions), and, therefore, our souls cannot purify themselves by deferring to prophets. Pure moral deference is always wrong because our redemption lies in digesting the truth through examination and investigation. Using the language of *The Philosophical Way of Life*, our redemption is in the imitation of God, and we would not be imitating God were we to rely on authorities.

Al-Rāzī does not seem to want to deny that we may learn true propositions by pure deference. So he is not an epistemic pessimist. He is a moral pessimist. He thinks that moral deference does not lead us to salvation. It is not clear what, in Rāzī's view, the difference is between learning by pure deference and learning by independent investigation. But it is clear that he thinks that there is a significant value in making up our minds and living in accordance with our own reasoning. Maybe the value of independent reasoning lies in acquiring *moral understanding*. When we acquire a belief through pure moral testimony, we don't know *why* the belief is true. We don't have moral understanding. Accepting something based on the testimony of an authority does not amount to understanding it, and we should live based on what we understand. But why is moral understanding important? In al-Rāzī's view, the goal of morality is redemption of the soul, and the soul can't be redeemed without understanding.

We might be able to express al-Rāzī's argument against pure moral deference without accepting his grand metaphysical view: morality is defined in terms of the good life. Moral actions are actions that are constitutive of the good life. Living well is similar to doing philosophy well, in that it requires depth, insight, originality, and rigor.[40] In the same way that we can't do philosophy well by purely deferring to other philosophers, we can't live well by deferring to other people. Living well requires us to make up our mind, and to act on the basis of our understanding of the world. Therefore, morality requires us to act in accordance with our own understanding. If we understand the good life to be similar to philosophical accomplishment, it would not be surprising to say that we should always distrust the pure reliance upon moral testimony. Even if we don't understand life to be like a philosophical project, there is still room to value our own independent moral reasoning. As contemporary moral pessimists explain, proper moral behavior involves,

---

[40] In order to explain why pure moral deference is morally problematic, David Enoch also compares morality to philosophy. Enoch, "Defense of Moral Deference."

in part, having appropriate affective and conative responses to situations. Acting on the basis of pure moral testimony looks very cold. So acting on pure testimony is not a moral achievement. To have moral achievement, the agent needs to have the right affective and conative response to the situation. Without them, moral pride would never be appropriate.

The difference between al-Rāzī and contemporary moral pessimists is that while al-Rāzī holds that acting on the basis of pure moral deference is never right, most contemporary moral pessimists think that we may act in certain situations on the basis of pure moral deference. For example, suppose that we lack not only moral understanding regarding a certain subject matter, but that there are also good reasons for this lack, reasons that explain why we cannot have moral understanding in this case. Suppose also that we have good reasons to believe that the someone else is reliable with respect to this subject matter. Given that we have good reasons to believe that the best option, that is, acting from understanding, is not available to us in the case, it seems that we should opt for the second-best option, that is, being guided by a moral expert. Or suppose that we need to make an urgent decision on an important matter without having enough time to think it through. It looks as if it would be permissible, or even required, to defer to a reliable moral expert in such a case. Hence, there might be cases in which we lack a complete understanding of the situation but would not be wrong to act on the basis of moral authority. Even if we think that our telos is to imitate God, there would be still room for justified moral deference. True, God would never defer to an authority. But this is because His epistemic perspective is not limited. Sometimes our epistemic standpoint is limited and we know that it is limited. This difference between God and us makes it rational for us doing things that would not be rational for God to do. Let me give you a few examples in which moral deference seems permissible.

> *The Soldier Case.* An artillery soldier sees some children playing in the street. His commander is standing watch in a tower ordering him to fire at the street immediately. If he fires, he will certainly kill some of the children. The soldier knows that the commander is in a position to see the children and has other relevant facts which may be inaccessible from his standpoint. He knows that the commander is well informed about ethical issues in war and takes them very seriously, as the commander is of good moral character and seeks always to act morally. The fact of the matter is that behind the children, unbeknownst to the soldier, there is an enemy

troop nearby about to fire a very destructive missile that would destroy a whole city full of noncombatant civilians, were he not to fire. Should he obey the commander's order?

The Doctor Case. A doctor in a hospital has a patient connected to a respirator. The ethics committee of the hospital says that she should remove the respirator from the patient, as there are other people in the hospital in need of it. She knows that the patient will die if she removes the respirator, and for this reason she finds the removal of respirator morally objectionable. However, she knows that she is completely naive about ethical complexities regarding the question of life and death in the hospital. While she has no legal obligation to accept the ethics committee's direction, she knows that the ethics committee is very reliable on ethical matters. Should the doctor act in accordance with the committee's direction?

The Case of Anne Elliot. Anne Elliot, an emotionally inexperienced nineteen-year-old girl, falls in love with a handsome young naval officer. Despite her eagerness to marry the young man, Anne is aware that she is young and inexperienced, that the commitment to spend the rest of her life with someone else is a significant step, and that she might not be in a position to make such a decision. She seeks, thus, the advice of her godmother, Lady Russell, whom she regards as wise and experienced. Lady Russell advises her not to marry the young officer, as it is imprudent of her to make such a commitment. Should she listen to Lady Russell?[41]

I think that the answer is yes in the doctor case and the soldier case. The case of Anne Elliot is more difficult. But it looks like she *may* listen to Lady Russell (I am not sure whether she should). In the soldier case, the soldier should obey the order because he knows his epistemic position is limited. He knows that he does not have access to all morally relevant facts, and the commander made his decision by considering a much larger set of morally relevant facts. In the doctor case, the doctor might know all morally relevant facts, but she can't assess the moral significance of those facts. She should hand over the moral assessment of the case to the ethics committee, as she does not have time to delve into the moral complexity of the situation. The case of Anne Elliot is very interesting. Unlike the soldier case and the doctor cases, in which an important decision must be made very soon, Anne is not

---

[41] The case is from Jane Austen's novel *Persuasion*. Thanks to Matthew Griffin to drawing my attention to this example.

under significant time pressure to make her decision. The problem is not that she does not have time to think. The problem is that she does not trust her own thinking on the matter. Moreover, the case of Anne Elliot is not about the morality of harming others. It is about what kind of life would be good for her. We might think that she may hand over the moral assessment of the situation to her mentor, as she is incapable of properly assessing the situation. The case is similar to the doctor case in that both agents do not see themselves as being capable of conducting the proper moral assessment of the situation because they find the ethical issues to be too complex. Anne Elliot is not capable of making a proper decision on the matter because she knows that she lacks the moral development necessary for such a decision. She will be able to understand the issues at stake later in life, when she gains more experience.

What is in common in all the three cases is that the agent knows that they lack moral understanding due to a defect in their epistemic standpoint. I think that it is very plausible to think that we should, or at least may, rely on the moral authority in such cases. Of course, those cases are not ideal cases of moral behavior. But refusing to rely on an authority's direction when we know that our assessment of the situation is defective might be irrational. Al-Rāzī's insistence of the necessity of independent investigation in all cases seems to be too high minded.

4. Moses and Impermissibility of Pure Moral Deference

As noted in the first section, most contemporary philosophers think that pure moral deference is sometimes permissible. While moral optimists think that pure moral deference is in general permissible, moral pessimists are willing to accept the permissibility of pure moral deference in nonideal cases. Howell writes that "it simply cannot be the case that the act of deferring is always wrong. Normal agents should certainly defer in extreme cases, when circumstances are exigent and the costs of inaction are dire."[42] Lewis restates Hills's view (who is a prominent moral pessimist) as follows:

> Hills (2009) argues that if you cannot acquire moral understanding of why p, but you can come to acquire knowledge that p via deference, then

---

[42] Howell, "Google Morals," 390.

you should defer. This is because knowing that p will help you do the right thing.[43]

The main argument for the permissibility of pure moral deference is that moral deference helps us to do the right thing (let's call this argument for permissibility of pure moral deference *the main argument*). Sliwa (who is a moral optimist) presents the main argument in slightly different terms: "[moral advice] is morally good because it helps us do the right thing in cases in which we might otherwise fail to do so."[44] She further argues that there is no distinction between moral advice and moral testimony. Wiland, another moral optimist, expresses the main argument in favor of permissibility of pure moral deference in terms of the following question:

> If someone is telling me the moral truth, isn't it better for me to believe them than to remain stubbornly wrong about what morality requires of me? Isn't it foolish to reject the chance to have more accurate moral views?[45]

According to the main argument, if I acquire a justified belief that I ought to φ, it would be irrational for me not to φ, so it should be permissible for me to φ. But the argument stated as such is too quick. To see the reason, we should bear in mind that moral testimony occurs in situations of moral uncertainty. When there is moral uncertainty, we want to know what we should do, given our evidence. To better understand the situation, it is helpful to recall that obligation is a function of the interaction of various reasons. We can think of obligation as the output, and reasons as inputs. The *objective ought* is the output determined by *all* the moral reasons for and against the action. However, if we limit the reasons that are considered as inputs of an ought judgment, we will have a *less objective* or *more subjective* ought. It is plausible to think that what is *rational* for us to do is a function of all reasons that are *epistemically accessible* to us. Now suppose that in light of reasons that I am aware of, I form the judgment that I ought *not* to φ. Suppose that a morally reliable person tells me that I ought to φ. Assume that we are epistemically optimist, that is, that it is possible to be justified in forming a belief on the basis of pure moral deference. Given that we are considering the *pure* case of moral deference, I have no information about why the morally reliable

---

[43] Lewis, "New Puzzle," 462.
[44] Sliwa, "Defense of Moral Testimony," 181.
[45] Eric Wiland, "Moral Testimony," *Oxford Studies in Metaethics* 12 (2017): 58.

person made that judgment. Our case might be like the soldier case, in which someone has access to reasons that I don't. Or it might be like the doctor case, in which someone has a more accurate assessment of the interaction of all reasons for and against the action. Either way, the moral expert is in a better position to make a judgment about the *objective* ought. The question that I am concerned with, upon hearing the judgment of the moral expert, is whether it is *rational* for me to perform φ, given all my evidence, which of course includes the testimony of the expert. *But from the fact that I have justification for the proposition that I objectively ought to φ, it does not immediately follow that I rationally ought to φ.* There is *a gap* between having justification for an *objective* ought and being subject to a *rational* ought in the main argument for the permissibility of pure moral deference that needs to be filled.

David Enoch seeks to fill this gap by appealing to a moral principle which says, everything being equal, we rationally ought to minimize the risk of acting wrongly (in the objective sense).[46] Enoch is a moral pessimist, and thus accepts that it would be morally nonideal to act on the basis of moral testimony. Nevertheless, he argues that it is safer, and thus rational, for us to act on the basis of the testimony of a moral expert, when there is a conflict between the moral expert's verdict and our own. The gap in the main argument is filled by the principle that, everything being equal, we rationally should minimize the risk of acting objectively wrongly—let's call this principle *the minimization of the moral risk*. We can illustrate how the main argument is supposed to work by applying it to the soldier case and the doctor case. The soldier should fire because he should minimize the risk of acting wrongly in a critical situation in a time of war; the doctor should disconnect the respirator because that makes it more likely that the right call is made on a matter of life and death, thanks to the verdict of the ethics committee. Of course, the moral responses of these agents might not be ideal. They might not have the appropriate affective responses to all morally relevant features of the situations. But that does not alter the question of what they (rationally) should do.

Enoch's principle of the minimization of the moral risk may well be true. The rationale behind the principle is that given my goal of acting morally, when there is moral uncertainty, everything being equal, I should rationally choose the morally safer option. One might, however, question whether the goal of acting morally is the only rational goal that we have. Rationality might require us to have *other goals* as well. Acting *prudentially* (i.e., acting

---

[46] Enoch, "Defense of Moral Deference."

in your own best interests) might be another rational goal. Given that we are concerned with the *morality* of pure deference, we can set prudential considerations aside, though. But our *moral* goals are not limited to the goal of acting morally. Some authors make a distinction between a *de dicto* concern to act morally, and a *de re* one. A *de dicto* concern is a concern to do the right action, whatever the right action turns out to be, whereas a *de re* concern to act morally is a concern to pursue the actual objects of morality, honesty, equality, and so on. Michael Smith explains the distinction as follows:

> Good people care non-derivatively about honesty, the weal and woe of their children and friends, the well-being of their fellows, people getting what they deserve, justice, equality, and the like, not just one thing: doing what they believe to be right, where this is read *de dicto* and not *de re*. Indeed, commonsense tells us that being so motivated is a fetish or moral vice, not the one and only moral virtue.[47]

The distinction can be better understood when we consider someone with a false moral belief. Imagine a person who firmly believes that one morally ought to kill as many atheists as one can. When he looks for a new atheist to kill, he is concerned to act morally in a *de dicto* way. He wants to do what he *believes* to be moral. But he does not care for actual morality *de re*; that is, he does not care about the things that actually constitute morality, for example, people's right to life. Given this distinction, one might think that our rational (moral) goals are not restricted to acting morally (understood in a *de dicto* way), but also include the pursuit of moral ends, such as causing less harm, bringing about more equality, treating others with respect, and so forth.

The principle of the minimization of the moral risk has the qualification of *everything being equal*. This qualification helps the principle to be neutral with respect to other things we rationally should pursue. The principle just says that when our situation with respect to other rational goals is equal, it would be more rational to minimize the chance of acting wrongly. But, given the qualification, the principle is applicable only to cases in which both options, that is, relying on our own judgment and deferring to the moral expert, fare equally vis-à-vis other rational goals. Enoch assumes that in cases of pure moral deference, this condition is met. It is not that one option promotes objects of morality to an important extent, whereas the other hinders them. For example,

---

[47] Michael Smith, *The Moral Problem* (Oxford: Blackwell, 1994), 75.

in the soldier case, the soldier knows that there are lives at stake. If he acts on the basis of his commander's judgment, some lives will be lost. If he acts on the basis of his own judgment, some other lives (and perhaps more lives) will be lost. Either way, some lives will be lost. The same goes for the doctor case. The main question in the hospital is who should be saved, given that either way, some lives will be lost and other lives saved. In both cases, the moral outcomes of my own judgment and that of the experts are more or less comparable.[48]

However, contrary to what Enoch says, I am not sure if the principle of the minimization of the moral risk vindicates the rationality of pure moral deference, in general. In fact, the principle might even speak against pure moral deference in the case of the testimony of Scripture. Consider, first, this artificial case: Suppose I am 80 percent confident that I should not φ. Suppose that a moral expert tells me that I should φ. I think that he is 99 percent reliable. I know that he is in a better epistemic standpoint than I am. So, on the basis of his testimony, I come to believe that I (objectively) should φ with a very high degree of confidence. This belief is justified on the basis of moral testimony. I am less likely to act wrongly if I act in accordance with the testimony of the expert. But rationally speaking, should I φ? Not necessarily. Suppose also that I have two other beliefs: I believe that if the expert turns out to be right (which is very likely), the consequence of not φ-ing is only *slightly* worse than the consequence of φ-ing. But I also believe that if the expert is wrong (which is admittedly very unlikely), the consequence of φ-ing is *vastly* worse than not φ-ing. If the moral expert is right, and I don't act on the basis of his verdict, my action will be slightly wrong. But if the expert is wrong, and I act on the basis of his verdict, I will make *a grave moral mistake*. In this case, it looks like I should not φ; that is, it is not rational for me to defer to the testimony of the expert. There are three points about this example:

(i) It is not clear whether the principle of the minimization of the moral risk applies to this case. Suppose that my beliefs about the asymmetry

---

[48] The principle does not seem to be applicable to the case of Anne Elliot. The life in which Anne Elliot does not marry the naval officer is very different from the one in which she marries him. We can't say that the consequences of both options are comparable. Even if she may listen to her aunt, and I think she may, the main argument does not explain why deference in this case is permissible. We might have a similar worry about the soldier case too. The outcome of the soldier's not shooting is much worse than his shooting. We might, then, think that Enoch's principle does not apply to the soldier case either, since the outcomes of different options are not comparable at all. However, the soldier might reasonably think that the outcome of acting on his own judgment is either comparable or worse than the outcome of deferring to the commander's judgment. This might justify the application of Enoch's principle (or a slightly revised version of it) to the soldier case.

of consequences of the options are correct. The asymmetry of moral consequences might show that everything is *not equal*, and thus the principle does not apply. This would be more obvious if we hold that rationality requires us to care about morality in a *de re* fashion. That is, if rationality requires us to nonderivatively care about moral consequences, among other things, then clearly everything between two options is not equal from a rational perspective.

(ii) Suppose that the principle of the minimization of the moral risk applies to this case. Wrongness is not just a binary property. That is, there are degrees of acting wrongly. Some actions are more seriously wrong than some others. If so, the moral risk of acting wrongly should be understood as the expected value of acting wrongly. When we understand the principle of the minimization of the moral risk in terms of the expected value of acting wrongly, the principle, in fact, speaks against acting in accordance with moral testimony in our example. If I want to minimize moral risk, the safer option would be to avoid the possibility of a grave moral mistake, and to opt for the possibility of a slight moral mistake.

(iii) Regardless of the applicability of the principle of the minimization of the moral risk, *intuitively* the rational thing to do in the example is not to act in accordance with moral testimony. Even though it would be less likely that I act wrongly if I act on the basis of testimony, I should not act on the basis of testimony, because, in this case, it is better to act with a high chance of being slightly wrong, than to act with a low chance of being very seriously wrong. Moreover, if we think that, in addition to not acting seriously wrongly, we should also care (in a *de re* way) about not bringing about very negative moral consequences, assuming that our beliefs about consequences are correct, we have further reasons to ignore the judgment of the expert.

Now we can see that the problem with the main argument for the permissibility of pure moral deference is not that Enoch's principle can't fill its gap. The problem is that the gap can't be filled at all. Wiland expresses the main argument in terms of this rhetorical question: "Isn't it foolish to reject the chance to have more accurate moral views?" While Wiland expects us to agree that it is foolish to act against what we think is the more accurate moral view, as the example shows, it is not foolish to do so, if the view we justifiably take to be more accurate is morally too risky. We have to be careful about the distinction between objective ought and rational ought. In cases with the same structure as our example, we may accept the more accurate moral view about the objective ought. But this does not imply that we *rationally ought* to act in accordance with the view that we take it to be more accurate about objective ought. Arguably, if it is rational to *act* in accordance with our own judgment in such cases, we should also *believe* that we *rationally* ought to act in accordance with our own moral beliefs in those cases. So, it is not foolish to hold that sometimes the more accurate view about the objective ought is not the more accurate view about the rational ought. This is true in cases in which we believe that while it is likely that we objectively ought to φ, we rationally ought not to φ.

Moral deference to Scripture is structurally similar to our example. Suppose, for the sake of argument, that Scripture says that you should beat your wife. Suppose you have a high degree of confidence that Scripture is God's words, and a high degree of confidence that you understand its meaning correctly. So, on the basis of what you take to be divine testimony, you come to believe that you (objectively) should beat your wife. But you also know that, as far as we understand things, beating one's wife is very seriously wrong. Suppose you have no idea why God says that you should beat your wife, so you are in complete darkness about what would be the justifying reason (if any) for beating one's wife. You know that if the testimony turned out to be false, because perhaps there is no God, or Scripture is not God's words, or you misunderstood its meaning, and you were to beat your wife, then you would make a morally horrible mistake. But if the testimony is true and you should beat your wife and you don't, it's not clear how wrong your action would be. So even though you might trust testimony and you might think justifiably that you (objectively) should beat you wife, you rationally should not act in accordance with your belief. This would be even more evident if Scripture only gives you *permission* to beat your wife. Here if the testimony is false, and you beat your wife, your action would be morally horrible. But if the testimony were true and you did not beat your wife, then you would not do anything wrong. So, again, even though you might believe that it is likely that you may (objectively) beat your wife, you should believe that you (rationally) should not act in accordance with this belief.

It is also important to note that you *know* that if the testimony is false, wife-beating would be seriously wrong. If the testimony is false and you beat your wife, it is not only that you do something that you merely *believe* is deeply immoral if the testimony is false—instead, you *actually* make a deep moral mistake (in a *de re* way). So it is not only the *de dicto* concern not to act wrongly that speaks against deferring to Scripture, the *de re* concern to act morally also speaks against deferring to Scripture. In other words, morality requires you to care about your wife, among many other things. If the testimony is true, and you don't beat your wife, it is not clear which moral object you have disrespected and to what extent, but if the testimony is false and you beat your wife, you have deeply disrespected her basic human dignity. So both *de dicto* concern for morality and *de re* concern for morality are considerations against moral deference to Scripture.[49]

There is a Qur'anic story which can be read as recommending the same kind of response to morally counterintuitive divine injunctions. The story has two main characters, Moses and Khidr, a sage with divine knowledge. When Moses meets Khidr, he asks, "Shall I follow thee so that thou teachest me, of what thou hast been taught, right judgment?" (Qur'an 18:66). But Khidr answers: "You will surely not be able to bear with me. And how can you have patience about a thing which you know not?" Moses, however, says that "thou shalt find me, if God will, patient; and I shall not rebel against thee in anything" (18:69). So Khidr agrees that Moses can come with him, on the condition that Moses does not question him about anything. They set out upon their journey, till they stumble upon a boat in a quay. Khidr then says that Moses should make a hole in the boat, to which Moses objects, "We should not make a hole in the boat to drown its passengers. This is an evil act!" (18:69–71).

It turns out Khidr did in fact have sufficient reasons to make a hole in the boat. No one was going to be drowned. The boat belonged to some poor people working on the river; and there was a king who would take every sound ship by force. By damaging the boat, Khidr in fact would have helped the poor people to keep their boat. Moses, however, did not have epistemic access to Khidr's reasons. He had only access to the testimony of Khidr, who, Moses believed, had moral knowledge concerning this matter.

---

[49] Elizabeth Harman thinks rationality and blameworthiness are not functions of our *de dicto* concern for morality. False moral beliefs, on her view, do not get us off the hook. She also argues that uncertainty norms involving expected utility calculation are false when the agent's moral beliefs are false. See Elizabeth Harman, "The Irrelevance of Moral Uncertainty," *Oxford Studies in Metaethics* 10 (2015): 53–79. However, in the kinds of cases we consider in this chapter assume the agent's moral belief is correct and justified. That is, the agent *knows* (as opposed to merely believes) that wife-beating is seriously wrong if the testimony is false. So Harman's argument against uncertainty norms doesn't apply to our discussion in this chapter.

While Moses refuses to act in accordance with Khidr's verdict, he does not question the status of Khidr as a sage with divine knowledge. The Qur'an appears to endorse, or at the very least refrain from condemning, Moses's decision, as it does not raise any moral objection to his actions. One way to read this story is to say that while Moses believes justifiably that Khidr is right, he also correctly believes that he (rationally) ought not act in accordance with Khidr's judgment. Instead, he thinks that he should act in accordance with ordinary human morality, so to speak, and not God's. God's morality is in fact true. Objectively speaking, he should make a hole in the boat. But it would be morally too risky for Moses to act upon this (true) judgment when he does not have access to the reasons that make it true. If Moses makes a hole in the boat and it turns out that he is wrong, he would be guilty of serious wrongdoing. Moses has no idea what will happen if he does not make a hole and it turns out that he should have. Moses could appeal to something like the following principle to justify his refusal to act in accordance with Khidr's testimony:

> *Moses's Principle.* If one receives very reliable testimony that one should φ, and the situation is such that one knows that if the testimony turns out to be wrong, one's φ-ing would be seriously wrong, but one has no idea of how wrong one's not φ-ing would be if the testimony turns out to be true, then one ought not to act in accordance with the testimony.

An easy way to capture the idea behind the Moses principle is this. Suppose the testimony says that Moses should φ. There are four possible scenarios.

	Moses makes a hole in the boat	Moses does not make a hole in the boat
The testimony is true	(1) Moses is fine	(2) Unclear.
The testimony is false	(3) Moses's action is seriously wrong	(4) Moses is fine

As the table indicates, in two possible scenarios (i.e., (1) and (4)), Moses is fine. Given that Moses finds the testimony reliable, he has good reasons to think that the testimony is correct (and thus he is in fact in either scenario (1) or scenario (2)). However, he can't ignore the possibility described in scenario (3). But one might wonder: Considering the possibility of being a serious wrongdoer (i.e., scenario (3)) and being in complete darkness about the seriousness of one's wrongdoing (i.e., scenario 2), why should Moses choose to avoid the possibility of being a serious wrongdoer? I think that there are three reasons for Moses to think that scenario (3) is worse than scenario (2).

First, there is an intuition that in terms of doing serious wrong and being engaged in wrongdoing to some an unknown extent, it is better to choose the latter. The latter option leaves us some hope that we will not be engaged in serious wrongdoing.

Second, we can argue that it is more reasonable for Moses to be guided by his concern for the poor people's property than to be guided by a concern to be right. Let me explain. Weatherson discusses a case in which Martha, who thinks that eating meat is probably morally permissible, refuses to eat meat because she thinks that she may do something seriously morally wrong if she eats meat. Weatherson objects to Matha's decision on the following grounds:

> Why should she turn down the steak? Not because she values the interests of the cow over her dining. She does not. And not because she should have that value. By hypothesis, she need not do so. . . . Rather, she has to care about morality as such. And that seems wrong.[50]

Weatherson thinks that something is wrong with caring about morality as such. We should care about the objects that morality cares about, not about morality as such. Sepielli convincingly argues that Weatherson's objection is mistaken in part because Martha is not purely concerned with morality as such; she is also partly motivated not to cause animal suffering.[51] But in the Moses case, while Khidr asks Moses to make a hole in the boat out of his concern for the poor owners of the boat, Moses has no idea why he requests this. So Moses's motivation to make a hole in the boat can't involve a concern for the poor owners in any way. If he does what Khidr asks him to do, it is because he is purely motivated by morality as such. The intuition that there is something wrong about caring for morality as such speaks against pure deference in this case.

---

[50] B. Weatherson, "Running Risks Morally," *Philosophical Studies* 167.1 (2014): 152.

[51] Andrew Sepielli, "Moral Uncertainty and Fetishistic Motivation," *Philosophical Studies* 173.11 (2016): 2951–68.

Third, given that the original rationale behind moral deference is lacking in this case, and that there is always something problematic about moral deference, it is better to avoid moral deference in this case. On al-Rāzī's view, morality is a redemptive enterprise, and redemption comes when one responds properly to the wrong-(or right-)making features of actions. Al-Rāzī was wrong because *sometimes* it is better to avoid a wrong action than to have the right moral response to the case. In cases in which two options have more or less the same consequences, by deferring to testimony, we minimize the chance of performing a wrong action at the cost of not having the proper response to the moral dimensions of a situation. But this is not possible for Moses. He does not know which option is morally safer. Now that the possibility of minimizing moral risk is closed, perhaps the best option is to let ourselves be guided by *actual* moral objects, and not morality as such. Perhaps this is why the Qur'an does not condemn Moses's choice. There is something rationally recommendable, and even humanly praiseworthy, in Moses's choice of sticking to what he understands in his high-stakes situation.

Let me finish this section by noting that it is interesting that some classic Islamic jurists show some awareness of the argument just given. Perhaps because of their different moral intuitions, they did not think that this argument applies to the injunctions of the Qur'an. However, they were willing to accept that sometimes we should not act in accordance with the content of an authentic Hadith. In the prologue, section 3, I explained that the received view in the Islamic tradition is that there is no difference between the authority of the Qur'an and that of an authentic Hadith. According to these jurists, there are cases in which we should not act in accordance with the content of a Hadith, even though we have no reason to reject the authenticity of the Hadith (and presumably if the Hadith is authentic, according to them, we have to believe that it is true). While they did not extend this conclusion to the Qur'an, given that they made no distinction, in terms of authority, between the Qur'an and authentic Hadiths, it is not clear why they should not extend their arguments to the case of the Qur'an.

In Shia jurisprudence, the orthodox position is that a "single-source Hadith" is authoritative. A single-source Hadith is a Hadith which is not *mutawatir* (successive). A single-source Hadith is a report of the saying of the Prophet or imams which is acquired through one or even multiple sources. But the number of narrators of a single-source Hadith is not significant enough for the Hadith to be *mutawatir*. A *mutawatir* Hadith is a well-established Hadith relayed by numerous narrators. Muhammad Bāqir as-Sadr (1935–1980), a leading modern thinker in Shia jurisprudence, reports the orthodox position of Shia jurisprudence on single-source Hadith as follows:

> The fourth [method of authentication of traditions] is the single-source account reported by a single authority who is reliable. . . . The way to judge such a report is that if the informant is reliable it is adopted and it is evidence, otherwise not. Such probativity is established on the basis of the divine law.[52]

Shia jurists, then, think that they are justified in accepting what is reported in a single-source Hadith (as long as the source is reliable enough). It is also agreed upon, in Islamic jurisprudence, that the punishment for a person who commits murder is execution (with some qualifications). There is a credible single-source Hadith which says, in the process of establishing the occurrence of murder, the testimony of children is admissible. Even though this Hadith proved to have a reliable source and, thus, should be believed by Muslims, jurists do not rule in accordance with it. For example, al-Muhaqqiq al-Hilli (1205–1277), a very influential Shia jurist, writes: "It is too risky to be audacious about killing on the basis of a single-source report."[53]

Al-Hilli's student, Hassan Yusofi, known as Fazel Abi, in his influential book on jurisprudence, *Kashf al-romuz*, written in 1273, extends the ruling of his mentor to matters of property as well. There is a Hadith which says that if one finds one dinar in a holy shrine, one should announce it, and if one does not find the owner, one should give it away. But if one finds the owner after having given it away, one should give one dinar to the owner. Even though Abi finds the source of Hadith reliable, he does not rule in accordance with it on the following grounds: "It is too risky to be audacious about people's properties the basis of a single-source report."[54]

Both al-Hilli and Abi think that it is too risky to rule in accordance with a reliable Hadith when the content of the Hadith sounds counterintuitive and the stakes are high. Notice that they don't want to challenge the reliability of the source of the Hadith. Nor do they want to question the orthodox view

---

[52] Muhammad Baqir as-Sadr, trans., *Lessons in Islamic Jurisprudence* (Oxford: OneWorld, 2003), 99–100.

[53] Al-Muhaqqiq al-Hilli, *Shara'i al-Islam fi Masa'il al-Halal wal-Haram*, vol. 4 (Tehran: Esteghlal, 1988), 910.

[54] Fazel Abi (Hasan ibn AbiTalib Yusofi), *Kashf al-Romuz fi Sharh Mokhtasar al-Nafe*, vol. 2 (Qom: Islamic Publications Office, 1997), 411.

that every single-source Hadith is to be believed. So they should hold that the content of the Hadith is correct. Nevertheless, they do not actually rule in accordance with the Hadith, because they find such a ruling to be too risky morally. This line of reasoning aligns with the Moses principle.

5. A Solution to the Problem of Prescribed Evil

Where does the argument of the previous section leave us with regard to the problem of prescribed evil? To recall, the problem of prescribed evil consists of a tension between three theses: *the divinity of Scripture, the existence of seemingly prescribed evil,* and *the reliability of our independent moral judgments* (see the prologue). The argument for strict adherence in Part I is an argument designed to deny the reliability of our independent moral judgments and to show that we ought to follow the apparent meaning of Scripture in moral matters. Does the argument for the impermissibility of moral deference vindicate the reliability of our independent moral judgments? Yes and no.

We defined the reliability of our independent moral judgments in terms of a thesis which says our independent moral judgments *reliably* represent moral values, moral duties, and moral permissions. The argument for the impermissibility of moral deference does not show that our independent moral judgments *accurately* represent objective moral values. The argument just shows that when our independent moral judgments are in conflict with Scripture, we *rationally* ought to act on the basis of our own judgments. It shows that our independent moral judgments are reliable in the sense that we should rationally be guided by them (call this the *rational sense*). The argument is silent about whether they are reliable in the sense that they correctly represent *objective* moral values (call this the *objective sense*). On the other hand, the argument shows that the premise of God's Reliability in the argument for the strict adherence does not imply that, in the case of the conflict between our own judgments and God's, we *rationally* ought to act in accordance with God's judgments. Therefore, contrary to the conclusion of the strict adherence argument, even if Scripture states that "φ-ing is obligatory" (or "φ-ing is permissible") and Scripture is God's words, we are not rationally required to do φ.

In this chapter, I did not argue for the reliability of our independent moral judgments in the objective sense (this is my task in the next chapter). I argued that *even if* the reliability of our independent moral judgments is false in the objective sense, it is true in the rational sense, and this is enough for our independent moral judgments to be our guide in our moral behavior. We have then a solution to the problem of prescribed evil: the theist can hold beliefs in the divinity of Scripture and the existence of seemingly prescribed evil, while doubting the objective reliability of our Independent moral judgments. While this solution looks like a Scripture-first solution to the problem of prescribed evil, it is not. For this solution does not say that we ought to act in accordance with the judgments of Scripture. Instead, it says that we rationally ought to act in accordance with our own moral understanding. That is, this solution has no theological ramification for our moral behavior. Notwithstanding, this is in fact a conservative solution to the problem of prescribed evil, for it does not require us to deny the apparent meaning of Scripture. Adopting this solution, modern conscientious Muslims should lead their moral life in accordance with their own moral understanding, while remaining open to the possibility that the apparent meaning of Scripture can be true.

The theist can withhold judgment regarding the reliability of our independent moral judgments in the objective sense, based on the premise that our ethical perspective remains inherently too limited to discern objective moral truths. Consequently, the theist can also withhold judgment concerning whether seemingly prescribed evil holds the status of genuine evil. The problem of prescribed evil can thus be dissolved. The act of withholding judgment about objective ethics would practically be untenable if it were to render us morally paralyzed. But it does not. Suspending judgment on the objective reliability of our independent moral judgments bears no implications for our moral conduct; we can still acknowledge the reliability of our independent moral judgments in the rational sense. Following this perspective, we should be guided by our own moral understanding, as al-Rāzī recommends. If we are in a Moses-like situation with regard to the injunctions of Scripture, no matter what our attitude is toward the truth of those injunctions, we should act like Moses.

5
The Reliability of Our Moral Judgments

Summary of the Chapter

Section 1. Overviewing the debate between the subjective view and the objective view on the nature of moral obligations, the section argues that the *Conscience Constraint** correctly identifies moral norms by actions that are dictated by moral conscience.

Section 2: The subjective obligation comes apart from objective obligation in the cases of ignorance and uncertainty. While ignorance seems not to be relevant to Scriptural injunctions, it can be argued that, if the Conscience Constraint* is correct, our *uncertainty* about Scriptural obligations implies that our independent moral judgments are reliable.

Section 3: Philosophical utilitarianism and the Kantian view are two different ways of looking at ethics. While philosophical utilitarianism implies that *ignorance* of the reasons behind Scriptural injunctions are not morally important, the Kantian view holds that moral obligation is not sensitive to inaccessible reasons (this is called the *Accessibility Constraint*).

Section 4: Two Kantian arguments for the Accessibility Constraint are offered (one based on the agency view, the other based on the justifiability view). The Accessibility Constraint implies that our independent moral judgments are reliable.

Section 5: The Conscience Constraint* and the Accessibility Constraint are in line with the spirit of the Mu'tazilites' view of morality. The section also describes the distinction between God's morality and humans' morality as well as its implication for the parallel evil argument.

Section 6: Abraham's sacrifice is discussed in light of the Conscience Constraint* and the Accessibility Constraint.

Our independent moral judgments, as defined in the prologue, are moral judgments obtained through careful a priori moral reflections and sufficient empirical observations, independent of Scripture. In the previous chapter, I argued that our independent moral judgments are reliable in the sense that we should *rationally* be guided by them. In this chapter, I will argue that there are good reasons to think that our independent moral judgments are reliable in the sense that they *correctly* represent our moral obligations. That is, I will argue that the reliability of our independent moral judgments, in the *objective* sense, is true.

The argument for strict adherence depends on God's Reliability as well as the denial of Moral Justification.[1] I argued in the last chapter that God's Reliability does not imply that it is always rational to defer to God in moral matters. In other words, from the objective reliability of God in moral matters, it does not follow that we *rationally* should always rely on God. In this chapter, I argue that our independent moral judgments are *objectively* reliable. If so, either God's Reliability is false or Moral Justification is true. That is, *either* we are not morally obligated (or permitted) to do an action against our independent moral judgments, *even if* God intends to convey that it is obligatory (or permitted) for us to do that action, *or* God would never intend to convey that it is obligatory (or permitted) for us to do an action, when that action is not obligatory (or permitted), according to our independent moral judgments. If either God's Reliability is false or Moral Justification is true, the argument for strict adherence fails.

1. The Debate on Objective and Subjective Ought

In previous chapters, we talked briefly about the distinction between objective and subjective obligation. A clear understanding of the distinction is vital for my arguments in this chapter. So, in this section, I am going to give an overall review of the contemporary debate on the objective view and the subjective view about moral obligation.

In *On What Matters*, Derek Parfit distinguishes three different notions of moral wrongness. Some act of ours would be

---

[1] To recall, God's Reliability says that, for any action φ, if God intends to convey that it is obligatory (or permitted) for us (or a certain group of people) to do φ, it is true that we (or those people) are morally obligated (or permitted) to do φ. Moreover, Moral Justification is the following thesis: there are moral reasons to interpret morally controversial passages nonliterally, as the literal understanding of the passages is inconsistent with a morally perfect God.

wrong in the *fact-relative* sense just when this act would be wrong in the ordinary sense if we knew all of the morally relevant facts,

wrong in the *belief-relative* sense just when this act would be wrong in the ordinary sense if our beliefs about these facts were true,

and *wrong* in the *evidence-relative* sense just when this act would be wrong in the ordinary sense if we believed what the available evidence gives us decisive reasons to believe, and these beliefs were true.

Acts are in these senses *right*, or at least *morally permitted*, when they are not wrong, and they are what we *ought morally* to do when all of their alternatives would be in these senses wrong.[2]

While Parfit thinks all these three notions are legitimate notions of moral wrongness, the debate between the objective view and the subjective view is about which of these notions properly characterizes the notion of moral wrongness. The objective view holds that our moral obligations are determined by facts about morally relevant properties. The objective view, then, holds that moral wrongness is the same as Parfit's wrongness in the fact-relative sense. The subjective view, on the other hand, holds that moral wrongness is determined by our epistemic attitudes toward morally relevant properties. This definition of the subjective view is broad enough to include *both* the view that moral wrongness is Parfit's wrongness in the belief-relative sense, and the view that moral wrongness is Parfit's wrongness in the evidence-relative sense. Some call the latter view the *prospective view*.[3] Most subjectivists think that moral wrongness is determined by our evidence—and not merely our beliefs—about morally relevant properties. In our discussion of the subjective view, I consider only the view which says that moral wrongness is wrongness in the evidence-relative sense.

It is essential to morality that morality is supposed to be action-guiding. The subjective view holds that the objective view about moral obligation is not action-guiding enough. Two sorts of cases are presented by the subjective view to illustrate the deficiency of the objective view: one involves *ignorance*, and the other *uncertainty*. There are many different examples in the literature for those cases. Since I am going to use Jackson's example for the case of

---

[2] Derek Parfit, *On What Matters*, vol. 1 (New York: Oxford University Press, 2011), 150–51.

[3] Michael J. Zimmerman, *Ignorance and Moral Obligation* (New York: Oxford University Press, 2014); Benjamin Kiesewetter, "'Ought' and the Perspective of the Agent," *Journal of Ethics and Social Philosophy* 5.3 (2010): 1–24.

uncertainty, to have similar examples, I present a variation of Jackson's example for the case of ignorance.[4]

> *The Ignorance Case.* Jill is a physician who has to decide on the correct treatment for her patient John. She has two drugs to choose from: drug A and drug B. Careful consideration of the literature has led her to believe that drug A is very likely to cure John's disease, whereas drug B will kill the patient. The fact is that drug A will kill the patient, whereas drug B will cure the patient's disease. What should Jill do?

The objective view (as defended by, among others, Thomson and Graham) says that Jill should give drug B, whereas the subjective view (defended by, among others, Lord, Zimmerman, and Kiesewetter) claims that intuitively the answer is that Jill should give drug A.[5] The objective view, on the other hand, holds that this intuition can be accounted for by saying that Jill would not be blameworthy for giving drug A, which is in fact the wrong action, since she was trying to do the right action. One might think that there is no one right answer here. We need fundamentally two notions of moral obligation—let's call this the *two-level view*.[6] According to the two-level view, Jill subjectively ought to give drug A, while she objectively ought to give drug B.

While the ignorance case is not enough to make progress on the debate, subjectivists think that the case of uncertainty can show that the subjective view is correct. The following case is taken directly from Jackson.

> *The Uncertainty Case.* Jill is a physician who has to decide on the correct treatment for her patient, John, who has a minor but not trivial skin complaint. She has three drugs to choose from: drug A, drug B, and drug C. Careful consideration of the literature has led her to the following opinions. Drug A is very likely to relieve the condition but will not completely cure it. One of drugs B and C will completely cure the skin condition;

---

[4] Frank Jackson, "Decision-theoretic Consequentialism and the Nearest and Dearest Objection," *Ethics* 101 (1991): 461–82.

[5] Peter A. Graham, ed., "In Defense of Objectivism about Moral Obligation," *Ethics* 121.1 (2010): 88–115; Judith Jarvis Thomson, *Normativity* (Chicago: Open Court, 2008); Errol Lord, "What You're Rationally Required to Do and What You Ought to Do (Are the Same Thing!)," *Mind* 126.504 (2017): 1109–54; Kiesewetter, "Ought."

[6] Parfit, *On What Matters*; Holly M. Smith, "Subjective Rightness," *Social Philosophy and Policy* 27.2 (2010): 64–110.

the other though will kill the patient, and there is no way that she can tell which of the two is the perfect cure and which the killer drug. What should Jill do?[7]

Following Zimmerman, we can represent the morally important features of the case by the following table:[8]

	Facts	Evidence
A.	Partial cure	Partial cure
B.	Complete cure	Either complete cure or death
C.	Death	Either complete cure or death

Based on the table, similar to the ignorance case, the subjective view says that Jill should give drug A, whereas the objective view says that Jill should give drug B. There is an important difference between the ignorance case and the uncertainty case. Contrary to the ignorance case, in the uncertainty case, Jill knows that giving drug A does not produce the best outcome. This feature can help us to see why the two-level view's response to the case is not sufficient. The two-level view says that Jill subjectively should give drug A, whereas she objectively should give drug B. Jill knows that she subjectively should give drug A, and that she objectively should not give drug A. But that does not settle her *deliberative* question, "What should I do?" asked from the first-person perspective: "I know that I objectively should not do A, and that I subjectively should do A, but then what should I do?" The subjectivist thinks that the uncertainty case can also show that the objective view is mistaken. For the objective view can't account for the intuition that Jill should give drug A to John by saying that she was trying to do the (objectively) right action; she wasn't. She knows that giving drug A would not be objectively right.

Zimmerman as well as other subjectivists (e.g., Kiesewetter) think that the uncertainty case can be used to reconstruct an argument against the objective view. An important step in the argument is to find a way to identify the sense of ought that truly captures the moral ought. To this aim, Zimmerman

---

[7] Frank Jackson, "Decision-Theoretic Consequentialism and the Nearest and Dearest Objection," *Ethics* 101.3 (1991): 462–63.

[8] Michael Zimmerman, "In Defense of Prospectivism about Moral Obligation: A Reply to My Meticulous Critics," *Journal of Moral Philosophy* 15.4 (2018): 444–61.

thinks that we should look for "the sense of 'ought' with which the *morally conscientious person* is ultimately concerned" (29). He uses the following principle to identify the moral sense of ought (33).

> *The Conscience Constraint.* It is necessarily the case that, if one acts morally conscientiously, then one does not deliberately do something that one believes to be overall morally wrong.

It is easy to see how the Conscience Constraint can be used to show that the objective view is incorrect. Jill, if she acts conscientiously, knows that she should not give drug B to the patient. According to the Conscience Constraint, it is thus not the case that she morally should give drug B to the patient, whereas the objective view says that she morally should give drug B to the patient. Therefore, the objective view is false.

While the objectivists accept that the moral ought is the one that the morally conscientious person is concerned with, they hold that the Conscience Constraint is mistaken.[9] The objective view accounts for the intuition that Jill should give drug A to John by saying that the morally conscientious person is not only concerned with doing the right action, but also concerned with *not doing the wrong action*. And there are various degrees of wrongness. It would be slightly wrong of Jill to give drug A to the patient, whereas her giving drug C to the patient would be seriously wrong. The morally conscientious person seeks to minimize the chance of being engaged in serious wrongdoing. In cases of uncertainty, the morally conscientious person calculates the expected value of moral wrongness for her different options and seeks to minimize it. In the uncertainty case, the objectivist holds, Jill knows that it would be slightly wrong for her to give drug A, while she also knows that her other option, which is to randomly pick either B or C, has a significant chance of making her guilty of serious wrongdoing. Therefore, she rationally should give drugs A to minimize the moral risk. The Conscience Constraint is false because it is not true that if she acts morally conscientiously, then she does not deliberately do something that she believes to be overall morally wrong. Jill gives drug A to the patient while knowing that this is wrong.

Graham (2021) presents a series of uncertainty cases in which the agent faces uncertain options with various degrees of wrongness (in his examples, options are wrong for different reasons). Graham successfully shows that the

---

[9] For example, Peter Graham, "In Defense of Objectivism."

morally conscientious person is always concerned with minimizing the risk of engaging in seriously objectively wrong actions. He concludes that "the morally conscientious person is concerned not to act objectively wrongly. When she asks, 'what would it be (most) wrong for me to do in this scenario?' she is inquiring into which of her options it would be objectively wrong for her to take."[10] Therefore, if the moral sense of ought is to be identified with the concern of the morally conscientious person, the objective ought truly captures the moral sense of ought. I think Graham is right that the Conscience Constraint, as formulated by Zimmerman, is false. I think he is also right that the morally conscientious person is concerned with not acting objectively wrongly. But this does not show that the objective view is correct.

There are two important points here. First, the subjective view is consistent with the thought that the morally conscientious person is concerned to act *objectively* rightly, and to not act *objectively* wrongly. Second, while the Conscience Constraint, as formulated by Zimmerman, is false, there is a grain of truth in the Conscience Constraint. It would be helpful here to consider the epistemic case.

The epistemically conscientious person is ultimately concerned with believing what is true, and disbelieving what is not true. Truth is the ultimate goal. Yet sometimes epistemically conscientious persons are *unable* to rationally believe what is true when they have no evidential access to truth. Epistemic norms are those norms that tell them what they should believe given their epistemic limitations. Similarly, Graham might be right that morally conscientious people are ultimately concerned to do *what they have most reason to*. Overall objective wrongness is determined by the balance of all moral reasons for and against the action. Their goal is to do what the balance of all reasons is in its favor, i.e., to do the objectively right or permissible action. Yet, given their epistemic limitations, sometimes they are *unable* to do the right (or permissible) action for the right reason.

Moral norms are those norms that specify what they should do, given their epistemic limitations. That is, the moral obligations of a conscientious agent are determined by reasons that are *available* to the agent. Morally conscientious people should do the action that is supported by the balance of reasons that are available to them.[11] The Conscience Constraint seems correct

---

[10] Peter A. Graham, "Two Arguments for Objectivism about Moral Permissibility," *Australasian Journal of Philosophy* 99.1 (2021): 112.

[11] The view I express here is very similar to Lord's: Errol Lord, "Acting for the Right Reasons, Abilities, and Obligation," *Oxford Studies in Metaethics* 10 (2015): 26–52.

insofar as it identifies moral norms by actions that are dictated by moral conscience. The problem with Zimmerman's formulation of the constraint is that he identifies the moral ought by the *content* of the morally conscientious person's beliefs. A better way to capture the truth behind the Conscience Constraint is to identify moral norms by rules that governs the *action* of the morally conscientious person.

> The Conscience Constraint*: the ought used in the morally conscientious person's *answer* to the deliberative question "What should I do?" when the person deliberates about a moral matter, is the moral ought.

Both notions of objective and subjective ought might be morally important. One specifies what the morally conscientious persons *aim at*, the other specifies *how they should act*. Recall that the two-level view says that Jill objectively should give B, whereas she subjectively should give A. Jill might know this. But this does not yet answer her deliberative question, "What should I do?" The two-level view should say which of these two oughts would answer her deliberative question. Intuitively, the answer to her deliberative question is that she ought to give drug A. That is, the subjective ought appears in her answer to the deliberative question. If so, given the Conscience Constraint*, the subjective ought is the moral ought. The subjective ought might be derived from the objective ought. That is, the ultimate goal of morally conscientious people is to do what they objectively should do, i.e., to do what they have most reason to. Because of their epistemic limitations, however, they might not be able to do what they have most reason to. The subjective ought specifies what they ought to do, when doing what they have most reason to do is not rationally achievable. The fact that the subjective ought is derivative from the objective ought does not make it morally less important, in the same way that epistemic justification is not less important than truth, insofar as we are concerned with epistemic norms. The moral ought is just the subjective ought, because it is the subjective ought that determines what morally conscientious people should do, when they deliberate about what they should do.[12]

---

[12] Nothing that I said here should be very controversial. Zimmerman himself thinks that the debate between himself and objectivists is purely verbal. They both agree that the ultimate goal is doing what is objectively right and avoiding what is objectively wrong. "As far as I can tell, therefore, *there is no substantive difference* between my position and that of my critics . . . they have merely adopted different terminology. Where I talk of achieving what is of value and avoiding what is of disvalue, they talk of doing what is right and avoiding what is wrong" (*Ignorance and Moral Obligation*, 45).

2. Scripture, Ignorance, and Uncertainty

The debate between the subjective view and the objective view, as discussed in the last section, is about which ought, subjective or objective, is the same as the moral ought. The debate is pressing when our judgments about subjective ought and objective ought come apart. There are two main cases of this type: *ignorance* and *uncertainty*. We are interested in the normative status of Scriptural injunctions. Do the cases of ignorance and uncertainty have any implication for the normative status of Scriptural injunctions? In this section, I will argue that ignorance *appears* to have no direct implications for the normative status of Scriptural injunctions, whereas the consideration of uncertainty offers us a rationale to maintain that our independent moral judgments are indeed reliable, even when they contradict Scriptural injunctions. Let's discuss ignorance and uncertainty sequentially.

Ignorance of the Justifying Reason

Consider the seemingly immoral action of φ-ing (e.g., wife-beating). Suppose we know that there are very strong reasons *against* φ-ing. Suppose also that there is no justifying reason for φ-ing that we are aware of. Imagine Scripture says that one may φ. According to the argument for strict adherence, henceforth the *Scripture-first view*, we have a moral permission to φ. The Scripture-first view argues that we are subjectively and objectively permitted to φ, and thus, according to both the subjective view and the objective view, we are morally permitted to φ. Let me explain how the Scripture-first view makes a case for this claim.

Consider this question. *Prior to Scripture*, did we have moral permission to φ, given our awareness of very strong reasons against φ-ing? According to the subjective view, *prior* to Scripture, we have a *moral* duty *not* to φ, since we *subjectively* ought *not* to φ.

What the objective view says about the question is more complex. According to the objective view, it is objectively wrong to φ if the balance of all reasons is against φ-ing. Prior to Scripture, did we have reasons to *believe* that the balance of all reasons is (probably) against φ-ing? The answer to this question depends on whether *skeptical theism* is true. In Chapter 2 I introduced skeptical theism as the conjunction of three theses

(ST1–ST3). We can express the gist of skeptical theism in terms of the following thesis:

> ST: We have no reason to reject this possibility: the moral reasons we know of are not representative of all reasons there are, or the relations we know of between different reasons are not representative of all the relations between different reasons.

Either ST is true or not. Suppose ST is false. If ST is false, then prior to our knowledge of Scripture, we are in a position to make a *probabilistic* judgment about our objective obligation regarding φ. It is probably objectively wrong to φ. However, there are three important points regarding the assumption that ST is false.

First, the falsity of ST can undermine the argument for strict adherence. If ST is false, it means that our independent moral reasoning is a good guide to objective moral truths. Our moral reasoning is reliable in the sense that our moral reasoning can reveal the objective normative status of actions, events and things. Therefore, if ST is false, the reliability of our independent moral judgments as defined in the prologue is true. Moreover, an important premise of the argument for Scriptural adherence is that we are not in a position to know whether God would make a mistake in saying that φ-ing is permissible. But if our independent moral reasoning shows that probably φ-ing is not objectively permissible, then God would probably make a mistake in declaring that φ-ing is permissible. Therefore, our knowledge of the objective moral status of φ-ing provides an important reason against interpreting Scripture at face value (that is, Moral Justification, stated in the beginning of the chapter, is probably true).

Second, the falsity of ST makes the classical problem of evil a very serious challenge to theism. In Chapter 2 we addressed the classical problem of evil. The seemingly pointless suffering of children and animals, according to the atheist, provides us with a reason against the existence of God. The theist's best move, I believe, is to say that the existence of *seemingly* pointless evils does not show that those evils are in fact pointless, because God might have justifying reasons, of which we are not aware, to let those seemingly evil things occur. But if ST is false, it means that we have good reasons to think that we are aware of all objective reasons. Therefore, we can know that there is no justifying reason for those seemingly pointless evils. They are genuinely pointless. Of course, the theist might still try to resist the classical problem of evil by trying to find a theodicy which shows that God has justifying reasons to allow those evil to occur; but this seems be an incredibly hard challenge for the theist.

Third, it is most likely that ST is true. We have in fact very good reasons to think that ST is true. Consider the case of Hitler. Hitler's actions result in many deaths. The estimation is that six million Jews died in the Holocaust. Around twenty million military personnel and thirty-four million non-Jewish civilians died in World War II. It is fair to say that Hitler is morally responsible for the death of those seventy-five million people. Given this, it seems that it is objectively justifiable for Hitler's mother to kill him when he was an infant, as she could save the lives of millions of people by killing him. But could she know that it was probably objectively permissible for her to kill his son? Of course not. She had no idea about that. It is implausible to think that our moral reasoning alone can provide us with the knowledge of objective moral truths. In Hitler's case, his mother is ignorant about the consequences of her action in the distant future. Consequences matter in determining what we objectively ought to do. We probably are very ignorant about the total consequences of our actions in the distant or even near future. The situation is even worse *for a theist*. A theist believes that there are other worlds beside the world that we know of. For example, there might be the world of angels. There might be other religious creatures of which we are not aware. There might also be natural nonearthly creatures. If we believe in nonlocal causality (which we should, given findings in quantum physics), our actions might have causal consequences across the universe. Our actions might also have consequences for other religious realms. For example, my action might have lethal consequences for some angels. We can't rule out these possibilities by reason alone. If we can't rationally rule out these possibilities, we are not in a position to know about the unseen and unseeable consequences of our actions in the near or distant future. It is thus unlikely that we have knowledge of objective moral truths. *For the rest of this chapter, let's assume that ST is true.*

If ST is true, *prior to Scripture*, I do not know that φ-ing is (probably) objectively wrong or permitted, everything considered.

Let's now discuss the situation *after* our knowledge of Scripture's permission to φ.

Assuming ST, we can't, in general, make a (probabilistic) judgment about objective wrongness, everything considered, unless a fully informed person informs us about it. And Scripture might be the best way for us to have access to the judgment of a fully informed being. Scripture, then, can inform us that we *objectively* may φ, everything considered. Therefore, *if the objective view is true*, *after* our knowledge of Scripture, we have reasons to believe that we morally may φ everything considered.

What happens to our *subjective* obligations *after* our knowledge of Scripture? According to the Scripture-first view, God, through Scripture, informs us that there is in fact a justifying reason for φ-ing. Subjective obligation is defined relative to *all* my evidence, and given this new evidence, I have to update my subjective obligations. Now, I have evidence that there is a justifying reason for φ-ing. I am not directly aware of the justifying reason to φ, I have evidence only of there being a justifying reason. The Scripture-first view might appeal to the following principle.

> *Evidence of Reasons.* Concerning one's moral obligations and permissions, there is (almost) no difference between evidence of *a fact that is a reason* to φ with a certain weight and evidence of *the fact that there is a reason* to φ with that weight.[13]

According to Evidence of Reasons, evidence of a fact that is a reason to φ with a certain weight is (almost) morally on a par with evidence of the fact that there is a reason to φ with that weight. They both create obligation or permission to φ, if the subjective view is true (and neither does if the objective view is true). If so, evidence of there being a morally justifying (or conclusive) reason for S to φ is evidence that S is morally permitted (or obligated) to φ. Evidence of Reasons is similar to the epistemological principle which says that evidence of evidence is evidence. The subjective view says that our moral obligations are determined by reasons that are *available* to us. Evidence of Reasons roughly says that evidence of there being a reason makes that reason available to us and thus makes it pertinent to our subjective obligations. The Scripture-first view, then, holds that Scripture, by making the justifying reason to φ available to us, creates a subjective permission to φ which amounts to a moral permission to φ, if the subjective view is correct.

Therefore, the Scripture-first view holds that, as long as we accept ST, the distinction between the subjective view and objective view with regard to Scriptural injunctions disappear. According to both of them, Scriptural injunctions express moral obligations and permissions.

---

[13] One might think that evidence of a fact that is a reason with a certain degree is slightly morally more important than evidence of the fact that there is a reason to φ with that weight. Everything that I say in this chapter is compatible with there being some differences between two pieces of evidence, providing that the difference is not very significant.

Uncertainty

While the lack of direct knowledge of the justifying reason might not work against the Scripture-first view, uncertainty does if we accept the subjective view. More specifically, assuming the subjective view, uncertainty about the moral implications of the action prescribed by Scripture provides us with a reason to hold that our independent moral judgments are in fact *reliable*.

In the previous chapter I argued for the Moses principle. Let me state it again.

> *Moses Principle.* If one receives very reliable testimony that one should φ, and the situation is such that one knows that if the testimony turns out to be wrong, one's φ-ing would be seriously wrong, but one has no idea of how wrong one's not φ-ing would be if the testimony turns out to be true, then one rationally ought not to act in accordance with the testimony.

The Moses principle is about the rationality of acting in accordance with our own moral judgment. In section 1, we discussed the Conscience Constraint*. The Conscience Constraint* identifies moral ought with our answer to the deliberative question. Consider the story of Moses and Khidr (Chapter 4). Suppose Moses asks himself what he should do, given Khidr's request that he make a hole in the boat. The Moses principle says that he rationally should act in accordance with his own judgment, that is, not make a hole in the boat. Applying the Conscience Constraint* to Moses's case, we may say that Moses *morally* ought not to make a hole in the boat. In other words, Moses's independent judgment about what he subjectively ought to do specifies what he morally ought to do.

In the argument for the rationality of Moses's disobeying Khidr's order, I set aside prudential considerations. The rationality of Moses's disobedience was established by considering only moral reasons. If the consideration of moral reasons makes it *rationally* obligatory for Moses to act in accordance with his own judgment, we could say that his moral conscience *dictates* acting in accordance with his own independent judgment. He would act against his moral conscience by acting otherwise. It is very natural to describe the dictates of his moral conscience as his moral obligation.

The objective view might say that the Conscience Constraint* is false. Moral obligations are objective obligations. But it is important to recall that it is *not rationally optional* for Moses not to make a hole in the boat.

A nonoptional requirement dictated by moral conscience is as important as a moral requirement whether or not we call it moral. Zimmerman makes a similar point in his response to the objective view regarding the Conscience Constraint.

> I frankly don't care whether the requirement to give John drug [A] in [the uncertainty case] is said to be moral, rational, reasonable, or something else, as long as it is recognized that it exists and that it is this requirement that is of ultimate concern to the conscientious person. Nonetheless, I should immediately add that it seems to me very natural to say that it *is* a moral requirement, in light of the fact that it is this requirement that is of ultimate concern, more particularly, to the *morally* conscientious person.... In Kant's terminology, the imperative that gives expression to the requirement is categorical, not hypothetical, *and it is recognized as such by the conscientious person himself.*[14]

Even if the objective view is correct and the Conscience Constraint* false, there is a categorical imperative for Moses not to make a hole in the boat. And if the Conscience Constraint* is true, as I believe it is, the categorical imperative would be a moral one.

The Moses case generalizes to morally controversial passages in Scripture. Suppose that Scripture says that one may beat one's wife when one fears that she is rebellious. The conjunction of the Moses principle and the Conscience Constraint* implies that a conscientious Muslim should think that it is *morally* impermissible to beat one's wife. The situation a conscientious Muslim faces vis-à-vis morally controversial passages is very similar to Jill's situation in the uncertainty case (section 1). They both know that what they should do might not be the best option, but their moral consciences call them to act according to their evidence, given the dire consequences that their mistakes would have in those cases.

In sum, the Conscience Constraint* reinforces the conclusion of the previous chapter by showing that deference to Scripture, when it contradicts our independent moral judgements, is *morally* impermissible. If so, then either God does not require or permit actions that conflict with our independent moral judgments or there can be cases where, despite God's intention to convey permissions for actions such as spousal abuse, one is morally

---

[14] Zimmerman, *Ignorance and Moral Obligation*, 46–47.

obligated not to do those actions. The Scripture-first view, then, needs to reject either the Moses principle or the Conscience Constraint*. Both principles look very plausible, though.

3. Ignorance Revisited

The debate between the objective view and the subjective view is about what creates moral obligation, morally relevant *facts*, or the *evidence* of them. The Scripture-first view holds that, since the facts that determine our objective obligations aren't affected by our *ignorance* of them, the ignorance of morally relevant facts underpinning Scriptural injunctions is irrelevant to the validity of the Scripture-first view, *if the objective view is correct*. It also holds that, since, as Evidence of Reasons states, there is no difference between the evidence of a fact that is a reason and the evidence of the fact that there is a reason, insofar as we are concerned with moral obligations, epistemic issues concerning ignorance have no impact on the validity of the Scripture-first view, *if the subjective view turns out to be correct*. Therefore, the Scripture-first view holds that, no matter whether the subjective view is correct or the objective view is correct, the ignorance of the reasons which underlie Scriptural injunctions is not morally important, insofar as obligations and permissions are concerned. While this might be true, if we have a particular picture of morality (which is admittedly very popular), I will argue in this section that there is an *alternative conception of morality* under which epistemic issues concerning ignorance works against the Scripture-first view.

Utilitarianism is an ethical theory according to which we are morally obligated to maximize the aggregate amount of happiness. Thomas Scanlon uses the term *philosophical utilitarianism* for a family of normative theories according to which fundamental moral facts are facts about individual well-being.[15] Philosophical utilitarianism can include nonutilitarian views. A philosophical utilitarian can be a nonmaximizer or even a nonaggregationist. As Scanlon points out, for many people it is hard to imagine how there could be any other starting points for morality besides facts about individual well-being. The debate between the objective view and the subjective view is best

---

[15] Thomas M. Scanlon, "Contractualism and Utilitarianism," in *Utilitarianism and Beyond*, ed. Amartya Sen and Bernard Williams (Cambridge: Cambridge University Press, 1982), 103–29.

understood when our picture of morality is philosophical utilitarianism. If philosophical utilitarianism is true, our objective obligations are determined by facts about individual well-being. On the other hand, we can define *philosophical expected utilitarianism* as a family of views according to which our moral obligations are determined by our evidence of facts about individual well-being. The distinction between the objective view and the subjective view corresponds to the distinction between philosophical utilitarianism and philosophical expected utilitarianism.

I submit that if either philosophical utilitarianism or philosophical expected utilitarianism is the correct moral view, the epistemic issues concerning ignorance have no impact on the Scripture-first view. However, there is an *alternative conception of morality* which rivals philosophical (expected) utilitarianism. Let's call this alternative the *Kantian view*. I focus on two strands of Kantian view. Let's call them the *agency view* and the *justifiability view*. According to the agency view, moral facts are fundamentally about how well agents exercises their will. According to the justifiability view, fundamental moral facts are about what actions are unjustifiable to others. If the Kantian view of morality is correct, hidden moral facts, even if we have some evidence of their existence, cannot affect our moral obligations.

Contrary to philosophical utilitarianism, the Kantian view holds that epistemic considerations are relevant to the *individuation* of fundamental moral facts. The Kantian view is similar to philosophical expected utilitarianism in that they both say that epistemic states are important to determine the content of morality. But for the Kantian view, epistemic considerations are important to morality, not only because morality is supposed to be action-guiding, but also because it is in the very nature of morality that morality has something to do with our epistemic states. Consider the ignorance case in section 1. The Kantian view says that the objective ought used in the statement that Jill ought to give the drug B has *no moral content*.[16] That is, the unknown fact that drug B improves John's well-being is not actually a moral reason for Jill to give drug B to him. It is only *potentially* a moral reason. That is, it would be a reason if it were known or should be known.

Insofar as we are concerned with the validity of Scripture-first view, our main concern is not the cases of pure ignorance. We are concerned with cases in which while we are ignorant about facts underpinning the moral

---

[16] See Thomas M. Scanlon, *Moral Dimensions: Permissibility, Meaning, Blame* (Cambridge, MA: Harvard University Press, 2010), 48.

judgment of a morally reliable source, through the judgment of the morally reliable source, we have evidence of the existence of those facts. By appealing to Evidence of Reasons, philosophical expected utilitarianism argues that the ignorance of moral reasons is not morally important if the morally reliable source makes those reasons available to us by testimony. The Kantian view denies this claim, though. According to the Kantian view, there is an Accessibility Constraint on potential moral reasons that can contribute to the determination of our moral obligations.

> *Accessibility Constraint.* S's moral obligations (and permissions) are sensitive to a (potential) moral reason R only if S can in principle become aware of R by reflection or investigation.

The Accessibility Constraint says that potential moral reasons that are inaccessible to us cannot make any contributions in the determination of our moral obligations. Recall that, according to Evidence of Reasons, evidence of there being a moral reason to φ contributes to create a subjective obligation to φ. If the Accessibility Constraint is true, *Evidence of Reasons* can't be true as such. Rather, there should be a restriction on the scope of reasons to which Evidence of Reasons applies. That is, Evidence of Reasons is true *only of* reasons that are in principle accessible to the agent. In other words, according to the *restricted version* of Evidence of Reasons, evidence of there being a morally justifying (or conclusive) reason R for S to φ is evidence that S is morally permitted (or obligated) to φ only if R is in principle accessible to S by reflection or investigation. In the previous section, the argument of the Scripture-first view concerning the irrelevance of ignorance was underpinned by Evidence of Reasons. However, it's important to note that the Scripture-first view is unable to employ the restricted version of Evidence of Reasons to support its stance on the irrelevance of ignorance.

The Scripture-first view contends that Scripture, by providing strong evidence of there being a conclusive reason to perform certain action, creates a subjective obligation to perform that action. But if the Accessibility Constraint is true, Scripture could provide us evidence of a moral obligation only if the reasons that make up the obligation are in principle accessible to us. If the reasons behind Scriptural injunctions are inaccessible to us, Scriptural injunctions can't be evidence of moral obligations.

How does the Kantian view support the Accessibility Constraint? Before I present the Kantian arguments for the Accessibility Constraint, let me provide some *intuitive support* for it. We can start by Judith J. Thomson's case, Day's End, which is another version of a normal ignorance case.

> *Day's End.* B always comes home at 9:00 p.m., and as usual the first thing he does is to turn the light on by flipping the light switch. Because of extraordinary series of coincidences unpredictable in advance by B, B's flipping the switch causes a release of electricity in a neighbor's house. His neighbor, A, unfortunately, was in the path of electricity and thus badly burned.[17]

We should know by now that the objective view holds that while B is not blameworthy, B's flipping the switch was impermissible. On the other hand, the Kantian view, in line with the subjective view, holds that B's flipping was morally permissible. Now let's slightly change the case.

> *Day's End 2.* Everything is similar to the original Day's End except that B's friend, C, who, B correctly believes, is a genius scientist and an admirable moral agent, finds out by a series of quantum calculations about the causal consequence of flipping the switch. While driving in her car, C calls B before he gets home and tells him not to flip the switch. Unfortunately, before C can explain why B should not flip the switch, she dies in a car crash.

Is it morally permissible for B now to flip the switch? There is an intuition that he should not. On the assumption that it is in principle possible for B to find out that the switch will electrocute his neighbor, the restricted version of Evidence of Reasons explains why B should not flip the switch. B has evidence of there being a reason not to flip the switch, which creates a subjective obligation for him. Now consider the following variant of Day's End 2.

> *Day's End 3.* Everything is like Day's End 2. B does not flip the switch and spends the night in darkness. The next day, B hires a decent electrician to examine the switch thoroughly. The electrician does not find anything abnormal with the switch. B knows that C's knowledge is vastly greater than the electrician's knowledge. But there is nothing further that he can do to examine the safety of the switch for himself and others.

---

[17] Judith Jarvis Thomson, *The Realm of Rights* (Cambridge, MA: Harvard University Press, 1990), 229.

There is an intuition that, this time, B may flip the switch. Despite the fact that he knows that the electrician's knowledge is not comparable to C's, he has done everything he could to examine the situation and minimize the risk to himself and others. The Accessibility Constraint explains the intuition behind Day's End 3. Given that the fact that flipping the switch electrocutes his neighbor is in no way accessible to B, that fact is not a moral reason for B not to flip the switch. C's testimony is misleading evidence. It misled B into thinking that there is a moral reason for him not to flip. In Day's End 2, B mistakenly assumed that he could figure out why C asked him not to flip the switch with further investigations. Now he finds out that that assumption is mistaken. Further investigations proved useless to show anything. B is not morally obligated not to flip the switch because the potential reason to flip the switch is not accessible to him.

One might worry that C's testimony can make moral reasons accessible to B that were not already available. Perhaps B ought to have consulted with a series of quantum physicists and highly trained engineers given the testimony of his genius friend, knowing that the friend's prediction would be more sophisticated than the electrician's. Or B could have spent more time learning about such matters. It's only really when B exhausts such avenues that we get the intuition that the relevant knowledge is necessarily inaccessible to B. Without C's testimony B would not have known about where to look and would not have known that the electrician's assessment was inadequate. C's testimony does not mean that B's evidence is the same as C's, but makes accessible to B *different* and new evidence. The same can be said about Scripture. Scripture makes accessible to us evidence that would not otherwise be accessible.[18]

The objection stated in the last paragraph is compatible with the Accessibility Constraint. The objection assumes that in Day's End 3, B believes that C's judgment is based on her knowledge of quantum physics. As I will explain shortly, this is not how I imagine Day's End 3. But for the sake of argument, suppose B suspects that C's judgment has something to do with quantum physics. If so, B has reason to think that there are some morally relevant quantum facts that he should look into. Accordingly, as the objection states, he should consult with a series of quantum physicists and highly trained engineers to find the morally relevant facts. Of course, if quantum

---

[18] Thanks to the anonymous referee for Oxford University Press who raised this objection. The hugely positive impact of the referee on this chapter goes well beyond this point.

physicists and highly trained engineers find nothing wrong with the switch, C's potential reason remains inaccessible to B and thus extraneous to his obligation. The objection is correct that C's testimony provides new evidence for B that there might be some morally relevant facts that he should know, and this is enough to create a moral obligation for B *to investigate*. C's testimony provides a new reason for B to investigate the matter and to consult with some quantum physicists. But after a thorough investigation, B would have no evidence that there are morally relevant facts accessible to him, and thus B has no moral reason not to flip the switch.

The way I imagined Day's End 3 is different from the way that the objection does. I imagine that B has no clue whatsoever about the basis of C's request. As far as B understands, C might have made her judgment for a number of reasons. There might be an electrical problem with the switch. Perhaps C knows that it is spiritually better for B to spend some time in darkness. Perhaps the light in the room has some negative impact on the wildlife outside of the house. Perhaps by not flipping the switch, B's moral self-esteem increases. Perhaps it is an aesthetic or legal issue. Or perhaps there is a reason that only a beautiful mind can see. If the case is like this, C's testimony creates a moral obligation for B to rule out only harmful near possibilities such as the electrical problem or perhaps the environmental effect. But when those options are examined, B has no further obligation, epistemic or moral. The case of Scripture is similar to Day's End 3. Consider the scenario where Muslims take the Scriptural injunction about wife-beating seriously, yet lack an understanding of it underlying purpose. In this context, they might have an obligation to explore potential justifications. Could there be any reasons to morally justify the practice? When they fail to discover any morally justifying reasons for the practice, if the Accessibility Constraint is true, Scripture does not grant them moral permission for wife-beating.

4. Kantian Arguments for the Accessibility Constraint

Beside the intuitive appeal of the Accessibility Constraint, we have principled arguments for it. The Kantian view, in fact, supports the Accessibility Constraint. In this section, I will reconstruct two Kantian arguments for the Accessibility Constraint, one from the agency view, the other from the justifiability view.

The Agency View

According to the agency view, the object of moral assessments is primarily our willing. What *happens* is not morally important. We choose a maxim and act in accordance with the maxim. If the maxim is okay, our action is permissible. If not, the action is impermissible. The maxim of an action is determined by what we see or should see. We act morally if we respond properly to what we see or should see.

The agency view holds that our response to the situation does not happen at just one particular instance. It happens in a temporally extended period. For this reason, things that we don't see are also important for the moral assessment of our action, providing that we could do things in the temporally extended period that would help us to see those things. As Barbara Herman puts it: "The requirements of obligation may not begin at the time of the required action.... The earlier carelessness involves its own moral fault, one caught not in maxims of action or response but in maxims of *preparation*."[19] When the agent does not have a proper maxim of preparation, that is, is not prepared to take into account all morally relevant properties of the situation, the agent is at fault. For example, suppose an agent promises to repay a debt on a certain date. The agent

> can be said to have adopted "repaying the debt" as her end. She is thereby required to take reasonable steps to ensure that she will be able to repay it, for she must, if she is rational, intend some sufficient means to her end. There are steps one can take (and so maxims one ought to have) to ensure that owed money is available, not spent or lost through carelessness; there are things one can do to diminish the likelihood of forgetting. In short, maxims of sufficient means must be taken for the morally required end. When the agent fails to have such preparatory maxims, she is morally at fault.[20]

Sometimes we are not prepared enough to deal with a situation. Perhaps we don't have enough time to discover all morally relevant facts, or we have not thought about the situation well enough, or some vices of ours have clouded

---

[19] Barbara Herman, *The Practice of Moral Judgment* (Cambridge, MA: Harvard University Press, 1993), 100.
[20] Herman, *Practice of Moral Judgment*, 100–101.

our vision. In such circumstances, the testimony of a moral expert can help us to make the right call. The moral expert informs us about a reason that we would see, had we been prepared enough. When the agent is not prepared enough to deal with a moral situation, the testimony helps him to become more prepared. But when agents are prepared enough, they form the right maxim and respond properly to the situation. If they respond properly, they cannot make a moral mistake. Based on the agency view, we can reconstruct the following argument for the Accessibility Constraint.

(1) Moral agents who respond well to their maxim and who are prepared enough to deal with the situation cannot make a moral mistake.
(2) Were moral considerations inaccessible to a prepared moral agent to contribute to determine the moral obligation of the agent, the agent described in premise (1) could make a moral mistake.
(3) Therefore, moral considerations inaccessible to a prepared a moral agent do not contribute to determining the moral obligation of the agent.

In the previous chapter, we discussed three legitimate examples of moral testimony. The soldier case concerns a soldier who should listen to his commander and fire the artillery at the street where the children are playing. The doctor case concerns a morally uneducated doctor who should listen to the ethics committee of the hospital asking her to remove the respirator from the patient. The case of Anne Elliot concerns an emotionally inexperienced nineteen-year-old girl in love with a handsome young naval officer. She may listen to the advice of her wise aunt not to marry the young officer. These three cases are legitimate cases of moral testimony. They are all legitimate cases of moral testimony *precisely because the agent is not prepared enough* to respond properly to a grave moral situation.

In the soldier case, given that time is pressing and the soldier knows that his view is limited, he may rely on the testimony of his commander. He has evidence that there is a reason for him to fire. This reason is in principle accessible to him. He does not know the reason now because his sight is limited. His limitation, however, is ideally removeable by him. He could become more prepared for this situation. There are ways for him to be prepared to respond properly to the moral situation, but he just does not have time to perform those preparatory steps, and this is why he should rely on the moral testimony of his commander.

In the doctor case and the case of Anne Elliot, the testimony is legitimate because the agents know that their reasoning is defective, and they can make up for that by relying on the testimony. In these cases, too, the relevant reason is in principle accessible to the agent. If the doctor spent some time reflecting on ethical issues relevant to her work, she would know what to do in these situations. It is because of her lack of reflection that she may legitimately rely on the ethical committee of the hospital. She is not prepared to respond appropriately to the situation. Anne also is not prepared to think about the situation properly. She is too inexperienced and emotional. Her emotions cloud her judgment. She needs more time. By having more experience, she could see what her adviser can see now.

The case of Muslims in the wife-beating example is different from these cases. They don't believe that they could become more prepared about the case by more reflections or observations. In contrast to the soldier case, they are not restricted by time to prepare themselves to deal with the situation. Unlike the doctor case, they don't believe that they did not reflect enough on the situation. Muslims in such a situation have done everything in their power. They are prepared enough to form their maxim properly and respond to it.

The Justifiability View

According to the justifiability view, we are fundamentally interested in justifying our actions to others. The ultimate reason for us not to do a wrong action is not, contrary to what philosophical utilitarianism claims, that the action detracts from happiness; it is rather that we cannot justify such an action to others on the grounds that they are willing to accept. This is in fact a Kantian view of morality in the sense that morality is ultimately about respecting the rationality of ourselves and others. One particular conception of the justifiability view, which is popular among contemporary moral philosophers, is Scanlon's *contractualism*.[21] On Scanlon's view, the following principle gives an account of the nature of moral wrongness.

> *Scanlon's Principle.* An act is wrong if its performance under the circumstances would be disallowed by any system of rules for the general

---

[21] See Thomas M. Scanlon, *What We Owe to Each Other* (Cambridge, MA: Harvard University Press, 2000).

regulation of behavior which no one could reasonably reject as a basis for informed, unforced general agreement.

According to Scanlon's principle, when we formulate various general principles of behaviors, those which cannot be reasonably rejected by rational agents concerned to justify their actions to others are true principles of morality. I will argue that Scanlon's principle supports the Accessibility Constraint. Consider the following two general principles.

> *Allowing Known Harm.* We *may* significantly harm a group of people (e.g., beat rebellious women) solely on the basis of the fact that a morally reliable source says that we are permitted to harm that group of people, even when, after a thorough rational and empirical investigation, we find no evidence of the basis of the morally reliable source's verdict.
>
> *Rejecting Known Harm*: We *may not* significantly harm a group of people solely on the basis of the fact that a morally reliable source says that we are permitted to harm that group of people, when, after a thorough rational and empirical investigation, we find no evidence of the basis of the morally reliable source's verdict.

Rejecting Known Harm aligns with the Accessibility Constraint, whereas Allowing Known Harm contradicts it. According to Scanlon's principle, if one can reasonably reject any of these two principles, it can't be a guiding principle of morality. Can one reasonably reject Allowing Known Harm or Rejecting Known Harm? We have to examine first what group of people might find these principles objectionable.

Concerning Allowing Known Harm, the group of people permitted to be harmed by the principle—let's call them the Victims—find the principle objectionable. In the wife-beating example, the Victims are almost all women. Women who would lose their safety by this principle find the principle of wife-beating very objectionable.

It is harder to determine who finds Rejecting Known Harm objectionable. We don't know why the morally reliable source permits the harming of the Victims. There are at least two possibilities. Perhaps, the morally reliable person says that it is permissible to harm the Victims because harming them will greatly benefit them in the future (for example, beating women will help them to find a better place in heaven). Or perhaps the morally reliable person says that it is permissible to harm the Victims because harming them prevent *another* group of people—call them the X's—from being harmed. If so, the Victims or the X's should find Rejecting Known Harm objectionable since they would be affected by our not harming the Victims.

However, Victims can have various rational grounds to prefer Rejecting Known Harm to Allowing Known Harm even if there is a chance that Allowing Known Harm will benefit them in the future. For example, if the Victims are risk-averse, they have prudential grounds to prefer Rejecting Known Harm to Allowing Known Harm since it is rational for them to prefer not being harmed now to not possibly being benefited to an unknown degree in the future. Moreover, Victims might find Allowing Known Harm paternalistic. It is rational for them to honor their liberty and safety rather than to allow their freedom and safety to be restricted for an unknown benefit in the future. Therefore, Victims would not rationally reject Rejecting Known Harm in favor of Allowing Known Harm.

What about the X's? The X's might find Rejecting Known Harm objectionable because it imposes on them the risk of being harmed. In general, we should not *recklessly* impose a risk of being harmed on people. However, the risk that is imposed on the X's is *not* reckless. As the principle states, a thorough investigation has been made. In general, we cannot avoid all behaviors that involve risk. Consider the development and the use of a vaccine, the construction of a bridge, or the use of airplanes. They all involve risks. We know that it is very likely that some people will be killed during the construction of bridges, some people will be killed by planes crashing into their houses, some people will be killed by experiments necessary for new vaccines or medicines. Risks cannot be avoided in our life. However, as Scanlon notes, "Our idea of 'reasonable precautions' defines the level of care that we think can be demanded: a principle that demanded more than this would be too confining, and could reasonably be rejected on that ground."[22] Note also that the cost that people pay when a plane falls on their house is very high. It is their life. The cost that they pay is much greater than the benefit each of us gets from riding an airplane. In this sense, their complaint is stronger than the benefit of each one of us. Yet, as long as reasonable precaution is taken, they cannot reasonably reject a principle merely on the ground that the principle put their life at risk. Riding airplanes is part of our normal life.

---

[22] Scanlon, *What We Owe*, 209.

To reasonably reject Rejecting Known Harm, the X's should be able to say that the possible risk the principle imposes on them is known to be more significant than the definite harm the Victims will be subjected to by Allowing Known Harm. Can they? The X's might say that, given the reliability of the moral source, it is very likely that they would be harmed significantly greater than the Victims. But this is not true. It is unknown to what extent and to what group Rejecting Known Harm poses risks. For example, there is the possibility that the moral source's verdict is not because harming the Victims prevent anybody beyond the Victims from being harmed. It might be that harming the Victims now is good for them in the future. The point is that the X's are not in a position to know the *likelihood*, or the *magnitude*, of the possible burden that Rejecting Known Harm will impose on them. The X's are not in a position to claim that reasonable precautions have not been taken to avoid potential future harm. Therefore, it looks like that the Victims are in a better position to reasonably reject Allowing Known Harm than the X's are to reject Rejecting Known Harm.

The Victims can reasonably reject Allowing Known Harm on the grounds that while they would pay a *significant* price by this principle, the price that the X's pay would be *unknown* and *uncertain*, and that *extreme precautions* are taken to minimize the possible risk that Rejecting Known Harm might have for others.

If, as I have argued, Rejecting Known Harm cannot be reasonably rejected by the X's or the Victims, and Allowing Known Harm can be reasonably rejected by the Victims, Allowing Known Harm is not justifiable to others, and thus it is not a true principle of morality. If Allowing Known Harm is not true, then evidence of the facts that are not accessible to us by reflection and investigation cannot be taken as evidence of moral obligation. This establishes the truth of the Accessibility Constraint.

The above argument does not apply to legitimate cases of moral testimony such as the soldier case or the doctor case. The soldier case and the doctor case are different, at least, in two important respects. First, due to time constraints, the agent cannot take necessary precautions to minimize risk in these cases. Second, the soldier's and doctor's background information indicates that the moral expert is judging death versus death. In other words, both choices of the doctor or the soldier would cause the victims almost the same amount of harm. The lack of necessary precautions and the knowledge of almost equal degree of harms to victims of either choice make the soldier case and the doctor different from the case discussed above. Because of the lack of precautions and the knowledge of almost equal degrees of harm caused by either choice, the above argument does not apply to the soldier case or the doctor case.

5. Moral Knowledge Optimism and the Muʿtazilites

Let's summarize what we've learned so far. Suppose you are a philosophical expected utilitarian. There are good reasons for you to accept the Conscience Constraint*. The Conscience Constraint* (together with the Moses principle) implies that conscientious Muslims, due to their uncertainty about the reasons behind Scriptural injunctions, have a moral duty to act in accordance with their own independent moral judgments. On the other hand, if you espouse a Kantian understanding of morality, the Accessibility Constraint looks very plausible. The Accessibility Constraint implies that when the reasons behind Scriptural injunctions are inaccessible to us by investigation or reflection, Scriptural injunctions can't determine the content of our moral obligations. So there are good reasons for both philosophical utilitarianism and the Kantian view to hold that our independent moral judgments—when they are made after sufficient empirical and ethical investigations—are *objectively* reliable in the sense that they *accurately* represent our moral obligations.

What is at the core of the arguments for the reliability of our independent moral judgments is that when the agent conscientiously, thoughtfully, carefully, responsibly and with enough preparation and investigation makes a moral judgment, that judgment is not morally mistaken. This picture of morality is in fact congenial to the Muʿtazilites' idea of morality. As we discussed in Chapter 2, the fundamental ethical notion for the Muʿtazilites' is the notion of *blameworthiness*. ʿAbd al-Jabbār built his whole ethical view on the notion of blameworthiness. If we define moral obligations in terms of blameworthiness (as ʿAbd al-Jabbār does), then the subjective view is correct; Jill in the ignorance case is not blameworthy to act in accordance with her own judgment. More importantly, if the notion of blameworthiness defines moral obligations, the Conscience Constraint* would be undeniable. In the uncertainty case, Jill would be blameworthy to give "the right" drug. Therefore, the Conscience Constraint* is certainly true on ʿAbd al-Jabbār's view. Moreover, while it is very hard to know if ʿAbd al-Jabbār's ethical view is more in line with philosophical expected utilitarianism or the Kantian view, the fact that he does not believe that we have a general duty to promote happiness, and the fact that the notion of desert is a right-making aspect on his theory suggests that Kantian intuitions are not alien to 'Abd al-Jabbār's ethical view. True, he says that we are not blameworthy if we act in accordance with Scriptural injunctions when they are in conflict with our independent moral judgments. But it is hard to see why we *would be* blameworthy to act on the basis of our own judgments, assuming that we are morally prepared enough and that we act responsibly enough by considering moral principles that nobody can reasonably reject.

In the case of the killing of animals, 'Abd al-Jabbār thinks that while reason prohibits us from killing animals, revelation defeats this prohibition of reason (see Chapter 2). However, there are other cases of the conflict between reason and revelation where 'Abd al-Jabbar seems to be on board with relying on reason. A notable example is the case of the torture of the children of pagans. A question that is often addressed in the theological books of the Mu'tazilites is whether God would torture pagans' children. The Ash'arites see no problem in this. They hold that the Qur'anic passage about Noah's Ark supports their view. The passage suggests that the prophet Noah says that the children of pagans are unbelievers and thus they will go to hell. Noah said, "My Lord, do not leave of the unbelievers a single dweller on earth. If You leave them, they will mislead your servants, and will breed only wicked unbelievers" (71:26–27). In response, 'Abd al-Jabbār discusses the nature of torture at some length and concludes that it would be in fact wrong to torture someone for the wrongdoing of someone else and that God would never commit such wrongdoing.[23] There is a consensus among Mu'tazilites and Imāmiyya theologians that the Qur'anic passage just cited should be interpreted in a way that does not imply that children may go to hell when they are children.

Concerning the torturing of children, 'Abd al-Jabbār thinks that reason can discover the moral nature of the torture and there is nothing hidden about the matter that God could inform us about. We might ask ourselves, however, what the difference is between the case of the torturing of children and the case of the killing of animals. Why does 'Abd al-Jabbār downplay the judgment of reason in one case but not in the other? It might be because the Qur'anic passage 71:26–27 is not clear, whereas the permissibility of

---

[23] 'Abd al-Jabbār, *Sharh al-usul al-khamsah* (Cairo: Maktabat Wahbah, 1996), 477–83.

meat-eating in the Qur'an is very clear—that is, 'Abd al-Jabbār has *linguistic* reasons to deny the Ash'arites' literal interpretation of 71:26–27. But 'Abd al-Jabbār does not rely solely on *linguistic* reasons. He justifies his interpretation by first presenting a moral argument against the permissibility of torturing children. I suspect that 'Abdal- Jabbār's discriminatory treatment of these two cases is the result the fact that he is truly convinced that torturing children is very wrong, whereas he does not have such a strong conviction when it comes to meat-eating.

'Abd al-Jabbār's ethical theory shows that he is optimistic about the power of reason in discovering moral truths. He thinks that the human mind can grasp the bases of all evil and that the cognition of aspects is what should guide us in our moral behavior. From here, it would not be such a huge leap to say that humans are blameworthy only for not responding to moral aspects they can see. It is in the spirit of his moral theory to deny that evidence of moral features that are humanly inaccessible to us can create moral obligations for us.

Another notable example of Mu'tazilites' and Imāmiyyas' optimism about the power of reason in discovering moral truths concerns the notion of God's assistance (*lutf*). God's assistance is God's help for people to achieve the highest possible good. The Mu'tazilites and the Imāmiyya believe that there are many instances of God's assistance. One clear instance of God's assistance is his sending prophets to guide us. According to the Mu'tazilites and the Imāmiyya, sending prophets is an instance of God's assistance (*lutf*) through which God helps people to act morally and achieve the highest good. According to the Mu'tazilites and the Imāmiyya, God's sending prophets is morally obligatory for God because it is something that helps God to achieve His morally good ends. But a challenge for the Mu'tazilites and the Imāmiyya is this: How do we know that there aren't hidden wrong-making aspects in sending prophets? In the following passage, al-Hillī (1250–1325), an Imāmiyya theologian, whose moral theory is highly influenced by the Mu'tazilites, responds to this objection:

> Given that having a good making aspect is not sufficient for an act to be obligatory, one might object that God's assistance is morally obligatory only when it has no wrong-making aspect. How do you know that there is no unknown wrong-making aspect in the act of God's assistance? Answer: We know all wrong-making aspects. If a wrong-making aspect were unknown, we would not be obligated not to do it, and thus it would

not be a wrong-making aspect. This is not an argument for the knowledge of non-existence from the non-existence of knowledge.[24]

Al-Hilli's argument is simple: if we don't know P is a moral reason against φ-ing, P can't be a reason against φ-ing. The argument is just an endorsement of the subjective view. But the interesting thing about the argument is that it is an argument against the possibility of God's having unknown moral reasons. The argument does not only say that *our* obligations are not sensitive to reasons unknown to us. It also says that *God's* obligations are not sensitive to reasons unknown *to us*. While the argument is insufficient to establish the latter view, the Mu'tazilites and the Imāmiyya need that claim to prove God's obligation to send prophets. At this point, we might think the Mu'tazilites and the Imāmiyya optimism about moral knowledge goes beyond the Accessibility Constraint. What they might have in mind is the denial of skeptical theism (ST) (see section 2). If ST is false, as we discussed in section 2, we are in a position to make judgments about objective wrongness, everything considered. The ability to make judgments about objective wrongness, everything considered, can directly establish the reliability of our independent moral judgments and block the argument for strict adherence.

On the other hand, as I explained in section 2, the denial of ST makes the classical problem of evil a very hard problem for theists. I discussed the *parallel evil argument* in Chapter 2 (section 5). The argument's conclusion was this: *either* the appearance of pointless evil undermines the belief that there is an omniscient, omnipotent, and omnibenevolent God, *or* our intuition that a certain action is immoral provides us no reason to think that it would be against God's nature to say that the action is morally right. By rejecting ST, we accept the conclusion's first disjunct, that is, that the appearance of pointless evil undermines the belief in God.

There are *three different ways* to establish the truth of the reliability of our independent moral judgments. One direct way is to deny ST. The other two ways involve endorsing either the Accessibility Constraint or the Conscience Constraint* (in conjunction with the Moses principle). The advantage of the latter two solutions for a theist is that they are consistent with ST. As well as being plausible, ST helps the theist to respond to the classical problem of evil. A theist who accepts either the Accessibility Constraint or the Conscience

---

[24] Allāmah al-Ḥillī, *Kashf al-murād fī sharḥ Tajrīd al-i'tiqād* (Bayrūt: Mu'assasat al-A'lamī, 1988), 304. *Kashf al-Morad* was written by al-Hillī to explain and comment on the short book by another Imāmiyya theologian, al-Tusi (d. 1274), called *Tajrid al-Itiqad*.

Constraint* can appeal to ST to respond to the classical problem of evil, saying that although we don't know whether God's allowing a seemingly pointless evil is in fact wrong, we do in principle know *our* moral obligations. That is, our knowledge of human morality has no implication about our knowledge of God's morality. If so, the theist could deny that natural evil and prescribed evil are parallel.

The main premise of the parallel evil argument in Chapter 2 is that natural evil and prescribed evil are parallel in the sense that if the appearance of pointless natural evil is compatible with God's having a hidden justifying reason for allowing it, then our independent moral judgment that an action prescribed by Scripture (e.g., wife-beating) is immoral is also compatible with there being a hidden justifying reason for us to perform that action. By accepting either the Accessibility Constraint or the Conscience Constraint* (in conjunction with the Moses principle), theists can deny this parallel. That is, they can say that the reliability of our independent judgments about our moral obligation has no implication for the reliability of our judgments about God's obligations. While God may have hidden reasons to allow natural evil, we may not accept Scriptural commands that are incompatible with our independent moral judgments. Accepting either the Accessibility Constraint or the Conscience Constraint* also allows us to hold that either Moral Justification is true or God's Reliability is false. That is, either God, for some moral reasons, did not intend to convey seemingly immoral injunctions, or we are not morally permitted to go against our independent moral *even if* God has commanded us to do so. If either Moral Justification is true or God's Reliability is false, then the argument for strict adherence collapses.

In sum, the main claim of this chapter is that when an agent conscientiously, thoughtfully, carefully, responsibly, and with enough preparation and investigation makes a moral judgment, that judgment is not morally mistaken. This view is in fact congenial to the Muʿtazilites' idea of morality. Although there is evidence that the Muʿtazilite and the Imāmiyya endorse the Scripture-first view (see Chapter 2), given that their view is congenial to the Accessibility Constraint, the Conscience Constraint*, and even the denial of ST, it is in the spirit of their views to accept the reliability of our independent moral judgments. The Muʿtazilites did not distinguish between optimism about our knowledge of human morality and optimism about our knowledge of God's morality. In light of the Accessibility Constraint and the Conscience Constraint*, we are able to be optimistic about our knowledge of human morality without having to be optimistic about our knowledge of God's morality.

6. The Case of Abraham

A very well-known example of the conflict between morality and revelation is the case of Abraham's sacrifice. I finish the chapter by applying the conclusions of the chapter to the case of Abraham. God asked Abraham to kill his son. The Old Testament tells us that Abraham wanted to sacrifice Isaac, whereas most Islamic thinkers believe that in the Islamic version of the story, the son to be sacrificed is Ishmael.[25] In conformity with the Islamic version, I will refer to the son that Abraham wanted to sacrifice as Ishmael.

I assume that, independent of the moral content of the command, Abraham has good epistemic reasons to think the revelation is from God. It might be epistemologically hard to have a very high degree of confidence that God has spoken to you. But I am not concerned with the epistemology of religious experience. I just assume that Abraham has conclusive reasons to believe that the source of his revelation is God. The question is whether God's command could provide a justification for Abraham's sacrifice in a *testimonial manner*, that is, whether God's words would justify Abraham's believing in an obligation that was *already* in place *without* God's command. For example, God might know that Ishmael would become a Hitler-like figure in the future, and killing him now would be the only way to prevent a future moral catastrophe. In this scenario, God knows that killing Ishmael is required, independent of His command, and His command would inform Abraham about the existence of such an obligation.

However, as I have argued, as long as God's reasons are completely unknowable to Abraham, there can be no existing obligation for Abraham to kill his son. Abraham's morality is not affected by hidden facts that he is unable to know. To illustrate, we can apply the Moses principle to Abraham's case. If Abraham kills his son and it turns out that he should not have, he has made a horrendous mistake. But if he does not kill his son and it turns out that he should have, he has no idea how serious his wrongdoing would be. The Moses principle says that it would be more rational for Abraham to act with his own understanding in this situation. According to the Conscience

---

[25] There are Islamic scholars, however, who believe that the "great sacrifice" was Isaac. See al-Tabarī, *Tafsīr al-Tabarī*, ed. 'Abd Allah b. 'Abd al-Muhsin al-Turki et al., vol. 19 (Cairo: Dar Hajar, 1422/2001), 587–92.

Constraint*, this requirement is a moral requirement. Morality, then, demands that Abraham not kill his son.

The Accessibility Constraint also implies the same conclusion. Abraham's obligation is not sensitive to reasons that are in principle inaccessible to him. The reasons that speak in favor of Abraham's killing his son (if there are any) are beyond Abraham's intellect. Abraham's lack of knowledge of those reasons is not due to a failure of reasoning or a lack of precaution or investigation on his part. According to the Accessibility Constraint, then, Abraham is not permitted to sacrifice his son. Therefore, God's command to kill Abraham's son cannot provide moral justification, through testimony, for him to kill his son. If so, it might be reasonable for Abraham to appeal to Moral Justification and to doubt whether he should take God's words literally. This is what Kant thinks about Abraham's sacrifice.[26]

> Abraham should have replied to this supposedly divine voice: "That I ought not to kill my good son is quite certain. But that you, this apparition, are God—of that I am not certain, and never can be, not even is [if] this voice rings down to me from (visible) heaven."[27]

Kant thinks the content of revelation undermines the reasons Abraham has for the authenticity of revelation. I *assumed* that Abraham had strong reasons for the authenticity of his experience. If Abraham had good reasons that the revelation was from God, an option for him is to question whether God really meant that he should kill his son.

The story itself suggests that God did not in fact command Abraham to kill his son. The story tells us that God ultimately stopped Abraham from killing Ishmael, which implies that God did not want Abraham to kill his son in the first place. This understanding of the Qur'anic passages is not unfamiliar to the Islamic tradition. For instance, *Tafsīr al-Tabarī*, which is the earliest major commentary on the entire Qur'an, written by Muhammad ibn Jarīr al-Tabarī (838–923), suggests that Abraham was not commanded to kill his son. During the reign of the Samanid king Mansur ibn Nuh, scholars tasked

---

[26] Robert Merrihew Adams also defends the same position in his book *Finite and Infinite Goods: A Framework for Ethics* (New York: Oxford University Press, 1999), especially on 284–92.

[27] Immanuel Kant, *The Conflict of the Faculties*, trans. Mary Gregor (Lincoln: University of Nebraska Press, 1975), 115.

to translate and summarize al-Ṭabarī's commentary distilled his view on Abraham's sacrifice as follows:

> And the other possibility is that this sacrifice was not commanded by God to Abraham, if it was, Abraham should have done it. It was Abraham's vow to God, the Almighty and God, the Almighty, tested him to see if he kept it. . . . And blessed and holy God did not demand that he kill his son; He only asked for his heart and willingness to keep his word. This is why the Angel Gabriel did not come to speak with him, a dream sufficed.[28]

The story was never about Abraham killing his son, according to this understanding. Killing the son was never commended. The dream was rather a test of Abraham's sincerity.

The Islamic story of Abraham's sacrifice is different from the one told by the Old Testament in a very important moral respect. While the issue of Isaac's consent in the Old Testament is unclear, the Islamic story explicitly says that Ishmael consented to his being sacrificed for God.

> Then, when he was old enough to accompany him, he said, "O My son, I see in a dream that I am sacrificing you; see what you think." He said, "O my Father, do as you are commanded; you will find me, God willing, one of the steadfast." (Qur'an 37:102)

If al-Ṭabarī is right about Abraham's dream being a test of sincerity, Abraham's best strategy was to look at whether he could fulfill his vow without engaging in any immoral behavior. This is exactly what Abraham does in the Islamic story; he asks for Ishmael's opinion on the matter and proceeds with the sacrifice only after Ishmael consents to it. Ishmael's consent may remove some moral objections to Abraham's killing. If it is permissible for one to sacrifice oneself for God upon one's belief that God has so requested, then it is permissible for Abraham to sacrifice Ishmael on his behalf. In other words, if Ishmael has the moral power to sacrifice himself, he can vest this power in someone else. If so, Abraham might not wrong Ishmael by sacrificing him. Of course, there is a worry that Ishmael might be too young to give consent to being sacrificed. There is also a worry that Abraham might transgress his parental duty by involving his son in the situation. But the fact that Abraham

---

[28] Tarjume-yi tafsīr-i Ṭabari, ed., Ḥabīb Yaghmā'ī, vol. 6 (Tehran: University of Tehran, 1960), 1529.

seeks Ishmael's consent mitigates significantly his possible transgression of morality.

To sum up, God's command could not provide a justification for Abraham in a testimonial manner to kill his son. But could God's command provide a justification for Abraham to kill his son in *a nontestimonial manner*? I will return to this question in the last section of the next chapter.

In this chapter, I argued that, contrary to arguments presented by the Scripture-first view, we have good reason to accept the reliability of our independent moral judgments. This is not by itself sufficient to solve the problem of divinely prescribed evil, since the problem is generated by the tension between three theses: the divinity of Scripture, the existence of seemingly prescribed evil, and the reliability of our independent moral judgments. We assumed the truth of the divinity of Scripture. I argued for the existence of prescribed evil in the prologue and I argued for the reliability of our independent moral judgments in this chapter. Given the truth all three theses, the only possible way, then, to solve the problem of prescribed evil is to argue that the theses are in fact compatible with each other, and this is what I am going to do in the next chapter.

6
The Hermeneutics of Scripture

Summary of the Chapter

Section 1. There are two ethics-first solutions for the problem of prescribed evil. According to the second solution, the problem arises only if we have a *moral* interpretation of Scriptural injunctions and can be removed once we reject that interpretation in favor of a *legal* interpretation of Scriptural injunctions.

Section 2. This section discusses Ibn Tufayl's philosophical tale, *Hayy ibn Haqzān*. This story can help us to understand the social function of religious laws and why it is rational to legislate immoral rules under nonideal conditions.

Section 3. The debate between legal positivism and the natural law theory, in light of the moral language of law and the normativity of law, is explained. The planning conception of law is a promising way to make sense of the normativity of law under nonideal conditions.

Section 4. Based on the planning conception of law, an argument for Legal Interpretation is offered. This argument reveals that there is a grain of truth in the contextualization view.

Section 5. This section discusses the moral functions of Scripture in our modern world.

1. Ethics-First Solutions to the Problem of Prescribed Evil

The thesis of *the existence of seemingly prescribed evil* asserts that there are some actions prescribed or permitted by the best linguistic interpretation of Scriptural passages which seem immoral, according to our independent moral judgments. As discussed in the prologue, there are two strategies adopted by modern Islamic scholars to deny that thesis: the *reinterpretation view*, and the *contextualization view*. The reinterpretation view attempts to find *linguistic* reasons to reconcile morally controversial passages with our modern moral sensibilities, while the contextualization view seeks to limit the application of morally controversial passages to the time and the context of revelation. As we saw in the prologue, the major problem with the reinterpretation view is that our moral consciousness is forever broadening, which results in constant alterations in our moral judgments. Given the constancy of the text, and linguistic constraints on how best to interpret it, it is thus implausible to think that at any given time our independent moral judgments and the best interpretation of the text must coincide. On the other hand, the contextualization view faces two serious worries. First, according to our modern moral sensibilities, some actions prescribed by morally controversial passages seem to be wrong *even at the context of revelation*. Second, the contextualization view needs to justify why the application of the Scriptural passages should be limited to the context of revelation, and why those prescriptions are not still binding on us. Nevertheless, contextualization has a grain of truth to it that I will return to shortly.

In the previous chapter I argued that we have good reasons to think that *the reliability of our independent moral judgments*—according to which our independent moral judgments accurately represent our moral duties and moral permissions—is correct.[1] Assuming the divinity of Scripture, we might think that the reliability of our independent moral judgments is in tension with the existence of seemingly prescribed evil, because God is truthful: if God does not lie in Scripture, Scriptural injunctions cannot be false, in which case they would seem to communicate moral truths inconsistent with our independent moral judgments. To make the inconsistency clearer, it helps to see that the reliability of our independent moral judgments and the existence of seemingly prescribed evil appear inconsistent because the following thesis seems to be true:

Moral Interpretation. Actions prescribed or permitted by the best interpretation of a Scriptural passage are morally obligatory or permitted.

Moral Interpretation is justified on the grounds that, first, God or the Prophet uses *moral language* to express Scriptural injunctions and, second, that they

---

[1] In the prologue, I defined our independent moral judgments as moral judgments obtained through careful a priori moral reflections and sufficient empirical observations, independent of Scripture.

are truthful. If Moral Interpretation is correct, then, Scriptural injunctions should be regarded as expressing moral truths. But if the reliability of our independent moral judgments and the existence of seemingly prescribed evil are correct, some actions prescribed or permitted by Scriptural injunctions appear to be *immoral*. This seems to yield a conflict: the moral truths expressed in Scripture contradict the moral truths revealed by our independent moral judgments.

One way to resolve the tension between the reliability of our independent moral judgments and the existence of seemingly prescribed evil would be to say that it is morally permissible for God (or the Prophet) to utter falsehoods in Scripture. That is, the contradiction could be avoided if God's justice is consistent with the possibility of His lying. In fact, we can make a distinction between God's *act* of prescribing a rule and the *content* of what is prescribed by God. If God is just, what He *does* must be just. But from this it does not follow that *what is said by God* must be necessarily true. After all, there are such things as justified lies, and God may have reasons which justify His saying false things. It is not theologically inconsistent to say that Scripture is the word of a tri-omni God yet contains some falsehoods. This response may have some merit, but from a theological standpoint, it would be more desirable to find a solution that doesn't imply that God lies (even justifiably). Thus, I believe a better strategy for a believer is to reject Moral Interpretation altogether, in favor of Legal Interpretation.

> *Legal Interpretation.* Actions prescribed or permitted by the best interpretation of a Scriptural passage are *legally* obligatory or permitted, according to religious law. But God or the Prophet may legislate legal obligations or permissions that deviate from *moral* ones.

The importance of making a distinction between the legal and moral interpretations of Scriptural passages can also be found in the work of Fazlur Rahman. He observes that "in understanding the Qur'an's social reforms, however, we will go fundamentally wrong unless we distinguish between legal enactments and moral injunctions. Only by so distinguishing can we not only understand the true orientation of the Qur'anic teaching but also solve certain knotty problems with regard, for example, to women's reform."[2] If Legal Interpretation is correct, there would be no

---

[2] Fazlur Rahman, *Major Themes of the Qur'an* (Chicago: University of Chicago Press, 2009), 30–31.

inconsistency between the reliability of our independent moral judgments, the existence of seemingly prescribed evil, and the divinity of Scripture. Legal Interpretation does not imply that God or the Prophet is not truthful. Rather, it only states that God can use Scriptural injunctions to issue legal obligations and permissions, and that legal permissions do not entail moral permissions. In other words, Legal Interpretation allows the theist to claim not only that *what God does* can be just (if He has sufficient reason to issue those legal prescriptions), but also that *what is said by God* is true under a legal interpretation, since the fact that Scriptural injunctions do not coincide with our independent moral judgments does not imply that they are false.

I presented *an ethics-first solution* to the problem of prescribed evil in Chapter 4, which involved suspending judgment about the reliability of our independent moral judgments in the objective sense while maintaining it in the rational sense. Put it differently, the first solution suggests that when it comes to morally controversial Scriptural passages, we find ourselves in a Moses-like situation in which we rationally should live according to human morality while suspending judgment about whether human morality captures the extension of true morality. Legal Interpretation opens up the possibility of *another ethics-first solution* to the problem of prescribed evil. According to this solution, while all of our three main theses are true, there is no inconsistency between them. The appearance of inconsistency is generated by Moral Interpretation. Once we reject Moral Interpretation in favor of Legal Interpretation, the inconsistency disappears.

Legal Interpretation also helps us to see the grain of truth in the contextualization view. Legal permissions and obligations are designed to solve the social problems of a community. When the structure of the community changes radically, new positive laws are needed. So it is very plausible to think that legal permissions and obligations specified in morally controversial passages need not extend to our modern societies. The contextualization view is correct, then, to limit the application of morally controversial passages to the context and the time of revelation; its error is in failing to distinguish moral permissions and prescriptions from legal ones. Once that distinction is made, we can argue that legal permissions and prescriptions by the Prophet do not entail moral ones, and this is what Legal Interpretation claims. The main question of this chapter, then, is how we can defend Legal Interpretation.

2. Lessons from a Philosophical Tale

Islamic philosophers such as al-Fārābī, Avicenna and Averroës held that human reason is capable of acquiring all truths (see Chapter 3). Ibn Tufayl (1105–1185), an Andalusian philosopher and a physician and counselor to the caliph, wrote his philosophical novel, *Hayy ibn Haqzān* (Living, Son of Awake), to illustrate how that might be possible. Ibn Tufayl's novel, however, is not only about the power of reason to discover the fundamental structure of reality, but also about the relationship between philosophy and religion, and this is where the novel can teach us a very important lesson about Scriptural injunctions.

Let me start by briefly describing the story for you. Hayy ibn Haqzān is a child raised alone on an equatorial island. Initially nursed by a doe, he gradually develops a sense of the world and learns to make things to satisfy his needs. Facing the death of his stepmother doe, and in hopes of finding a way to bring her back to life, he starts to learn about biology. The knowledge he gains in biology sets him on a path toward discovering more truths in psychology, metaphysics, and theology, and his spiritual journey also helps him to discover some moral truths about how to live.

When he considers what he may eat and what he may not, for instance, he realizes that eating other beings "would unavoidably cut them off from their own fulfillment and prevent them all from achieving their intended purpose. This would mean opposition to the work of the Creator and defeat the whole aim of drawing near Him and becoming like Him." On the other hand, he knows that he needs to eat, as matter of necessity for perfecting his soul. So, he decides that, when there are options, he should follow the following dietary practice:

> He would have to decide carefully what to eat so as to bring about the least opposition to the work of the Creator. Thus he could eat such things as the meat of fully ripened fruits, with seeds ready to reproduce, provided he was certain not to eat or harm the seeds or throw them in places unfit for vegetation—among rocks or in salt flats or the like. If it was hard to find fruit with nourishing meat, such as apples, plums, and pears, then he would have to eat either fruits in which only the seed had food-value, such as nuts and chestnuts, or else green vegetables—on condition that he pick only the most abundant and prolific and be sure not to uproot them or destroy the seeds. If none of these were available, then he must

eat meat or eggs, again being careful to take only from the most abundant and not root out a whole species. So much for his notion of what he should eat.³

Hayy decides that he should be a vegan eating fruits and nuts. Eating meat or eggs is permitted only if vegan options are not available. This practice is already in tension with the orthodox Islamic view on the ethics of eating, according to which eating the flesh of certain animals is not objectionable, providing that those animals are killed in an Islamic manner.

Later in the story we find that there is a nearby island on which a society of "the followers of a certain true religion" live. In particular, among them is a right-minded theist, called Absāl, who decides to travel to Hayy's island in search of some solitude. Absāl finally meets Hayy and teaches him his language. Upon hearing the story of Hayy's life and his findings, Absāl becomes certain that "all the traditions of his religion about God, His angels, bibles and prophets, Judgment Day, Heaven and Hell were symbolic representations of these things that Hayy Ibn Yaqzān had seen for himself."⁴ Absāl now is convinced that Hayy is a man of God, and that he should serve as his disciple and follow his example.

Hayy was also curious to learn about Absāl and his religion. When he hears about Absāl's religion, Hayy finds out that the prophet of Absāl's religion is a true messenger sent by God. "Hayy believed in this messenger and the truth of what he said. He bore witness to his mission as apostle of God."⁵ There were, however, two things that Hayy did not understand. First, he did not understand why the prophet used symbolic and metaphorical images to portray the divine world. This could increase the possibility of misunderstanding the truth. Second, he could not understand some rituals and moral truths brought by the prophet. The second worry is particularly relevant to our goal in this section.

> Second, why did he confine himself to these particular rituals and duties and allow the amassing of wealth and overindulgence in eating, leaving men idle to busy themselves with inane pastimes and neglect the Truth. Hayy's own idea was that no one should eat the least bit more than would keep him

---

³ *Ibn Tufayl's Hayy Ibn Yaqzan: A Philosophical Tale*, trans. Lenn Evan Goodman (Chicago: University of Chicago Press, 2015), 112–13.
⁴ Ibn Tufayl, *Hayy Ibn Yaqzan*, 145.
⁵ Ibn Tufayl, *Hayy Ibn Yaqzan*, 146.

on the brink of survival. Property meant nothing to him, and when he saw all the provisions of the Law to do with money, such as the regulations regarding the collection and distribution of welfare or those regulating sales and interest with all their statutory and discretionary penalties, he was dumbfounded. All this seemed superfluous.[6]

Hayy does not find the prophet's rulings about eating or trading very convincing. Nor does he find the symbolic language of the prophet helpful. In an effort to help others to find the Truth, Hayy and Absāl go to Absāl's island so that Hayy can teach them. They first choose a group of people who are Absāl's friends. The goal is to see whether Hayy could succeed in teaching this rather small group of people. The result turns out to be disastrous. The group resents Hayy and finds his teachings repugnant. Hayy's teachings make them even worse. In the end, Hayy despairs of helping the people on the island and gives up his hope of teaching them the truth.

Hayy had no knowledge of how people in Absāl's island would want to live their lives. This failed attempt to teach the truth to the people of the island, however, made him realize that humans are distracted by greed, that they are full of ignorance, and that they are corrupted by their passions. Teaching them the truth only makes them more pig-headed.[7] Ibn Tufayl concludes:

> Hayy now understood the human condition. He saw that most men are no better than unreasoning animals, and realized that all wisdom and guidance, all that could possibly help them was contained already in the words of the prophets and the religious traditions. None of this could be different. There was nothing to be added. . . . Any attempt to impose a higher task on them was bound to fail. The sole benefit most people could derive from religion was for this world, in that it helped them lead decent lives without others encroaching on what belonged to them. . . . If ever they were to venture beyond their present level to the vantage point of insight, what they had would be shattered, and even so they would be unable to reach the level of the blessed. They would waver and slip and their end would be all the worse.[8]

---

[6] Ibn Tufayl, *Hayy Ibn Yaqzan*, 148.
[7] Ibn Tufayl, *Hayy Ibn Yaqzan*, 151.
[8] Ibn Tufayl, *Hayy Ibn Yaqzan*, 154–55.

Having learned that the Truth is of no use to the people of Absāl's island, Hayy and Absāl leave Absāl's island and return to Hayy's island, where they live happily ever after.

The two islands in the story represent two different conditions: Hayy's island is the *ideal* island in which everybody—consisting of only two persons—wants to find the truth and live in accordance with it; Absāl's island, on the other hand, is the *nonideal* island in which people are full of greed and ignorance; they would not do "a single action that did not amount to seeking one of these vile, sensory aims: money making, pleasure seeking, satisfying some lust, venting rage, saving face, performing religious rites for the sake of honor, or just to save [their] neck[s]."

Ibn Tufayl's conclusion is that the rules governing in ideal conditions should be different from the rules governing in nonideal conditions. In ideal conditions, Hayy could, and should, live by the *correct* moral principles, for example, he should be a vegan. However, correct moral principles cannot be the governing laws in nonideal conditions. Sanctioning moral truths as the law of the nonideal island would make everybody worse off. Given this, it would be better for the corrupt people of the nonideal island to follow the teachings of their prophet. The function of the laws of the prophet is mainly to solve the social problems of the islanders: "The sole benefit most people could derive from religion was for this world, in that it helped them lead decent lives without others encroaching on what belonged to them." Let me express Ibn Tufayl's conclusions as follows:

> *The Social Function of Religious Laws.* The function of religious laws in a nonideal society is to solve the social problems of the community.
> *The Permissibility of Immoral Laws.* The best laws to solve the social problems of a community consisting of corrupt people are not necessarily correct moral principles.

Absāl's island is a place in which religious laws are legal laws. But when religious laws are legal laws, religious laws should play the same role as legal laws: they should regulate communal life. Ibn Tufayl's real insight lies in the understanding that religious laws, in their capacity as legal laws, can't function as the guiding principles for ideal conditions; instead, they are the laws that serve in nonideal circumstances to make communal life possible. Although Absāl's island exists within the realm of fiction, the Islamic society that emerged during the time of the Prophet draws parallels to it. The legal laws governing the Islamic society at the time of revelation were the religious laws legislated by the Prophet. Consequently, Ibn Tufayl's understanding of the role of religious laws on Absāl's island similarly extends to the nascent Islamic society during the era of the Prophet.

To comprehend the role of religious law in such societies, a clear grasp of the nature of legal law is important. The next section explores two major contemporary approaches to understanding law's nature: legal positivism and natural law theory.

3. The Nature of Law

John Austin has famously said that "the existence of law is one thing; its merit and demerit another."[9] The two major contemporary views about the relationship between morality and the law, that is, legal positivism and natural law theory, can be understood with reference to Austin's claim. According to *legal positivists*, Austin is correct, and the existence and the content of the law does not depend on the merits of the law (the contemporary advocates of this view include Hart, Raz, and Shapiro, among others).[10] Their opponents, *the natural law theorists*, disagree: our conception of law is not detached from its moral or rational merits.

There is an important distinction among two kinds of natural law theory, though. According to the *strong* natural law view, the *existence* of law depends on its rational or moral merits. The *weak* natural view says that the existence of law does not depend on its rational or moral merits, its *nondefectiveness* does. To see the difference, consider the "laws" of an unjust authoritarian country. Are they laws? According to the strong natural law view, they are not real laws, whereas according to the weak view, they are actually laws, but they are *defective*. Finnis calls them "peripheral," "watered-down," or "borderline" instances of law. On the face of it, the strong natural law view is not very plausible. It certainly seems false to say, for instance, that nondemocratic countries have no laws. For this reason, while the strong version has its proponents

---

[9] John Austin, *The Province of Jurisprudence Determined*, ed. Wilfrid E. Rumble (Cambridge: Cambridge University Press, [1832] 1995), 157.
[10] H. L. A. Hart, *The Concept of Law* (Oxford: Clarendon Press, 1961); Joseph Raz, *The Authority of Law* (Oxford: Clarendon Press, 1979); Scott Shapiro, *Legality* (Cambridge, MA: Harvard University Press, 2013).

(e.g., Moore), the leading natural law theorists espouse the weak version of the natural law theory (e.g., Finnis, Murphy).[11]

The debate between positivists and natural law theorists is quite complex, but insofar as the debate bears on our purpose in this chapter, it will be helpful to understand them in terms of how they account for two general observations about laws. The first observation is this:

The Moral Language of Law. Legal texts use normative terms that are very similar to (and possibly identical to) moral terms.

Legal texts are full of normative terms such as 'ought', 'obligation', 'wrongness', 'guilty', 'punishment', 'offense', 'authority', 'right', and so on. Legal normative concepts are very similar to, if not identical with, moral ones. Legal claims guide and evaluate our conduct. They make demands and justify punishments. We might be legally obligated to join the army, an obligation that requires us to make great sacrifice for the sake of others. We are legally obligated to pay taxes (despite our self-interest). We would be *guilty* if we avoid paying taxes for our own self-interest. We would *deserve* punishments for failing to do these other-regarded actions. And, like moral authority, legal authority is *compulsory*; that is, it does not need consent for its applicability. For instance, that you do not agree with current tax laws does not excuse you from paying taxes.

The natural law view easily explains the moral language of law. Legal normative concepts look like moral concepts because legal laws are ideally moral laws. Contemporary legal positivists, however, can also take the moral language of law onboard. According to Hart, legal normative concepts are normative concepts, but they are *not* moral, because, from the fact that you legally ought to φ, it does not follow that you morally ought to φ. Other positivists (e.g., Raz and Shapiro), however, think that legal normative concepts *are* moral concepts, and that the law makes moral claims. On their views, the best way of understanding a legal claim that you ought to φ is to understand it as this: *from the point of view of the legal system of S, you morally* ought to

---

[11] Michael S. Moore, "Law as a Functional Kind," in *Natural Law Theory: Contemporary Essays*, ed. Robert P. George (Oxford: Oxford University Press, 1992), 188–242; Moore, Michael, "Law as justice," *Social Philosophy and Policy* 18.1 (2001): 115–45; Mark Murphy, *Natural Law in Jurisprudence and Politics* (Cambridge: Cambridge University Press, 2006); Mark Murphy, "The Explanatory Role of the Weak Natural Law Thesis," in *Philosophical Foundations of the Nature of Law*, ed. Wil Waluchow and Stefan Sciaraffa (Oxford: Oxford University Press, 2013), 3–21; John Finnis, *Natural Law and Natural Rights* (Oxford: Oxford University Press, 2011).

φ. If so, Hart is right that from the fact that you legally ought to φ, it does not follow that you morally ought to φ, but this does not make legal concepts nonmoral; instead, by using the term "legally," we are qualifying the moral claims made by specifying a legal system according to which those moral claims are true. With respect to the moral language of law, the difference between legal positivism and the natural law view is therefore less significant than it might initially look.

The natural law view holds that law has a moral function (Moore, Murphy). Some recent legal positivists (e.g., Shapiro) also hold that it is constitutive of law that it aims to solve the moral problems of social life. Even the laws of nondemocractic governments reflect the government's approach to addressing the moral problems of societal life. Contrary to the strong natural law theory, both recent legal positivism and weak natural law views maintain that the failure of a legal system to fulfill its moral goal does not destroy the legal status of the legal system. It is just that the legal system would fail by its own terms because it fails to achieve its goal.

There is an important related observation about the nature of law that any theory of law should accommodate. As we noted, legal positivists can account for the moral language of law by saying that legal texts express moral laws from the perspective of legal systems. But the fact that from the perspective of the legal system S, one is obligated to φ is a descriptive fact. Social scientists can investigate the moral claims of different legal systems. They can make a list of legal systems which accept that one is obligated to φ and legal systems which do not. There is nothing normative here. However, *within a legal system*, things look different. Within a legal system, judges, officials, and legislators make normative judgments. They *must* issue certain rulings. The law has normative force for them. So there is normativity within a legal system, and this is the second observation.

> *The Normativity of Law.* The law has normative force over participants in a legal system (e.g., officials and judges).

It initially appears that the natural law view is in a better position to account for the normativity of law. But this is not the case. The strong natural law view says that legal laws are normative because legal laws are just moral laws. The weak natural law view holds that nondefective legal laws are normative because they are moral laws. But the issue becomes difficult when we consider the laws of an unjust society. According to the normativity of law, the laws of an unjust society have normative force. It is intuitively true that the officials within an unjust legal system must issue certain rulings. They law make certain demands on them. But the natural law theory can't explain the normativity of the laws of an unjust society. The strong view would deny that there is any law in the unjust society and thus would deny the normativity of law in an unjust society. The weak view would say that the laws of an unjust society are not normative in the same way that the laws of a just society are. That is, the normativity of law in an unjust society cannot be explained by appealing to moral laws. So the weak view needs either to say that it is a *mistake* to think that officials *must* perform certain actions and issue certain rulings, or to provide *another* account of the normativity of law in unjust societies.

However, according to legal positivists, at least those who accept the normativity of law, in just and unjust societies it should be explained in the *same* nonmoral way. For example, Hart appeals to "the internal point of view" to explain the normativity of law. On his view, officials are *committed to treat* certain social facts as having certain weight in their practical deliberations. In other words, officials are committed to treat certain descriptive social facts as normative.

Another influential approach to explaining the normativity of law is Scott Shapiro's planning conception of law. He seeks to explain the normativity of law in terms of the normativity of *instrumental reasoning*. According to Shapiro, the law is essentially a *social plan* designed to solve moral problems that are *complex* and *contentious* and that involve *arbitrary* elements. By "contentious" problems, he means problems that people have different preferences about. Problems with arbitrary elements are those problems that involve coordination problems. If the law is essentially a shared plan, then participants in the plan, including judges and officials, have *instrumental* reasons to carry out the plan, and this is why they should treat the law as having normative authority.

The normativity of instrumental reasoning is different from the normativity of morality. Suppose my plan is to do A. Suppose that in order to do A, I should do B. If so, it is *instrumentally necessary* for me to do B to do A. But from this it does not follow that I *morally* ought to do B, or that I *morally* ought to do A. Suppose my plan is to kill someone, and the only way for me to kill him is to shoot him. So, given my plan to kill him, it is instrumentally necessary for me to shoot him. But it is not the case that I ought to shoot him. Morality requires me to abandon my immoral plan altogether. To give another example, suppose that I have the morally neutral plan of having a certain object. But now suppose that the only way for me to have that object is to kill its owner. So, given my plan to have the object, it is instrumentally necessary for me to kill the owner. Yet I morally ought not to kill the owner. Morality demands that I abandon my plan in this case too. There is a large literature about how we should understand the normativity of instrumental reasoning.[12] But no matter how we understand the normativity of instrumental reasoning, it is very different from the normativity of morality. Shapiro's important insight is that the normativity of law should be explained in terms of the normativity of instrumental reasoning and not in terms of the normativity of morality. Of course, in an ideal society in which the law presents the correct solution to the moral problems of the society, we have also moral reasons to abide by the laws of the society.

The debate between the natural law view and legal positivism has many other elements that we have not discussed, and there are important distinctions *within* natural law views and legal positivist views that we have not considered. I discussed the debate between the natural law view and legal positivism with respect to the two observations mentioned because these observations are also true of Scriptural injunctions: Scriptural injunctions use moral language and have authority over believers.

And, although I have shown that, with respect to the two observations made, the difference between the weak natural law view and recent legal positivist views is not significant, I find Shapiro's way of accommodating the normativity of law more convincing than the weak natural law theory. Thus, in the next section I will use Shapiro's view to argue for the truth of Legal Interpretation. It is important to point out, however, that my choice here is a practical one. It would be easier, more elegant, and more insightful to formulate my argument for Legal Interpretation in terms of Shapiro's account, but my defense of Legal Interpretation is not essentially dependent on Shapiro's view.

---

[12] A promising way to explain the normativity of instrumental reasoning is to appeal to rational wide-scope requirements. For example, when the only way to achieve my goal A is to do B, it is true that I rationally ought to [do B, if I plan to A]. The object of my rational requirement is the whole conditional. From the fact that I have a wide-scope rational requirement to [do B, if I plan to A], it does not follow that I rationally ought to do A or that I rationally ought to do B. The literature on wide-scope rational requirements is vast. For an excellent discussion of the topic see John Broome, *Rationality through Reasoning* (Malden, MA: John Wiley & Sons, 2013).

4. Legal Interpretation Defended

In all other chapters of the book, we have assumed that Moral Interpretation is correct. Scriptural injunctions express moral claims. The tale of Hayy ibn Haqzān, however, teaches us about the social function of religious laws. In a society where religious laws are the governing laws, Scripture plays a legal role in solving the social problems of the society. As noted, this was the case for the newly formed society at the time of revelation. Scriptural injunctions were the governing laws of the society at the time of the Prophet. This becomes especially important when we consider that many morally controversial passages in the Qur'an are *Medinan*.

There is a well-established distinction between two types of verses in the Qur'an: *Meccan* verses and *Medinan* verses. Meccan verses are revealed to the Prophet before his migration to the city of Medina in 622 CE (Hijra) to establish his Islamic government. Medinan verses, on the other hand, are those verses revealed to the prophet after Hijra. The Medinan verses state the positive laws of the Islamic society formed in Medina. All examples of morally controversial scriptural passages given in the prologue, section 2, are Medinan verses. The Prophet, however, did not design the legal system of the newly formed Islamic society from scratch. The Prophet adapted some of the pre-Islamic laws of Arabia that he found to be effective, either entirely or in part. Even the small Muslim community in Mecca before Hijra adapted some laws from pre-Islamic times.

According to Shapiro's planning conception of law, legal activity is an activity of social planning. Scriptural injunctions determine the laws of the Islamic society at the time of the prophet, laws which were partially or entirely adapted from the pre-Islamic laws or entirely new to the society. Given the planning conception of law, Scriptural injunctions reveal the social planning of the Prophet to solve the social problems of the newly formed Islamic community. Similar to any new society, the newly formed Islamic society had many social problems, including issues concerning property, trade, the resolution of disputes, and so on. Scriptural injunctions specify the plan adopted by the Islamic community to address those problems, problems that were complex and contentious and involved arbitrary elements.

As asserted by the moral language of law, any legislating body employs moral language. Hence, like any other legislator, the Prophet used moral language to express his plan to solve the problems of the society. Therefore, the presence of moral terms and concepts in Scriptures does not entail that

Moral Interpretation is correct. Legal Interpretation is consistent with the moral language of Scripture.

The planning of the Prophet to solve the social problems of his community is reflected in Islamic law. One important point about the rationality of planning, though, is that it is not rational to have plans that we know are not *feasible*. In order to make a plan, the planner should believe that it is possible, and indeed likely, to execute the plan successfully. This *feasibility condition* places a constraint on the rationality of our activity of planning, including social planning, and could sometimes make it rational to legislate *nonoptimal* moral rules. If we knew that the correct moral principles had no chance of being followed or of solving the problems of the society, it would not be rational to legislate them in order to solve our problems. Let me give you an example.

The Geneva Conventions are international laws that aim to regulate human behavior during war. According to these conventions, a military combatant may intentionally kill another military combatant, but a military combatant may not intentionally kill a civilian. The Geneva Conventions make no distinction between the combatants of the conflicting parties. In recent years, prominent moral philosophers, including Jeff McMahan and Helen Frowe, argue that the Geneva Conventions are fundamentally wrong.[13] The combatants on the just side are *not* morally on a par with combatants on the unjust side. Killing unjust aggressors is morally defensible, whereas killing soldiers who are engaged in a legitimate act of self-defense is not permissible. So there is a moral *asymmetry* between the combatants on the just side and those on the unjust side. These philosophers also find the distinction between combatants and civilians problematic. Some soldiers' role in war is minimal—they might do just some administrative work, while some civilians have a huge role in supporting the war.

If McMahan and Frowe are right, the Geneva Conventions are seriously morally wrong. They permit the unjustified killing (basically murdering) of innocent people. Still, you might think the ethical claims of McMahan and Frowe are too utopian to be practical. In practice, there will be always unjust wars. Powerful countries launch unjust wars and rationalize their behaviors. Enforcing correct moral principles in these cases is not feasible, and legislating them will have disastrous results. If our concern is to minimize the

---

[13] See, for example, Jeff McMahan, *Killing in War* (New York: Oxford University Press, 2009); Helen Frowe, *How We Fight: Ethics in War* (New York: Oxford University Press, 2014).

damage, it might be better not to draw a distinction between just and unjust sides. Moreover, the distinction between combatants and civilians helps us to minimize the atrocities in wars. The Geneva Conventions might be morally incorrect, but they minimize the damage. Also, it might be more practical to avoid controversial disputes, possibly unresolvable, about which side is the "just" side. So it would be irrational to legislate the correct moral principles that McMahan and Frowe offered as international laws. It would be rational to solve the problem of the atrocities in wars by legislating the morally incorrect principles of the Geneva Conventions.

The tale of Hayy is another example in which legislating the correct moral principles is irrational. When most people act immorally and find correct moral principles repugnant, one can't solve social problems of the society by legislating the correct moral principles. The lesson we learned from the tale of Hayy is that there could be reasons to maintain the permissibility of immoral laws. Sometimes the best way to solve the social problems of a corrupt community is through legislating morally incorrect principles. In a society in which racism, sexism, and other moral vices are deeply ingrained, in a society in which sexism and racism are firmly believed to be correct, it might not be feasible to solve those social problems by legislating egalitarian principles. Legislating egalitarian principles might even make the situation worse. In such cases, nonegalitarian laws might help the society to move gradually toward equality. It could even be the case that morally incorrect principles present a *Pareto improvement* solution with respect to the current situation *and* with respect to the situation in which morally correct rules are legislated. By a "Pareto improvement" solution, I mean a solution in which everybody is better off and nobody is worse off, when compared to other alternatives.

Let me state the argument for Legal Interpretation. At the time of revelation, Scriptural injunctions were the laws of the society. Therefore, given *the planning conception of law*, they represent the Prophet's planning to solve the social problems of the society. The *feasibility constraint* on social planning makes it the case that in some circumstances it is rationally necessary to legislate immoral laws to solve social problems (the permissibility of immoral laws). Assuming that the Medinan community is such a case, the Prophet would be in principle justified to legislate nonoptimal moral laws, through Scripture, to solve their social problems. Therefore, Legal Interpretation is true; that is, while actions prescribed or permitted by the best interpretation of a Scriptural passage are *legally* obligatory or permitted, according to religious law, they may not be morally obligatory or permitted.

With respect to morally controversial passages, I think the contextualization view is correct that we have to understand them in the context of revelation. And so, while the laws prescribed in those passages might not be the optimal moral principles, they might have presented the best available plan to solve some social problems of the newly formed society. Barlas is basically right that "at a time when men did not need permission to abuse women, this Ayah [i.e., the wife-beating verse] simply could not have functioned as a license; in such a context, it could only have been a restriction insofar as the Qur'an made *daraba* [to strike] the measure of last, not the first, or even the second, resort." We can assume that this plan made sense in the context of revelation and probably helped the women to be protected against unhinged violence. It *could* even be the case that this plan produced a Pareto improvement in women's situation.

The mistake of the contextualization view, however, is that it assumes that the action permitted by Scripture was *morally justified* in the context. The contextualization view is also correct that the social legislation that was suitable for the Medinan community at the time of the Prophet might not be suitable for our community now. We now have an explanation of why this is so. Assuming that our independent moral judgments are reliable (as shown in the previous chapter), Scriptural injunctions presented a morally suboptimal plan to solve the social problems of the society at the time of revelation. While the permission for wife-beating as a last resort might be a good plan to improve a deeply misogynistic community, it would be a terrible plan to solve our social problems today, given the broad understanding of the wrongness of sexism in our society.

The planning conception of law implies that when the structure of a society radically changes, laws (including Scriptural social laws) suitable for the older society might not be suitable for the new society. If God is just and if Scripture is divine, then the central message of Scripture cannot go against justice. In fact, the essential characteristics of a Muslim, as stated in many passages of the Qur'an, are having faith (in God) and acting justly (see the Qur'an 2:25, 2:82, 2:277, 3:57, 4:57, 4:122, 4:124, 5:9, among many others). If so, as Fazlur Rahman notes, "To insist on a literal implementation of the rules of the Qur'an, shutting one's eyes to the social change that has occurred and that is so palpably occurring before our eyes, is tantamount to deliberately defeating its moral-social purposes and objectives."[14] No one with a

---

[14] Fazlur Rahman, *Islam and Modernity: Transformation of an Intellectual Tradition* (Chicago: University of Chicago Press, 1984), 19.

clear conscience can insist that the Scripture's permission of slavery should be maintained today—it contradicts the Qur'an central call for Muslims to act justly. The same goes for other morally controversial passages. In time, hopefully the moral consciousness of the community broadens, and thus it would be only reasonable and in line with the Qur'an's central message of justice to abandon the discriminatory laws that were suitable for a community with a very narrow moral consciousness for a new set of laws that are morally improved. Of course, there might always be a distance between correct moral principles and proper legal laws, as the example of the Geneva Conventions shows. But, as time passes, the legal laws should come closer to correct moral principles.

5. The Moral Functions of Scripture

If our independent moral judgments are reliable, what moral function could Scripture have in our modern world? In her excellent paper "How to Be a Feminist Muslim," concerned with the problem of the conflict between morally controversial Scriptural passages and feminist values, Amijee presents an epistemic version of Euthyphro's dilemma:

> Do Muslims recognize these norms because the Quran prescribes them, or does the Quran appear to prescribe certain norms to Muslims because they already (independently) recognize those norms? Put differently, is the ultimate "detector" of these norms the Quran, or Muslims?[15]

She finds the second horn implausible on the following ground:

> If Muslims are the ultimate detector of norms, then the Quran is redundant: we already know how we ought to live our lives, and so what point is there in looking to the Quran? (10)

Amijee's project, then, is to find a way of reconciling controversial Scriptural passages with feminist values without renouncing that the Qur'an is the ultimate detector. Mahmoud Muhammed Taha and his student An-Na'im argue

---

[15] Fatema Amijee, "How to Be a Feminist Muslim," *Journal of the American Philosophical Association* 9.2 (2023): 193–213, https://doi.org/10.1017/apa.2022.9.

that an Islamic reformation ought to be based on the Meccan message.[16] Amijee finds this idea promising and seeks to find a plausible foundation for it.

> The distinction between Meccan and Medinan verses maps onto a distinction between norms that govern how to be, and norms that govern what to do.... Some examples of norms that tell us how to be are those expressed by 'be just', 'be kind', and 'be pure'. By contrast, some examples of norms that tell us what to do are those expressed by 'take an eye for an eye', 'do what maximizes greatest happiness for all'. ... Let us call the norms that prescribe how to be 'thick norms', and the norms that prescribe what to do 'thin norms'. ... I claim that the two types of norms differ in that Muslims should treat thin norms as having a normative force that is conditional on the social milieu in which the verses prescribing them were revealed, and thick norms as having unconditional normative force. Thin norms thus have normative force in the social milieu of 7th Century Arabia, but need not have normative force in any other social milieu in 7th Century Arabia. By contrast, thick norms have a normative force that holds at all times and in all places, regardless of when and where the relevant verses were revealed. They thus have universal normative force. (15)

I find Amijee's overall project very appealing. But neither the distinction between Meccan and Medinan verses, nor the distinction between thick and thin norms, I believe, is key for reconciling controversial Scriptural passages with moral values. Considering that many Medinan verses express the positive law of the Muslim society at the time of the Prophet, the distinction between Meccan and Medinan verses may be helpful in addressing the problem of the conflict between moral values and Scripture. Yet there are some Meccan verses that are morally controversial, especially those that presuppose or endorse pre-Islamic laws. The Prophet assumed some pre-Islamic laws to regulate the small Muslim community in Mecca. For example, consider the following example of a Meccan passage in which the preexisting law of permissibility of having a sexual relation with a slave is presupposed.

> Prosperous are the believers, who in their prayers are humble, and from idle talk turn away, and at almsgiving are active, and guard their private parts,

---

[16] See Abdullahi A. An-Na'im, "The Islamic Counter-reformation," *New Perspectives Quarterly* 19 (2008): 29–35.

save from their wives and what their right hands own [i.e., their slaves] then being not blameworthy. (Qur'an 23:1–6)[17]

The Meccan verses that presuppose pre-Islamic laws functioned to regulate the small Muslim community and solve their social problems. Similar to morally controversial Medinan verses, those Meccan verses can also be understood in accordance with Legal Interpretation. On the other hand, as I will explain shortly, not only Meccan verses, but also Medinan verses, may play an important moral function for Muslims: they may provide a religious extension of our moral consciousness that has normative force at all times and in all places.

I find the distinction between thick and thin norms less helpful than the distinction between Medinan and Meccan verses in addressing the problem of prescribed evil. Let's define a proposition as a priori *knowable* if it can be discovered by reason alone through reflection. One immediate worry for the proposal to understand the Qur'an's message in terms of think norms is that thick norms are a priori knowable. Amijee's thick norms (e.g., "be kind") are imperatives involving thick terms. These imperatives can be analyzed as normative propositions which predicate a thin concept, such as "goodness" (or "ought"), of a thick concept, such as being kind. For example, "be kind" can be understood as "one ought to be kind" or "being kind is good." But, as we discussed in Chapter 2, section 2, there is a *conceptual* connection between thick and thin concepts. That is, the evaluative component of a thick concept, say kindness, contributes to its semantic value. Accordingly, it is conceptually true, and thus a priori knowable, that a thick concept instantiates the corresponding thin concept. For example, *being kind is good (in some respect)* is in fact only a conceptual truth, which is a priori knowable.

If the Qur'an is "the ultimate detector" but its main messages consist of thick norms, given that the thick norms are only conceptual truths, "the ultimate detector" has no substantial function. For example, one of Amijee's main Qur'anic examples of a Meccan thick norm is "be not excessive" (15). But *that being excessive is bad* is just an a priori knowable conceptual truth. Rather than making the Qur'an "the ultimate detector of norms," Amijee's view implies that the Qur'an' moral message is no more than conceptual truths that are not very substantial and that are already knowable through pure reflection.

---

[17] The translation is by Arthur John Arberry.

Amijee's view also faces another related concern. Either Amijee's view is a Scripture-first view, or it is an ethics-first view. That is, either our independent moral judgments play a role in discovering the message of the Qur'an or not. As discussed in Part I, Islamic theologians such as al-Ghazālī argue that we can't assume our independent moral judgments, especially when they are in conflict with the apparent meaning of Scripture. Scripture has epistemic authority over our independent moral judgments. If Scripture has epistemic authority over our independent moral judgments (or, as Amijee puts, Scripture is "the ultimate detector" of norms), the strict adherence argument *forces* us to take morally controversial passages at face value (assuming that there aren't textual reasons to do otherwise). In other words, I cannot see how one can hold that Scripture is the ultimate detector of norms while resisting the literal interpretation of at least some of the morally controversial Scriptural passages.

On the other hand, if Amijee's view is an ethics-first view, then our independent moral judgments would have authority over our understanding of Scripture (this is the view that I argued for in Part II). But if so, Scripture would not be the *ultimate* detector of values, and this is the second horn of Amijee's epistemic Euthyphro dilemma. Amijee denies this option on the ground that it makes the Qur'an "redundant."[18] In fact, Amijee's epistemic Euthyphro dilemma is very similar to an old objection to prophecy raised by Barahima regarding the relation between reason and revelation.[19] Almost all Islamic classic books of theology address this objection and provide a response. This is how al-Ghazālī's formulates the objection:

---

[18] Interestingly, at the end of her paper, Amijee says that modern feminist values should influence our understanding of the Qur'an's message (and so it appears that, contrary to what she said earlier, on her own view, the Qur'an is not the ultimate *detector* of values). But she says that "independently acquired background values do not affect what one takes to be the meaning of particular verses, but instead influence the status of the norms prescribed by particular verses i.e., influence whether we take the norms in question to be ideal or merely 'stepping-stone' norms." But there are problems with this suggestion. First, to connect this response to her earlier discussion, we have to assume that her distinction between ideal and stepping-stone norms maps onto the distinction between thick and thin norms. But, as I already pointed out, what she calls "ideal norms" of the Qur'an may not be very substantial and also a priori knowable. Second, Amijee does not explain why and how feminist values change the status of Qur'anic thin norms. But, given that on her view feminist values do not change the meaning of the Qur'anic prescriptions in any way, she is committed to the Moral Interpretation of Medinan verses. But then, as she acknowledges, these moral prescriptions are false. This entails that, on her view, God (and probably the Prophet) is a *liar*, He *knowingly* prescribed false moral norms, and this brings a significant theological cost to her view. Third, as I will explain shortly, not only Meccan but also Medinan verses may expand our moral consciousness, and thus Medinan verses can also prescribe optimal moral rules.

[19] As I explained in a note in Chapter 1, the people referred to as Barahima may have no connection to Indian Barahima. Theists who didn't believe in prophecy were called Barahima by Islamic thinkers.

If a prophet is sent to relate something that agrees with the intellect, then it is dispensable for the intellect. In this case the sending of the prophet is a frivolity; and this is impossible for God. If he is sent to relate something that does not agree with the intellect, then it would be impossible to believe and accept it.[20]

Islamic philosophers and rationalist theologians all agree that the second option is unacceptable: Scripture is in agreement with reason. Therefore, Barahima's objection boils down to this: if Scripture agrees with reason, then Scripture is redundant (Amijee's objection to the view that Scripture is not the ultimate detector of norms is basically the same). Applying this objection to our discussion, the worry is that if our independent moral judgments are reliable, and if they take priority over Scripture, then it is not clear whether Scripture has any moral function.

To Barahima's objection there are two basic responses, one provided by Islamic philosophers such as al-Fārābī and Averroës, the other by rationalist theologians such as al-Ghazālī and 'Abd al-Jabbār. I think both are adequate responses to Barahima's (and Amijee's) objection. Let's begin with the philosophers' response.

As discussed in Chapter 3, al-Fārābī and Averroës hold that all theoretical and practical truths are discoverable by reason alone. Religion cannot extend the findings of reason. However, the power of reasoning of most people is imperfect, and that's why religion has a function for most people (see Chapter 3, sections 2 and 3). Religion can help most people to learn about theoretical and practical matters. That is, religion provides *epistemic assistance* for most people. Therefore, a moral function of Scripture is to provide epistemic assistance. We can explain this moral function of Scripture as follows:

(A) *Epistemic Assistance.* Scripture's moral teachings about benevolence and justice can help ordinary people to learn about the high demands of morality. Our vices sometimes cloud our moral reasoning, and self-interest might prevent some people from knowing what moral obligations they have. Scripture can help many people across the world to know about their moral duties and obligations. Consider these (Medinan and Meccan) verses of the Qur'an: "You will not

---

[20] Abu Hamid M. b. M. al-Ghazālī, *Al-Ghazālī's "Moderation in Belief,"* trans. Aladdin M. Yaqub (Chicago: University of Chicago Press, 2014), 189–90.

attain virtuous conduct until you give of what you cherish" (3:92). "And to be of those who believe, and advise one another to patience, and advise one another to kindness" (90:17). Ideally, we should know by reason that virtue requires sacrifice, and that we have an obligation to be kind to one another. But verses like these are very reassuring and instructive for people who might have reservation about how they should live their lives.

Epistemic assistance is not the only moral assistance that Scripture can provide. Al-Fārābī correctly observes that knowing the right action does not guarantee that one will be motivated to do it. Religion can provide us with *motivational assistance* to do the right action. The second moral function of Scripture is then motivational assistance.

(B) *Motivational Assistance.* Scripture can provide us with motivational assistance for moral behavior. In fact, the Muʿtazilites held that an instance of divine grace (*lutf*) is God's motivational help for us to act morally. Various studies have shown that the belief in the existence of an outside observer motivates people to act morally. Belief in the cosmic punitive system also might provide extra reasons or incentives for people to act morally. One might think that the afterlife incentive is the wrong kind of reason to act morally, but as various philosophers have argued, believers need not act morally *purely* out of self-interest. Afterlife can play a supplementary role for moral behaviors.[21]

Islamic theologians such as al-Ghazālī and ʿAbd al-Jabbār provide a different response to Barahima's objection. To explain, let's distinguish between two types of moral propositions: propositions that are a priori *knowable* and propositions that are *not* a priori knowable and that are *compatible* with our independent moral judgments. While Islamic philosophers hold that all practical truths are ultimately a priori knowable, Islamic theologians believe that there are moral truths that don't disagree with reason but which cannot be discovered through reason alone. In the same vein, we can hold that there are moral truths that are not a priori knowable and that are compatible with

---

[21] See, for example, Kelly James Clark, *Religion and the Sciences of Origins: Historical and Contemporary Discussions* (New York: Palgrave Macmillan, 2014), chap. 10, for a helpful discussion of the role of religion to increase moral behavior.

our independent moral judgments. If there are such moral truths, Scripture may expand our moral consciousness by teaching us about them. In other words, Scripture can provide us with a *religious extension* of morality. This extension is religious because even though it contains moral teachings, it can only be accepted by someone who believes in Scripture. The Scripture would not be morally redundant if it can expand morality in this way.

But how can Scripture expand morality? In what follows, I will offer some suggestions for the religious extension of morality. Although the suggestions expand the moral function of Scripture beyond epistemic and motivational assistance, they are not intended to be exhaustive of all the moral functions of Scripture.[22]

(C) *The Possibility of the Highest Good.* Kant famously identified the highest good with "happiness distributed [to persons] quite exactly in proportion to [their] morality (as a person's worth and his worthiness to be happy)."[23] The highest good, for him, is neither merely being happy nor merely acting morally, but rather being happy because of our moral behaviors. The Muʿtazilites had the exact same conception of the highest good. According to them, the value of receiving heavenly rewards because of one's efforts is much higher than the value of receiving some favor of God when one has done nothing to deserve it. In Kant's view, while morality would be pointless if the highest good were not attainable for us, we cannot show that it is attainable—we can only *hope* that it is. Scripture can reassure believers that the highest good is attainable.

(D) *Solving Coordination Problems.* The possibility of performing collective actions is dependent on solving various coordination problems. In general, coordination problems for collective action can be solved by authorities. In a religious context, Scripture can help us to perform collective religious actions. For example, we might think that whatever value there is in prayer is magnified when many individuals are required to pray together. The nature and the value of prayers can

---

[22] Sara Aronowitz, Marilie Coetsee, and I discuss values mentioned in (D)–(G) in more details here: Sara Aronowitz, Marilie Coetsee, and Amir Saemi, "The Problem of Arbitrary Requirements: An Abrahamic Perspective," *International Journal for Philosophy of Religion* 89.3 (2020): 221–42. My discussions of these four religious requirements are taken from that paper.

[23] Immanuel Kant, *Critique of Practical Reason*, trans. Werner S. Pluhar (Indianapolis: Hackett, 2002), 111.

be transformed when done in a coordinated group. In this Medinan verse, the Qur'an exhorts us to pray collectively: "O Mary, be devoted to your Lord, and bow down, and kneel with those who kneel" (3:43). But collective prayer requires coordination on the location and timing of prayer. In this way, Scripture can make new values available to us by making it possible to perform collective religious actions.

(E) *Spiritual Requirements*. Spiritual requirements are those requirements that help us to grow spiritually. Scripture can teach us about spiritual requirements. In particular, some spiritual requirements might not be precisely translatable into empirical requirements. For example, consider the history of praying toward the qiblah (direction of prayer toward the Kaaba, the House of God, in Mecca). We can think of the qiblah as a spiritual requirement (prayer figuratively oriented toward God) translated into an empirical requirement of literally facing Mecca. Praying itself might be another spiritual requirement. The specific way that Islamic prayer is performed (e.g., five times a day in a specific manner) is a translation of the spiritual requirement into an empirical requirement. The same can be said of other Islamic rituals. Scripture can teach us empirical requirements that correspond to spiritual requirements.

(F) *Valuing Our Relationship to God*. Suppose my mother asks me to do something. My special relationship to my mother gives me a reason to do her bidding—regardless of whether there are any other, independent reasons to do the thing she asks me to do. My decision to do as she asks in this instance allows me to demonstrate that I value my special relationship to her for its own sake. Similarly, to do God's bidding allows one to show that one holds one's relationship with God in special esteem, for its own sake. For instance, if God asks me to go above and beyond the call of duty and perform certain supererogatory or ritualistic actions, I may show that I value my relationship to God (for its own sake) by following this command. I do what God asked me to do in part *because* He asked me to. I do God's bidding because I value my relationship to God (this provides a reason for a believer to adhere to the requirements of praying, fasting, and pilgrimage found in many Medinan verses).

(G) *Devotional Value*. Religious requirements can help us to develop religious virtues. For instance, the Buddha is reported to have compared the dharma to a raft that disciples might use to cross a river—only to then leave it behind as they progress further along the path to Enlightenment.[24] To give another example, a practitioner might be directed to recite a certain text an arbitrary number of times. Obedience to such a directive might be necessary for teaching the practitioner to moderate his compulsive need for personal control over his circumstances, and that (in turn) may be necessary for him to progress toward liberation and salvation. Scripture can specify requirements involving devotional values.

(H) *A Basis for Nonanthropocentric Expansion of Morality.* Many of us believe that our moral duties are not only *to* humans; we have duties *to* nonhuman animals as well. Some environmental ethicists believe that we have also duties to nonliving objects, including ecosystems, mountains, rivers and the earth itself. But it is hard to figure out what the basis of our duties to nonliving things would be. A popular approach in environmental ethics is to hold that the self is part of the natural world and that the earth, from a moral point of view, should be treated as a living thing. But it is hard to find convincing arguments for such views. Scripture can offer believers a divine view of nature and its connection to the self. As a result, Scripture can provide a more secure basis for a nonanthropocentric ethics in which we have duties to both living and non-living elements of the natural world.[25]

Spiritual values, the value of collective actions, devotional values, the value of our relationship with God and a divine view of nature provide genuine moral reasons for us to perform certain actions. These reasons—generated by Scriptural injunctions and grounded in these values—are not available to us before Scripture. Hence, Scriptural injunctions can create genuinely *new* obligations for us. These new obligations, however, are grounded in moral values recognizable by reason. For instance, reason tells us that self-improvement or special relationships are valuable. In this sense, new religious obligations are constructed on the basis of values already recognized by reason.

---

[24] John J. Holder, ed. and trans., *Early Buddhist Discourses* (Indianapolis: Hackett, 2006), 108.
[25] As far as I can see, the fascinating views on land ethic and deep ecology developed by Leopold, Naess, and others should appeal even more to religious believers. See, for example, Aldo Leopold, *A Sand County Almanac* (New York: Ballantine, 1970); Arne Naess, "A Defense of the Deep Ecology Movement," *Environmental Ethics* 6.3 (1984) : 265–70.

Different moral values can compete with one another. Religious requirements constructed out of the value of self-improvement or that of special relationship are no exception in this regard. These obligations might be in tension with some of our other moral obligations, and they may even override some of our other moral obligations. For example, I might have an obligation to be kind with a friend by welcoming her with tea. I can imagine situations in which obligations generated by those religious values (e.g., the obligation to perform my prayers on time) override my obligation to offer my friend a tea.

However, reasons created by religious values have limited power to override our obligations to others, especially our obligation not to harm them. For instance, consider the obligation created by the value of special relationships. If my father asks me to kill someone, I would not acquire an overriding reason to kill that person in virtue of the fact that I value my relationship with my father. It is plausible to say that obligations created by religious values can never undermine our *negative* duties to others, especially our duties not to harm them. Negative duties are duties that we have toward others not to do certain things to them. Similarly, negative rights are the rights that people have that we don't do certain things to them (e.g., not to harm them). For example, everybody has a negative right against me not to be killed. This means that I have a pro tanto negative duty toward each person not to kill them.

It would be bizarre to think that my special relationship with some people (or my spiritual improvement) would justify me in violating the negative rights of *other* people. By doing someone's bidding, we honor our relationship with them. But it is strange to think that I may violate a person's negative right (not to be harmed) to honor my relationship with someone else. My special relationship to someone should not come at the expense of other people. The same holds about my spiritual improvement. The cost of my spiritual development shouldn't be borne by others. Therefore, obligations created by religious values are not strong enough to override negative rights and duties. I would not acquire a duty to harm someone only because God has asked me to do so.

In the previous chapter, we discussed whether God's command could provide a justification for Abraham's sacrifice in a testimonial manner—by providing evidence of reasons that exist independently of God's command. It is now time to see whether God's command can provide justification for Abraham in a *nontestimonial manner*. As described above, God's commands can create *new* reasons for our actions in various ways. But can God's command create a new obligation for Abraham to kill his son, an obligation that in no manner exists independently of God's command?

Kierkegaard famously argues that while Abraham's killing would be morally wrong, there is a nonmoral religious value, derived from the value of a particular personal relationship with God, in acting in faith even when what is required by faith goes against morality.[26] On Kierkegaard's view, God's command creates an obligation for Abraham in a *nontestimonial* way. That is, God, through merely His command, creates a new obligation for Abraham to kill his son. Kierkegaard thinks that this new obligation, grounded in Abraham's particular personal relationship with God, is beyond morality.

However, on a broad understanding of morality, our personal relationship with others is yet another moral value. What I find strange, and in fact implausible, in Kierkegaard's view is his belief that the value of my personal relationship with God can justify me in violating significant negative rights of others. It would be selfish, and utterly immoral, to impose a great cost on others for the sake of my special relationships. The value of Abraham's special relationship with God, the value of Abraham's spirituality, or the value of Abraham's devotion to God cannot create a sufficient reason for Abraham to violate his son's right to life, just as self-interest and the promotion of one's own well-being are never justifying reasons for harming others. The nontestimonial moral values inherent in my deference to God's command tend to be self-involved. Consequently, they are not of the kind of values that can override our reasons to respect important negative rights of others, such as their right not to be harmed.

In sum, Scripture can have different moral functions as specified in (A)–(H). In particular, Scripture can expand morality by creating new obligations. But these new obligations are constructed out of values already recognized by reason. If my arguments for the reliability of our independent moral judgments are on the right track, the religious extension of morality cannot be incompatible with our considered independent moral judgments.

Let me finish the book by responding to one last worry: one might say that while Scripture may teach moral behaviors and promote other moral and religious values, it might also teach immoral behaviors through morally controversial passages. For example, someone might read Scripture and come to believe that he has permission to, say, beat his wife. So, wouldn't it be better to distrust Scripture's moral teachings altogether? I think this is not the

---

[26] Søren Kierkegaard, *Fear and Trembling*, trans. Alastair Hannay (London: Penguin, 1985).

right reaction to morally controversial passages in Scripture. Even conservative theists, if they are conscientious, can see that there is something very objectionable about mistreating their spouses; after all, they should have our modern moral sensibilities, too. Of course, the conservatives might *argue* that people of faith should ignore those intuitions and stick to Scripture's literal meaning. However, the arguments of this book, if successful, show that there are plausible ways to resist this conservative argument. As I have argued in the previous two chapters, we can recognize that no hidden fact can ever justify us in the belief that we possess rational or moral permission to engage in practices such as wife-beating or any form of discriminatory conduct against women or minorities. If the conservatives' argument fails, we should adhere to our independent moral judgments in our lives and in our understanding of Scripture. Guided by their independent moral judgements, humans with uncorrupted moral sensibilities are in a position to see which passages in Scripture can supplement morality, and which cannot.

Index

For the benefit of digital users, indexed terms that span two pages (e.g., 52–53) may, on occasion, appear on only one of those pages.

Abd al-Jabbār, 30, 67, 67n.1, 70, 70n.5, 71–72, 72n.7, 73–74, 73n.8, 75, 75n.10, 76, 77, 78, 79–80, 81, 82–93, 82n.18, 95, 98, 99n.31, 100–2, 197–99, 227, 228–29
Abraham, 3n.2, 3n.3, 5n.6, 171, 202–5, 233
Absāl, 211, 212, 213–14
absolutism, 75, 76, 79–80, 81, 83, 101
Abu Hatim al-Rāzī. *See* al-Rāzī Abu Hatim
Accessibility Constraint, 171, 187–88, 189–97, 200–1, 203
Acquired Intellect, 110–11, 113n.18
Active Intellect, 110–13, 115–16, 125, 126
Actual Intellect, 110
Adams, Robert, 72n.7, 117n.25, 203n.26
Adamson, Peter, xi, 38n.2, 70n.4, 107n.6, 143n.28–44, 150, 151, 151n.39
agency view, 171, 186, 190, 191–93
agent-neutral, 46n.11, 82n.20
al-Fārābī, 31, 32–33, 32n.30, 103, 104, 105–13, 105n.5, 107n.7, 108n.11, 109n.14, 111n.16, 113n.18, 114, 118, 119, 120, 121–34, 124n.34, 125n.35, 125n.36, 125n.37, 128n.42, 128n.43, 129n.44, 129n.45, 131n.46, 132n.47, 132n.48, 210, 227, 228
al-Fārābīan solution, 105–6, 113, 118, 120, 133–34
al-Ghazālī, 25–26, 31–32, 35, 37, 37n.1, 40, 44n.7, 44n.8, 45n.9, 47n.12–48, 48, 49, 50–53, 51n.13, 54, 55, 56–58, 59, 60–61, 60n.16, 60n.17, 60n.18, 62, 63–66, 63n.22, 68–69, 69n.2, 70, 71–72, 72n.7, 73–74, 90–91, 92–93, 100–2, 114, 116, 138, 226, 227, 227n.20, 228–29
al-Ghazālī's main claim, 53, 57–58, 59, 92

al-Hallaj, 3
al-Hillī, 199, 200n.24
al-Hillī, al-Muhaqqiq, 168–69, 168n.53
al-Iqtisād, 44–45, 44n.8, 45n.9, 47, 48–49, 50, 58–59, 61–62, 65–66, 68, 227n.20
al-Juwainī, Imām al-Haramayn, 37, 38, 39, 40–41, 41n.4, 42–44, 43n.6, 45–46, 50–52, 90
al-Madina al-Fadila, 110, 111n.16, 124n.34, 125n.35, 125n.36, 128n.42
al-Mughnī, 30, 75, 76, 82, 84, 85, 86, 88, 89, 90, 91
al-Rāzī, Abū Bakr Muhammad ibn Zakariyyā, 31, 32–33, 47n.12–48, 104, 137, 137n.1, 143–57, 143n.28–44, 147n.32, 149n.36, 149n.37, 167
al-Rāzī, Abu-Hatim, 150, 151, 152–53
al-Rāzī, Fakhr al-din, 44–45, 45n.10, 47n.12–48, 144
al-Tabarī, 202n.25, 203–5
Amijee, Fatema, 11n.12, 18n.22, 223–24, 223n.15, 225, 226, 226n.18, 227
Anne Eliot, 156–57, 161n.48, 192, 193
Argument for strict adherence, 25–27, 26t, 37, 52–53, 54, 57, 58, 59, 60, 66, 67, 71, 92–93, 92n.22, 94–95, 100–1, 102, 133–34, 138–39, 169, 172, 179, 180, 200, 201, 226
Ash'arites, 25–26, 30–32, 38–45, 38n.2, 47, 49, 51–52, 67, 68–70, 71, 72, 72n.7, 91
Averroes, 31, 32, 33, 103, 104–7, 108, 108n.12, 108n.13, 113–21, 113n.19, 210, 227
Avicenna, 31–33, 32n.30, 104, 106–7, 108n.13, 113n.19, 127–28, 127n.41, 138n.3, 210
awad, 91

236 INDEX

Barahima, 43–44, 43n.5, 43n.6, 226, 226n.19, 227, 228–29
Barlas, Asma, 11–12, 13–15, 13n.16, 14n.17, 19, 19n.23, 20, 20n.26, 222
Booth, Anthony, 51n.13, 107n.8, 107n.9, 107n.10, 108n.11, 126, 126n.38, 126n.39, 127, 127n.40, 128, 129
Burge, Tyler, 101, 101n.33

certainty, 107–8, 108n.11, 117, 127, 128
Chomsky, Noam, 15–16
classical problem of evil, 9–10, 24–25, 67, 68, 70, 91–92, 93, 180–81, 200–1
Conscience Constraint, 171, 176–78, 183–85, 197–98, 200–1, 202–3
Consequentialism, 25–27, 26t, 37, 45–46, 46n.11, 47–48, 47n.12–48, 49, 50–52, 51n.13, 55–58, 59, 61–62, 66, 68–69, 71, 72, 82–84, 82n.20, 85–86, 90–91, 92–93, 100–2, 175n.7
 self-centered, 45–46, 47–48, 47n.12–48, 49, 50, 55
 Universal, 45–46, 46n.11, 48, 49, 50–51, 55, 56
Consequentialization, 46n.11
contemplative life, 121, 122–23, 130
Contextualization view, 18, 20, 21–22, 206–7, 209, 222
Contributory Aspects, 80, 81, 87–88

de dicto, 159–60, 163–64, 164n.49
de re, 159–60, 161–62, 163–64
Decisive Treatise. See Fasl al-Maqāl
Deliverance from Error, 60
demonstration, 62, 65–66, 103, 105, 106–8, 108n.11, 109, 113, 114–17, 118–19, 120, 131–32
demonstrative method. See demonstration
demonstrative proof. See demonstration
discursive knowledge, 86, 87, 88–89, 93
divine command theory, 30–31, 37, 38, 38n.2, 40, 50–52, 68, 71–72, 72n.7, 138
Divinity of Scripture, 5, 6–7, 8–9, 10, 23–24, 28, 38, 102, 169, 205, 207, 208–9
Doctor case, 156–57, 158–59, 160–61, 192, 193, 196–97

emanation, 110, 112–13, 144–45
Enoch, David, 142n.17, 142n.19, 154n.40, 159–61, 159n.46, 161n.48, 162–63
Epitome of the Parva Naturalia, 108
Ethics-first, 25, 26t, 27, 135–234
eudaimonia. See happiness
Euthyphro's dilemma, 223
Evidence of Reasons, 182, 185, 186–87, 188
Existence of Seemingly Prescribed Evil, 23–24, 28, 54, 102, 169, 205, 206–9

falāsifa, 25–26, 31–32
Fasl al-Maqāl, 104–5, 105n.4, 106, 113, 114n.20, 117n.24
Faysal, 62, 63, 64, 115, 116
Fazel Abi, 8, 17n.21, 168–69, 168n.54
Feasibility condition, 220
felicity. See happiness
figurative, 37, 64, 65–66, 105, 114, 116
Frowe, Helen, 220–21, 220n.13

Geneva conventions, 220–21, 222–23
good for, 46
God's Reliability, 53, 57, 58, 59, 92, 100–2, 138–39, 169, 172, 172n.1, 201
good simpliciter, 46, 47–48, 47n.12–48
Graham, Peter, 176–77
Griffel, Frank, 44n.7, 45n.9, 60, 60n.16, 63n.22

Hadith, 6–8, 6n.7, 22, 168–69
 single-source, 167–69
Hamzah, 2
happiness, 27–28, 50, 56, 57–58, 103, 121, 122–23, 124–25, 126, 127, 127n.41, 128, 129, 130–33, 131n.46, 144–45, 147, 148–49, 185–86, 193, 197–98, 224
Hart, H. L. A., 214–16, 214n.10, 217
Hayy ibn Haqzān, 33, 206, 210, 219
Herman, Barbara, 191, 191n.19
Hourani, George, 41n.4, 43n.6, 44n.7, 70n.5, 79–80, 79n.17, 82, 82n.18, 82n.19, 83

Iblis, 3
Ibn Kathir, 17n.21

Ibn Tufayl, 28, 32–33, 206, 210, 211n.3, 211n.4, 211n.5, 212, 212n.6, 212n.7, 212n.8, 213–14
ignorance, 43, 48, 76, 77, 89, 120, 142, 171, 173–74, 175, 179, 185, 186–88, 197–98, 212, 213
Ihyā, 35, 61–62
Imāmiyya, 10–11, 30, 198, 199, 200, 200n.24, 201
Independent moral judgments, 8–9
Infallibility of the Prophet, 7
inner meaning, 115–16, 118–19
inseparability view, 78–79
intellectualized epistemology, 26t, 119
intelligibles, 110–13, 125, 126, 127
Ishmael, 202, 203–5

justifiability view, 171, 186, 190, 193

Kant, Immanuel, 184, 203, 203n.27, 229n.23
Kantian view, 27–28, 171, 186–88, 190, 193, 197–98
Khidr, 3n.3, 137, 164, 165, 166, 183
Kierkegaard, Soren, 233, 233n.26
Knowledge of Aspects, 87–88

Legal Interpretation, 206, 208–9, 218, 219–23, 225
legal positivism, 214–16, 217
Lord, Errol, 139n.5, 141, 141n.13, 141n.14, 142n.17, 142n.18, 142n.20, 142n.23, 174, 174n.5, 177n.11
lutf, 199, 228
lying, 58–59, 71–72, 74, 76, 77, 77n.12, 79–80, 83–84, 85–86, 88, 101–2, 208

McDowell, John, 78n.15, 124, 124n.31, 124n.33
McMahan, Jeff, xi, 220–21, 220n.13
Meccan verses, 219, 224, 225
Medinan verses, 219, 224, 225, 226n.18, 230
mimēsis, 111–13
minimization of the moral risk, 159–62
moral achievement, 141–42, 154–55
moral deference, 27, 137, 138–44, 140n.6, 140n.7, 141n.11, 141n.14, 142n.17, 142n.19, 148–49, 152, 153–55, 154n.40, 157, 158–59, 160–61, 162–64, 167, 169
pure, 139–42, 143, 155, 157, 158–59, 161
moral expert, 138–39, 140–41, 155, 158–59, 160–61, 191–92, 196–97
Moral Interpretation, 207–8, 209, 219–20, 226n.18
Moral Justification, 17, 18, 21–22, 24–25, 55, 92–93, 92n.22, 94–95, 100–2, 172, 180, 201, 203
Moral Language of Law, 215–16, 219–20
moral paralysis, 98
moral perception, 124, 128
moral risk, 159–62, 167, 176
moral skepticism, 98
moderate, 98
moral testimony, xi, 137, 140–42, 140n.8, 141n.11, 141n.12, 142n.26, 143–44, 154–55, 158–59, 161, 162, 192, 196–97
moral understanding, 141–42, 143, 154, 155, 157–58, 169–70
morally controversial passages, 5, 8–9, 10–12, 14–15, 16, 17, 19, 21–22, 33, 52n.14, 55, 65, 92, 102, 138–39, 172n.1, 184, 206–7, 209, 219, 222, 226, 233–34
Moses, 3n.3, 137, 157–69, 183, 184–85, 197, 200–1, 202–3
motivational externalism, 126, 127–28
mufassal (discursive), 86, 87
muhākāt. See mimēsis
mujmal, 15, 86, 87, 88
mutawatir, 167–68
Mu'tazilites, 25–27, 30–32, 38n.2, 41, 41n.4, 43–44, 43n.6, 67, 68, 70–81, 70n.4, 91, 92–93, 138, 171, 197–201, 228

natural evil, 91–102
natural law theory, 214–15
strong view, 214–15, 216–17
weak view, 214–15, 216–17, 218
Necessitating Aspects, 75, 81, 87–88
neo-Platonic, 104, 106
New problem of evil. See Problem of Prescribed evil

Nicomachean Ethics, 121–24, 128, 128n.43, 130
Normativity of Law, 216–17, 218

Objective view, 171, 173–74, 175–77, 179–80, 181–82, 183–84, 185–86, 188
obligation. *See* ought
optimism
  epistemic, 140–41, 158–59
  moral, 141, 142, 143, 157
  moral knowledge, 197–201
ought
  everything considered, 96–98, 120
  objective, 99, 158–59, 162–63, 172, 174, 176–77, 178, 178n.12, 179–80, 181, 186
  pro tanto, 96–98
  rational, 27, 158–59, 162–63, 169, 183, 218n.12
  simpliciter, 96–97, 96n.25
  subjective, 99–100, 99n.31, 158–59, 172, 174, 178, 179, 183
Our independent moral judgments. *See* Independent Moral Judgements

parallel evil argument, 93, 94–95, 95n.23, 171, 200, 201
pareto improvement, 221, 222
Parfit, Derek, 97n.26, 172, 173, 173n.2, 174n.6
Passive Intellect, 110–11
perfection, 110–13, 124–25, 126, 127–28, 127n.41, 129, 130–31, 144–45
Permissibility of Immoral Laws, 213, 221
pessimism
  epistemic, 140–41, 141n.10, 154
  moral, 141–43, 154–55, 157, 159
philosophical utilitarianism, 27–28, 171, 185–86, 193, 197
  expected, 185–87, 197–98
Philosophical Way of Life, 145, 146, 147, 147n.31, 147n.33, 148n.34, 149n.35, 153–54
phronesis, 123–24, 124n.31, 128, 130–31, 133
planning conception of law, 206, 217, 219, 221, 222–23
Plantinga, Alvin, 9–10, 10n.10, 25n.29

pointless evil, 24–25, 68, 91–92, 93, 94, 95, 96, 98, 180–81, 200–1
Posterior Analytics, 106–7
potential intellect, 110, 126
practical life, 121, 122–23, 130
practical wisdom. *See* phronessis
pro tanto
  ought, 96–98
  wrong, 67, 80–81, 82, 83, 85–86, 87–88, 90, 141
problem of prescribed evil, 1, 9–10, 16–17, 22, 23, 24–25, 26t, 27, 28–29, 32–33, 37n.1, 67n.1, 97–98, 102, 119, 133, 137, 143, 169–70, 205, 206, 209, 225
Proofs of Prophecy, 150, 150n.38
punishments, 4–5, 9, 49, 52–53, 55, 56–58, 65–66, 92–93, 149, 215

qabīh, 74, 77
Quinn, Phillip, 55

Rahman, Fazlur, 208–9, 222–23, 222n.14
Raz, Joseph, 214–16, 214n.10
Reinterpretation view, 11–18, 18n.22, 21–22, 206–7
Reliability of our Independent Moral Judgments, 1, 23–28, 26t, 37, 52, 53, 54, 102, 106, 119, 120, 137, 169–70, 171–72, 180, 197–98, 200–1, 205, 207–8, 209
  objective sense, 169–70, 171–72, 209
  rational sense, 169–70, 209
representative faculty, 110–11, 112–13
Rule of Figurative Interpretation, 60–66

sa'ada. *See* happiness
Scanlon, Thomas, 97n.26, 185–86, 185n.15, 193–94, 195
Scripture-first, 25, 26t, 35–134, 103n.1, 169–70, 179, 182, 183, 185, 186–87, 201, 205, 226
Seemingly prescribed evil, 9
separability view, 78–79
Shapiro, Scott, 214–16, 214n.10, 217–18, 219
Sharh, 73, 76, 81, 88–89
Shi'a, 6n.7, 10–11, 30, 143, 150, 167–69
skeptical theism, 95, 96, 98, 98n.28, 99–100, 179–81, 182, 200–1

Sliwa, Paulina, 142, 142n.26, 158
Smith, Michael, 78n.14, 159–60, 160n.47, 174n.6
Social Function of Religious Laws, 213, 219
Soldier case, 155–57, 159, 160–61, 192, 196–97
Spiritual Medicine, 143n.28–44, 145, 145n.30, 146–47, 149–50
Subjective view, 171, 173–74, 175, 177, 179, 182, 183, 185–86, 188, 197–98, 200

taqlīd, 60–66, 60n.16
testimony
 antireductionism, 101–2
 reductionism, 101–2, 101n.32
Textual Justification, 17, 18
The Condition of Certainty, 107–8
theological voluntarism. *See* divine command theory
theoretical knowledge, 51n.13, 105, 119, 127
theory of aspects, 74, 81, 82, 82n.18
 the epistemological role, 76, 78, 81
 the metaphysical role, 76, 80, 81

thick moral concepts, 76–77, 77n.13, 78–80, 81, 139–40, 225
thin moral concepts, 76–77, 78–79, 139–40, 225
Thomson, Judith Jarvis, 174, 174n.5, 187–88, 188n.17
two-level view, 174, 175, 178

uncertainty, 27–28, 158–60, 164n.49, 166n.51, 171, 173–74, 175–77, 179, 183, 184, 197–98

Wadud, Amina, 11–12, 12n.13, 13–15, 13n.14, 14n.18, 19, 20, 20n.27
Weatherson, Brian, 166, 166n.50
Wiland, Eric, 158, 158n.45, 162–63
wrong
 everything considered, 24, 67, 80–81, 88, 93
 pro tanto, 67, 80–81, 82, 83, 85–86, 87–88, 90, 141
wrong-making aspects, 74, 75, 76, 77, 78, 79–80, 81, 82–84, 85–86, 87–88, 90–91, 96, 99, 199–200

Zimmerman, Michael, xi, 173n.3, 174, 175–78, 175n.8, 178n.12, 183–84